# Date Due

# INFLUENCING
# HUMAN BEHAVIOR

BY

## H. A. OVERSTREET

Professor and Head of the Department of Philosophy,
College of the City of New York. Lecturer,
New School for Social Research

NEW YORK

W · W · NORTON & COMPANY, INC.

*Publishers*

PRINTED IN THE UNITED STATES OF AMERICA

THE VAIL-BALLOU PRESS
BINGHAMTON AND NEW YORK

# CONTENTS

*Foreword* . . . . . . . . . . . . vii

*Preface* . . . . . . . . . . . . 1

## PART ONE: INTRODUCTORY TECHNIQUES

CHAPTER

I. THE KEY PROBLEM: CAPTURING THE ATTENTION . . . . . . . . . 9

II. THE APPEAL TO WANTS . . . . . . 28

III. THE PROBLEM OF VIVIDNESS . . . . . 50

IV. THE PSYCHOLOGY OF EFFECTIVE SPEAKING . 71

V. THE PSYCHOLOGY OF EFFECTIVE WRITING . 87

VI. CROSSING THE INTEREST DEAD-LINE . . 110

VII. MAKING IDEAS STICK . . . . . . 125

## PART TWO: FUNDAMENTAL TECHNIQUES

VIII. HOW TO CHANGE PERSONS: THE ENTERING WEDGE . . . . . . . . . 143

IX. THE BUILDING OF HABITS: ASSOCIATIVE TECHNIQUES . . . . . . . . 159

X. OUR UNCONSCIOUS FABRICATION HABITS . 169

XI. THE PROBLEM OF STRAIGHT THINKING . 184

XII. DIAGNOSING THE PUBLIC . . . . . 201

XIII. TRAINING THE CREATIVE MIND . . . 217

XIV. CONFLICT AND INVENTION . . . . 238

XV. THE TECHNIQUE OF HUMOR . . . . 256

XVI. THE INDIVIDUAL AND HIS WORLD . . . 273

*The Listeners Speak* . . . . . . . . 279

*Index* . . . . . . . . . . . . 293

# FOREWORD

The following chapters are the substance of a course of lectures given last year at the New School for Social Research in New York City. In a number of respects the course was unusual. In the first place, it was requested by the students—men and women—and was given under the auspices of their Coöperative Association. In the second place, the manner in which the request was worded was significant. It came as a petition "for a course indicating how human behavior can actually be changed in the light of the new knowledge gained through psychology. We have in our group educators, social workers, lawyers, business men and women, and those describing themselves as having no vocation. We have in common an interest in understanding and improving social conditions. Besides this, and perhaps first of all, we desire to utilize as a part of our everyday technique of action such knowledge as modern psychology can furnish us. Our interest is not academic. We wish actually to function with such knowledge as we may gain."

From the outset, therefore, the course belonged to the students. Throughout the conduct of it, there was the closest coöperation between lecturer and class. Usually at least four discussion groups were meeting before the lecture hour; while one group met on another evening at the home of a member. The students were requested to coöperate actively in making observations and experiments and to report their findings. As a result, the lecturer became the much enlightened possessor of a large amount of valuable material contributed by the members of the class. It has not been possible to incorporate more than a small portion of this material in the present volume. Some of the material has been gathered together in a final chapter; in other cases it has been slipped into the body of the text. The writer wishes that far more of it might have been used; but the limits of space have forbidden.

The course was, to the lecturer, one of the most stimulating that it has been his good fortune to give. It strengthened his belief in the very great value (a value as yet scarcely realized throughout the country) of serious and systematic study on the part of men and women who can contribute out of the maturity of their experience to the urgent problems of human behavior.

It seems invidious to single out any one person for special mention. But the course, in its inception and continuance, was so indebted to Mr. Daniel Cranford Smith for unflagging interest and intelligent devotion that I cannot forbear giving him my thanks. Also, I should like to make one other exception—in favor of my wife, who ought to be acknowledged as the unofficial lecturer on more pages than can easily be counted.

H. A. OVERSTREET

# PREFACE

The object of these chapters is to discover how far the data of modern psychology can be put to use by each of us in furthering what is really the central concern of our lives. That central concern is the same whether we be teachers, writers, parents, merchants, statesmen, preachers, or any other of the thousand and one types into which civilization has divided us. In each case the same essential problem confronts us. If we cannot solve it, we are failures; if we can, we are—in so far, at least—successes. What is this central problem? Obviously, it is to be, in some worth-while manner, effective within our human environment.

We are writers? Then there is the world of editors, some of whom we must convince as to our ability. If we succeed in doing that, then there is, further, the reading public. It is a bit of sentimental nonsense to say that it makes no difference at all if a writer convinces not even a single soul of his pertinence and value, so be it only that he "express" himself. We have a way of being over-generous with so-called misunderstood geniuses. True, this is a barbarian world; and the fine soul has its hard innings. But the chances are that a writer who can convince no single person of the value of what he writes, probably has nothing of value to write. At any rate, as his manuscripts come back, he might well cease putting the blame on philistine editors and public long enough to ask himself whether, indeed, he is not deficient in the very elementary art of making the good things he has to say really understandable.

We are business men? Then there are the thousands of potential customers whom we must induce to buy our product. If they refuse, then bankruptcy.

We are teachers? Obviously, we are not teachers by right of sitting on a platform. We are teachers only when something of what we intend takes place in the lives before us. If we are invariably confronted by indifference, boredom, hostility, hatred, we had best earn our salaries at another undertaking.

We are parents? It may seem somewhat far fetched to say that the chief concern of a parent is to be accepted by his children. "What!" we cry, "aren't they *our* children; and aren't children required to respect their parents?" That, of course, is all old philosophy; old ethics; old psychology as well, coming from the day when children, like wives, were our property. Nowadays children are persons; and the task of parents is to be real persons themselves to such an extent that their children accept them as of convincing power in their lives. Hence the parent is no parent simply by right of his or her procreative power. For parent, in unnumbered cases, substitute "tyrant," "autocrat," "sentimentalist," "boor."

We need not specify further. As individuals, our chief task in life is to make our personality, and what our personality has to offer, effective in our particular environment of human beings. Nor need this connote undue egoism on our part. Lincoln had to make his personality, and what his personality had to offer, effective in his environment. So did the Nazarene, to the extent that folk gave up their all and followed him. So did Socrates. Neither Jesus nor Socrates, to be sure, could persuade the greater part of their human environment; and so they both met a tragic fate. But they persuaded enough of their fellows, profoundly enough, to make the impress of their personalities last through succeeding centuries.

We call lives like these successful, because they go on being increasingly accepted by the world of human beings. These lives, to use our modern slang, have in reality "got across," and continue still to "get across." As a consequence they have succeeded in profoundly influencing the behavior of their fellows.

However, we are not writing these chapters in order to show how we may become Lincolns or Socrateses or Christs. Before the wonder of personal greatness, psychology still bows its head. We are simply trying to come to some manner of understanding about what is the central concern for us, as it was for these superb spirits. Life is many things; it is food-getting, shelter-getting, playing, fighting, aspiring, hoping, sorrowing. But at the centre of it all it is this: it is the process of getting ourselves believed in and accepted.

That is what love making is. To make love to one who will not be persuaded, is a fool's game, albeit much indulged in. That is what trading is. The man who can persuade no one to believe in his goods is a business failure. That is what preaching is. The preacher who is a joke to his pew-holders is either a coxcomb or a fool.

To get people to think with us! It is an art—the supreme art. The blunderer in life is he who, wishful to capture the interests and enthusiasms of people, to get them to think and work along with him, is able only to capture their indifference or antagonism. The blundering parent, the blundering teacher, the blundering business man, the blundering reformer—herein lies their essential weakness.

Must this art—this major art of life—be simply hit or miss? Or may we be fairly intelligent about it? The position taken in these chapters is that we can be intelligent, and to such an extent, indeed, as to increase very materially the effectiveness of our life enterprise.

How are we to become intelligent about this? Obviously by addressing ourselves concretely to the problem. Not by talking vaguely about goals and ideals; but by finding out quite specifically what methods are to be employed if the individual is to "get across" to his human fellows, is to capture their attention and win their regard, is to induce them to think and act along with him—whether his human fellows be customers or clients or pupils or children or wife; and whether the regard which he wishes to win is for his goods, or ideas, or artistry, or a great human cause.

"Whenever we take ends without regard to the means, we degenerate into sentimentalism," says John Dewey. In these chapters we are studying the means to accomplish the central end indicated. In that sense we are doing what should go hand in hand with all fruitful ethical inquiry.

In this search after means, we shall find no little help in what modern psychology has to offer. The business man has already discovered, in a measure, what psychological understanding can do for him; the factory manager is beginning to discover it. Education, in its more progressive aspects, is pushing vigorously into psychological fields in order to make teaching comport more thoroughly with the needs and possibilities of human nature.

The difficulty about human life is that it still knows so poorly how to pursue its own best interests. The autocratic parent is perfectly sincere; but he is often so pitifully stupid. And in being stupid, he makes such an unfortunate waste of both his own and his children's lives. How much better if all of us who are parents really knew how to handle our children. The same is true of the autocratic employer or factory manager or foreman—sincere but blundering. The same is true of many an honest business man. Earnest, but unknowing of his public. And so a good life largely gone to waste!

The salvaging of human life consists not simply in having high ideals. It consists as much in having the knowledge "how." We need, in short, to know how to interest our fellows; how to arouse their expectation; how to build up habits of favorable response; how to lead and adjust and control. All this is the groundwork of our human ethics. To become skilled artists in the enterprise of life—there is hardly anything more basically needful than this. It is to this problem that we address ourselves.

The book is divided into two parts. In the first part, the relatively simpler and more frequent techniques for influencing human behavior are discussed. The comparative simplicity of these techniques should not, however, blind the reader to their real value both in the superficial give and take of everyday life and in those profound situations in which a deeper influencing is desired. In the second part, the discussion proceeds to the more difficult matters of actual psychological reconstruction. How, we ask there, can we influence human behavior not only in fleeting and surface ways, but in ways that are fundamental and permanent? How, in short, can we actually change individuals—ourselves as well as others—into personalities more apt for our human enterprise?

# PART ONE

# INTRODUCTORY TECHNIQUES

# CHAPTER I

## THE KEY PROBLEM: CAPTURING ATTENTION

In the delicate matter of influencing human behavior, most of us fall short, not so much from a profound ignorance of human nature—such ignorance does, unfortunately, exist—as from a failure to use the simplest and most obvious techniques. It is surprising how largely this is true. After one has become aware, for example, of the more elementary methods for securing attention, arousing and holding interest, one notes how greatly they are honored in the breach. Let us, in this chapter, consider a number of these simpler but far too neglected techniques.

*What we attend to controls our behavior. What we can get others to attend to controls their behavior.* In these two sentences we have the key to the influencing of human behavior.

"Tell me what you habitually attend to and I will tell you what you are." There is no doubt about this. If it is your constant habit to watch the facial expressions of people, their manner of speech and gesture, their behavior toward each other, one can safely wager that you are, to a noticeable degree, an analyst of human character. If, on the other hand, you habitually watch the ups and downs of the stock market, one can wager that you are, to an extent, an analyst of finance. If, again, your attention is constantly attracted by wheels, pistons, levers, etc., one can safely assume that your absorbing interest is in machinery. You are, in short, that to which you habitually attend.

The differences in peoples is likewise to be found in that to which they habitually attend. The Eskimos, for example, can hardly attend to crops of corn; nor can the inhabitants of Arabia attend to seals and polar bears. It is obvious that the Eskimos are what they are by reason of the peculiar type of objects that continually occupy their attention. They are blubber eaters; hunters of seals and fish; users of dog trains. One would hardly expect among them an appreciation of Beethoven or Rembrandt. Why? Because the objects that occupy their attention have no relation whatever to the interests and values out of which these have sprung. The Arabian, on the other hand, is occupied with herds and horses; with desert heat and sand-laden winds. He writes poetry; he sings songs; he builds camps; he carries on feuds;—all in ways that are peculiarly his own, for the simple reason that the objects and situations which occupy his attention are different from those which occupy the attention of any other people.

In the case of peoples, the major attention is largely involuntary; that is, it is chiefly what it has to be by reason of environment and historic conditions. And yet even in the case of peoples, a change in the object of attention can often be brought about which, more or less materially, modifies their behavior. To take an apparently trivial example, the Americans are now a clean-shaven people. There can be little doubt that the vanishing of facial adornment was much hastened by the type of pictures to which the American people were brought to attend in the early years of the century. The "Gibson man" was clean-shaven; and Gibson pictures, because they had humor and were technically

of high quality, came to be the rage.   Other artists followed; until a type of square-jawed, broad-shouldered,
clean-shaven man became the accepted ideal of young American manhood.   To be sure, had the condition of the techno-
logical arts been such that no easy way of shaving was possible, even Gibson pictures would have had no effect.   They
themselves would not have been drawn.   But given easy
deliverance from the barber, Gibson pictures were a powerful means of capturing attention and modifying habits.

We might paraphrase the well-known remark about the
songs of a people:   "Let me capture the attention of a people and I care not who makes their laws."

## Who is it that Wins?

The person who can capture and hold attention is the
person who can effectively influence human behavior.
What, we may ask, is a failure in life?   Obviously, it is
a person without influence; one to whom no one attends:—
the inventor who can persuade no one of the value of his
device; the merchant who cannot attract enough customers
into his store; the teacher whose pupils whistle or stamp or
play tricks while he tries to capture their attention; the poet
who writes reams of verse which no one will accept.

Woodrow Wilson captured the attention of Europe for
a time; captured and held the attention of his own people.
Then Wilson disappeared into secret session.   Attention
wavered.   Other stimuli were brought to bear.   The issue
was fogged.   Wilson emerged a defeated man.

Americans are at present indifferent or actively hostile to
entering the League of Nations.   Why?   Because for a
number of decades they have learned to attend to a certain

other idea: "no entangling alliances." Full, wholehearted
attention to a plan for internationalizing the world apparently cannot be secured as long as the attention holds to
an idea which is supposedly antagonistic. Two courses are
open; either to prove quite clearly that the doctrine of "no
entangling alliances" is not antagonistic to the idea of a
League of Nations; or to prove that the need of internationalization is so tragically pressing as to make it impossible for Americans not to attend. Neither of these ways
of capturing the attention of the American people has as
yet been successful. And therefore the League still goes
a-begging.

### The Kinetic Technique

How, now, does one capture attention? There are a
number of basic considerations. In the first place, suppose
one tries to hold one's attention immovably to a dot on the
wall. It is quite impossible. The eyes insist upon wandering. In fact, if the attention is held for very long, there is
every likelihood that one will induce in oneself a state of
hypnosis. One will, in short, have put his waking, vari-
ously attending mind to sleep.

There must, in other words, be *movement* if we are to
hold attention for very long. Hence, if one wishes to capture and hold another person's attention, he must be sure
that what he offers by way of stimulus moves. We might
call this the *kinetic* requirement—perhaps the most fundamental of all requirements.

One walks down the street and comes upon a crowd gathered about a shop window. One may take a safe wager
that something is happening there. A girl is writing with a

fountain pen; or a young man is demonstrating patent neck-ties. Doubtless it is all of a piece with the primitive curi-osity in us which responds instantly to a change of condi-tion—the rustling of a leaf, the dropping of a twig. "What is happening?" or "What is going to happen?" ( If one can stir either of these questions in the minds of people —students or prospective customers, or voters, etc.—he has in so far captured their attention. )

It is for this reason that a story almost invariably holds us. The story obviously moves. Something is happening; and we wish to know the outcome. Nor is the story just a rambling movement—unless it is a poor story. It is move-ment *towards*. It carries us along—*to something*.

## The Chase Technique

It is not, let us repeat, mere movement which captures and holds attention. It is dramatic movement. It is movement *towards* something; but also, it is movement which cannot in all its details be predicted. The move-ment which can be infallibly predicted soon bores us. In front of one of the dance halls in New York is an electric figure of a man and woman doing their dance steps. The movements are always the same. The light snaps on and snaps off in precisely identical ways. Only a moron could continue to stare fascinated at that sign.

Unpredictability, then, is one of the chief ingredients of attractiveness—in story, essay, drama, in human beings. We know, of course, that the human being whose every act can be foretold—the wife who infallibly uses the same phrases; the husband who, with exact precision, tells the same stories—is a bore. Success of personality consists at least—if we may so phrase it—in "keeping people guessing."

Listen to the dull speaker. Does he keep his audience wondering? Or do they not already see the tiresome path he has laid out for himself, along which he will dutifully tread? Or, even if they do not know the long path he will take, has he aroused them even to wish to know how and to what end he will proceed?

We have the impulse of the hunt deeply in us. We love to be after a quarry. He who presents an idea, therefore, had best present it as a quarry if he wishes to capture his audience. Just to hand out the idea is too mild a procedure. Therein lies the weakness of many a lecturer. He tells things, one after the other. After a while, the surfeited audience goes to sleep. He does not get them chasing after ideas.

Woodrow Wilson did not set the Americans—Congress and the rest—chasing after the idea of a League of Nations. He handed it to them. And they handed it back!

Much of the weakness of our educational methods lies in the absence of the "chase" technique. Students are assigned so much to learn. They learn, but under protest and with wandering minds. The more progressive schools now increasingly utilize the "chase" technique. The student is induced to run down a quarry, either by himself or with a group of his fellows. A lesson, then, is not something to be learned. It is something to be captured. Where such a method is employed, there is no difficulty about securing the attention of the students. We may take the Dalton method as an example, where a week's assignment is given to each child, and where the child is permitted to take up the work in any order or manner he pleases. I once asked one small English girl how she liked the method. "It's fine," she said.  "You can figger things out for yourself when you're on your own."  The chase!  As one sits among those children, one sees no lack of attention.  There is, indeed, a concentration that is wholly thrilling!

### Like Begets Like

But it is not enough to get attention.  A rowdy can do that.  What kind of attention do we wish to attract?  "It is what people are that gets across, not what they try to inculcate," writes Miss Colcord.[1]  Our minds are like vibrating strings.  If the A string on my violin is set vibrating, it will set A vibrations going in my piano.  If one comes to an audience with gloom on his face, one can hardly expect to arouse much pleasant anticipation.

Like begets like.  It is most important, therefore, that the person who wishes to influence others should ask himself in what ways he is unconsciously influencing them himself—by his appearance, his voice, his manner, his attitude. For we influence very largely in ways far more subtle than we suspect.  We shake hands; and instantly we are condemned.  Too limp!  We speak with raspy, querulous voice; and our auditor is all on edge to get us out of the room.  We make a timid approach; and we are turned down flat.  We make a boastful approach; and we arouse the bristling egoism of our listener.  We proceed with a frank, cheerful manner; and we get frank cheerfulness in return.

There is nothing, apparently, that parents and teachers

[1] "The Fabric of Family Life"; by Joanna C. Colcord.  *The Family*: Nov. 1924.

need more deeply to learn.   Parents and teachers have this advantage over business men: their prospects are completely at their mercy.   If the parents had to win their children; if they were in danger of losing their custom, we should doubtless have a vast improvement in our homes in the tone of voice and manners used towards our children. There are no places on this earth where more wretched techniques are used for influencing human behavior.   And since, "as the twig is bent, so the tree grows," there is a large indictment to be placed against the home.

But so, also, is the indictment to be placed against the school.   Querulous, raspy teachers, irritable, domineering, unjust—they bring out in children those qualities with which our social life can most easily dispense.

We capture attention, then, by what we are.   What kind of attention do we wish to capture?   Interest, frank approval, enthusiasm?   Then there must be in us the qualities that elicit these responses.

We might call this the *homeogenic* technique.   If we wish one kind of attention, and get another, it is probably due to the fact that we have given no thought to those qualities in us which subtly awaken in our audience the very responses—the unfortunate responses—which are akin to our own manner and attitude.

## Yes-Response Technique

The canvasser rings the doorbell.   The door is opened by a suspicious lady-of-the-house.   The canvasser lifts his hat.   "Would you like to buy an illustrated History of the World?" he asks.   "No!"   And the door slams.

House to house canvassing is perhaps the lowest estate

to which man can fall; nevertheless in the above there is a psychological lesson. A "No" response is a most difficult handicap to overcome. When a person has said "No," all his pride of personality demands that he remain consistent with himself. He may later feel that the "No" was ill-advised; nevertheless, there is his precious pride to consider! Once having said a thing, he must stick to it.

Hence it is of the very greatest importance that we start a person in the affirmative direction. A wiser canvasser rings the doorbell. An equally suspicious lady-of-the-house opens. The canvasser lifts his hat. "This is Mrs. Armstrong?"

Scowlingly—"Yes."

"I understand, Mrs. Armstrong, that you have several children in school."

Suspiciously—"Yes."

"And of course they have much home work to do?"

Almost with a sigh—"Yes."

"That always requires a good deal of work with reference books, doesn't it—hunting things up, and so on? And of course we don't want our children running out to the library every night . . . better for them to have all these materials at home." Etc., etc.

We do not guarantee the sale. But that second canvasser is destined to go far! He has captured the secret of getting, at the outset, a number of "yes-responses." He has thereby set the psychological processes of his listener moving in the affirmative direction. It is like the movement of a billiard ball. Propel it in one direction and it takes some force to deflect it; far more force to send it back in the opposite direction.

The psychological patterns here are quite clear. When

a person says "No" and really means it, he is doing far
more than saying a word of two letters.  His entire organism—glandular, nervous, muscular—gathers itself together into a condition of rejection.  There is, usually in
minute but sometimes in observable degree, a physical withdrawal, or readiness for withdrawal.  The whole neuro-
muscular system, in short, sets itself on guard against acceptance.  Where, on the contrary, a person says "Yes,"
none of the withdrawing activities take place.  The organism is in a forward-moving, accepting, open attitude.
Hence the more "Yesses" we can, at the very outset, induce, the more likely we are to succeed in capturing the
attention for our ultimate proposal.

It is a very simple technique—this Yes-Response.  And
yet how much neglected!  It often seems as if people get
a sense of their own importance by antagonizing at the
outset.  The radical comes into a conference with his conservative brethren; and immediately he must make them
furious!  What, as a matter of fact, is the good of it?
If he simply does it in order to get some pleasure out of
it for himself, he may be pardoned.  But if he expects to
achieve something, he is only psychologically stupid.

Get a student to say "No" at the beginning, or a customer, child, husband, or wife, and it takes the wisdom
and the patience of angels to transform that bristling negative into an affirmative.

### Putting-It-Up-To-You Technique

Our chief object in capturing attention, as we have indicated, is to "start something going" in the listener or be-
holder.  Here is a pamphlet on "Habit Training for Chil-

dren." It asks questions: "Does your child fuss about his food?" "Is your child jealous?" "Does your child have temper tantrums?" Suppose these questions had been put in the form of positive statements: "Many children fuss about their food." "Many children are jealous." "Many children have temper tantrums." How mild and uninteresting!

But does *your* child have temper tantrums? Ah, that is different! Here is something aimed directly at *you*. You are asked a question. You are expected to reply. *Does* your child have temper tantrums? Why it surely does. What about it?

And so you ask a question in turn. You have therefore been induced to do two things—to answer a question and to ask one. Note the difference in attention-arousing value between the following two versions of the same idea:

*"Nervousness"*                                    *cause others*

"Do I literally cause my child to be nervous? By—
Being nervous myself?
Telling him about it so I may have his sympathy?
Constantly reminding him how nervous he is?
Telling other people in his presence how nervous and queer and odd he is?
Worrying over his health and habits?
Coddling him physically and mentally?
Denying him independence of thought and action?
Expecting too much from him and driving him all the time?"

Compare the above with the following:

"From early infancy some children are 'nervous.' They are fussy, irritable babies; delicate, sensitive, easily upset children; they become easily flustered, excitable adults. Such children demand the utmost in placidity and patience from their parents.

"Most 'nervous' children are, however, the product of the management given them. Their parents do all or some of the things listed above. Nervous parents expect, and so cause, nervous children. They constantly remind the child of this. In their own nervousness they set an example—and it usually is imitated. They communicate their worries to the child, who increases them many fold. Etc."

The latter version uses the expository method. It tells the reader something. The trouble with the expository method is that the sense of superiority is all on the side of the expositor. It is he who is telling. Now, let the expositor ask you a question—not for quizzing's sake, but because he is interested to know your answer. The implication is that you can answer it. The situation is therefore reversed. It is you, now, who are momentarily the superior. The speaker is deferring to you.

We might indicate this by a diagram:

*Expository Method*
 Speaker      +        active          ↓
 Listener     —        receptive

*Putting-it-up-to-you Method*
 Speaker   ( + — )     actively receptive    ↓ ↑
 Listener  ( — + )     receptively active    ↓ ↑

In the expository method, therefore, the movement, as the arrow indicates, is altogether in one direction—from speaker to listener. The listener therefore is merely receptive. In the putting-it-up-to-you method, the movement is in both directions. Both speaker and listener are active and receptive.

To refer again to the Dalton method of teaching, the spirit is essentially that of putting-it-up-to-you. "Can you manage your own time, or must we manage it for you?" The old fashioned expository method says: "This is what we are telling you. At nine o'clock you do arithmetic; at nine-thirty, grammar."

### "Challenge" Technique

A minister preached Sunday after Sunday to a fairly good-sized and attentive audience. Then, one day, he threw down the gage of battle—not to his audience, but to a fellow minister. He challenged him to a public debate. The debate was held to a crowded house and was reported as first page news in the newspapers. The challenging minister lost the decision of the judges; but his plucky, clever speech won him a wide public adherence. Thereafter seats in his church were at a premium!

Ghandi flings a challenge to the British Empire and becomes a figure of foremost interest in the world.

We all wish, quite rightly, to get rid of the stupid futility of war; but we still respond to a fight. All new ideas fight with the old. All changes in organization, all modifications of practice mean that a new method either wholly or partially ousts an old. That is what progress means.

That is why we read Wells' "Outline of History" with eagerness. We know that Wells is fighting old traditions of history writing. That is why we read James Harvey Robinson's "Mind in the Making." That is why, a number of years ago, we responded to William James' "Pragmatism." We may not have known much about phi-

losophy. That did not matter. Here was a genial, belli-
cose, American professor who was hopping about delightedly, delivering body blows at the solemn thing that was
called philosophy. That is why "Behaviorism" gets its
hold upon most people. It is a "fight against;" and therefore it has every promise of stirring up an interesting time.

"A man going into a new line of business often needs
to excite some competition before he can get his own business moving, and the two competing get more than double
the business one could get." [1]

Challenge, then, is powerful as an attention-arousing
technique. But challenge must be fair or it misses the
mark. Note the following from an article called "Junk":
"I am convinced that up to this month of May, in the year
of our Lord 1923, all philosophy, all theology, all ethics
and all moral science, most sociology, all political science,
the greater part of history, most economics, most law and
pedagogics, and a large part of psychology—foot up to
just so much junk."

My own instant inclination is to respond with the good
American word "bunk"! Here is a challenge indeed, but
one which obviously overshoots the mark. A good deal of
this kind of exaggerated challenge is the stock-in-trade of
the Smart-Aleck type of writer. He knows it all! Everything before him is really quite negligible! And as for the
poor creature we call the Public——!

Note the modesty and yet the fine firmness with which
John Dewey issues his challenge in his little book: *The
Reconstruction of Philosophy*. "Being invited to lecture
at the Imperial University of Japan . . . I attempted an

---

[1] Cody, Sherwin. *How to Deal with Human Nature in Business;* p. 43.
Funk & Wagnalls.

interpretation of the reconstruction of ideas and ways of thought now going on in philosophy." He might have done it in this way: "Philosophy has been on the wrong track for a good many years. It is time, now, that it be put on the right track. In the following pages, I am going to indicate what new direction philosophy must take if it is to be rescued from its present lamentable futility."

Note the insufferable egotism of the latter; its assumption that the writer is doing it all!

Challenge, therefore, must be fair. It must show good sportsmanship. It must give even the opponent his due. But above all, it is most powerful when it enlists others in the fight. Not, "Come, see me wipe up the earth with this false prophet;" but rather, "Come, let's join in the fight."

The very essence of all power to influence lies in the ability to get the other person to participate. The mind that can do that has a powerful leverage on his human world.

### The Magic of the New

Little need be said about the very real effectiveness of having something to offer that is new. The new psychology, the new education, new schools, the latest styles, the newest plays. To indicate at once that what one is offering is not antiquated, or out-of-date, or already-well-known is to have at the start a strong hold on the attention. And yet, what is offered can easily be too new. Our understanding and acceptance of anything is conditioned by what we already have in our consciousness—by what the older psychologists called our "apperception mass." Introduce something that has no connection whatever with our past experience and we are not interested—for example, speak

of the electronic theory of atoms to an Andamanese Is-
lander; or read Gertrude Stein's poetry to persons for
whom poetry means something that has meaning! The
psychological rule is that there must always be a large
ingredient of the *familiar in the unfamiliar*.

This is the reason why so many proposals for economic
reconstruction fail to convince the man-in-the-street. They
seem to him like a complete overturn of all that has been
secure and familiar. The wise proponent of a new idea
will make sure that the new is sufficiently tied to the old
to be at least interesting as well as acceptable.

Of course, the new may disappoint us. Not every flower
is born to blush in pride. The exultantly new may have
its day and cease to be. Nevertheless—granting that we
are fairly critical in our appraisals—it is all to the good
to keep a sharp lookout for what is new—new to our children, new to our wedded mates, new to our customers and
our audiences. There is magic in the new that never grows
old—until the new itself grows old!

## Respect the Attention Limits

Here is a small grocer. He is industrious, honest, pains-
taking; but one suspects that he will never be anything but
a small grocer. There are a number of reasons why.
The most obvious is this: his windows and store are plas-
tered over with all manner of signs. Special sale of this;
so much a dozen for this; best brand of that; etc. So
many signs that one looks at none of them. The grocer
has not learned the most elementary principle of the art
of business, that to capture the public one must draw their
attention to a focus.

The artist—whether pictorial or musical or dramatic—knows that. A picture cannot have just a variety of beautiful things in it. It must capture the eye and lead it infallibly to one spot. There must, in short, be a dominant element in the composition.

Offer the attention too much; and it gets nothing, as the following fable indicates:

### The Monkey and the Nuts.[1]

A monkey (Aesop speaking) tried to take a handful of nuts from a small-necked jar, but he grabbed too large a handful and couldn't get his hand out, nor did he until he dropped some of the nuts.

The attempt to grab too much of the public's attention often makes a monkey of what might be a good advertisement.

A layout is made of a simple, strong, effective page. But the president wants another display line, the production manager wants the trade mark larger, the secretary wants the package in, the sales manager wants a paragraph addressed to dealers, the advertising manager thinks the slogan should go at the top of the ad, the treasurer insists on smaller space and the branch managers want the addresses of all the branches.

A good handful.

Only the neck of the jar is exactly as large as the public's interest—and no larger.

To get your hand out, to get the public to look at and absorb any of the advertisement, you must drop a few nuts.

### Watch People

With that admonition—"Respect the attention limits"—we close this chapter, lest we ourselves overstep the very rules we have laid down for others.

[1] Published by Calkins and Holden, Advertising Agents, 247 Park Ave., New York.

It will be a worthwhile enterprise for the reader to take the suggestions developed above and watch in how far they are observed in lectures, sermons, writings, parental admonitions, pedagogical techniques, selling methods, etc. It is rather important that one accustom oneself to this kind of psychological observation. It is almost better than observing oneself. For one can be at least drastically honest about the weaknesses of others!

Observing, then, a lecturer, writer, teacher, salesman, one might ask: Does the presentation *move?* Do I feel that I am being carried along? Am I being lulled into somnolence because nothing, apparently, is happening? (Kinetic Technique)

Is it moving towards something? Is my expectation keenly aroused? Am I all on "tenterhooks" to know what the outcome is to be? Or do I already see the end in the beginning? Has the whole story been given away? Is there a great deal of repetition; or an aimless going around in circles? (The Chase Technique)

Am I strongly irritated by something in the manner or attitude of the speaker or writer or salesman? Does his own lack of enthusiasm strike me cold? Does his boastfulness rouse my antagonism? Is he limp? Is he insincere? Is he a conceited coxcomb? (Homeogenic Technique)

Is the first response evoked a negative one? Am I being rubbed the wrong way? Or is the person first winning my approval, leading me through successive affirmations to an ultimate agreement with his main point? (Yes-Response Technique)

Am I pleasantly aroused by the fighting quality of the speaker or writer, etc.? Does he make me feel like joining in the fight? Or is he unfair? Boastful? Does he think he is doing it all himself? Is he a Smart-Aleck? (Challenge Technique)

Is there anything new in this sermon or speech or writing? Is it so new that I cannot make head nor tail of it? Or is the new cleverly linked on with what I already know and approve? (Novelty Technique)

Am I being deluged with facts? Do my ears buzz with endless details? Do I feel like a lost babe in the woods? Or does one dominant point stand out so clearly that I shall not forget it? (Respect-The-Attention-Limits)

Look for these simple matters of technique. There are revelations in store for the alert observer!

# CHAPTER II

## THE APPEAL TO WANTS

"If you turn to the 'Great Didactic'," writes Dr. Keatinge,[1] "the remarkable treatise on education written by Comenius in the seventeenth century, you will find an attitude towards the subject of attention that is characteristic of the older psychology. Comenius describes his ideal classroom. The boys in it sit in rows in a large room. It makes no difference what their number is, for Comenius believed that if a teacher's method was a sound one, one teacher could teach an unlimited number of boys. The teacher sits on a raised platform at the end of the room, and the boys, in the words of Comenius, 'place their attention like a wide-mouthed phial beneath the words of wisdom that flow from his lips!' Here you have the doctrine of the mind as merely passive and receptive. It makes little difference whether the analogy of a wide-mouthed phial is used, the pupils' mug being filled from the teacher's jug, or that of a blank sheet on which the teacher inscribes the subject matter of instruction. In either case the implication is the same, that of an inert mind which is operated on by external stimuli."

Modern psychology, with its doctrine of original impulses, has turned completely away from this older theory

[1] *Psychology and Education.* In *Psychology and the Sciences;* edited by William Brown, p. 114. A. and C. Black, London.

of the inert and receptive mind. Hence the "pouring in" technique, whether in the schools, the home, politics, or in any other relationship, is being increasingly discredited.

"Give the people the facts" has been a slogan much in use by persons interested in better politics. But giving the people the facts, has been, for the most part, an enterprise fraught with a surprising amount of disappointment. Usually when that technique has been used, something has been unaccountably missing. What is it that has been missing?

So, likewise, something is missing when parents conscientiously "instruct" their children, admonish them, pour into them the wisdom of the older generation. The little mugs move out from under the solemn jugs!

The mere giving of information, apparently, will not answer. What further is needed? "Imagine," continues Dr. Keatinge, "that you are reading an interesting novel and *ex hypothesi* are absorbed in it; what are the conditions and the nature of your mental process? You have just read the following passage: 'My God!' he said in a hushed and trembling whisper, and she gave no sign that she heard. She might have fainted but that her eyes glittered out of the shadow straight and steadily into his!' Why, instead of leaving off, do you go on to read the paragraph that follows? Because you want something. You want to know if she actually had heard, if she actually did faint and how long her eyes continued to glitter into his. Supposing these wants to be satisfied, do you continue to read or do you not? If the novel is well constructed, you do not lay it down at the conclusion of the short episode; you continue to the end of the chapter. The reason is that another want has asserted itself, the want to know how the sub-plot, with which the chapter is concerned, ends.   When you have finished the chapter, do you throw the book away? *Ex hypothesi* you do not.   Another want that has been lurking in the background makes itself felt, the want to know how the problem with which the novel began is solved in the last chapter.   You know the way in which stories of a certain type begin.   The scene is at Monte Carlo.   The hero and a friend drive to a well-known restaurant.   The hero goes in to see if there is any room, and on returning to the taxi, finds his friend has gone, and in his place a lady in evening dress, stabbed to the heart.   Here at once is formed the want which carries you through the sleepier portions of the story, the want to know how the mystery is cleared up at last.   'What I like about your stories, old man,' says one character to another in a recent American novel, 'is that the hero never grabs the girl till the last page.'   In other words the want is kept going to the end."

We capture attention when what we say or do is in response to people's *wants*.   There, apparently, is at least a clue!

## When Facts are Wanted

And that, apparently, is why so much "fact giving" is usually without avail.   People do not want facts—for the facts' sake.   True, if they want a particular thing badly, they will want the facts.   The assumption of the fact-givers is that if the facts are supplied, people will want what the facts indicate.   Nothing is psychologically farther from the truth.   Give a boy a pile of facts about health.   He is quite indifferent.   But suppose he wants badly to win the mile race. He will go into training and simply lap up the facts about health!

During the last election in America a vigorous campaign was carried on to get people to vote against the predatory interests. The campaign was unsuccessful; for the people overwhelmingly voted to return the party that had been denounced as the aider and abettor of the predatory interests. Why was this? One would suppose that good citizens would wish to keep the country safe from marauders. As a matter of fact, while, in a kind of a vague way, they doubtless wanted that, there was something which they wanted far more immediately, far more fervently. They wanted prosperity. Prosperity was something which was of immediate interest to everybody. The predatory interests might be bad; but they were very distant; they made practically no difference to one's grocery store or butcher shop.

The party which won the election talked consistently and persistently to that vividly felt and universal want. Its most vigorous efforts were directed toward showing that the victory of the anti-predatory party would mean such a panic in business as would bring about depression and business failures—disaster for everybody.

We are not interested—here at least—in the relative values of these two political positions. The defeat of the anti-predatory party may or may not have been unfortunate. But whether it was or was not, there can be no doubt whatever that the more effective psychological technique triumphed.

Of course, we are now opening ourselves to grave objections. To one who disapproves of the above-mentioned political victory, it will doubtless seem highly reprehensible that "the people" permitted their more immediate personal want for prosperity to take precedence in a situation apparently fraught with grave danger to the country. "The people should have had a finer sense of citizenship." Perhaps. But, one may properly ask, how are they to be trained to the type of want which is the sign of a finer, more impersonal sense of citizenship? By scolding them? Scolding makes the scolder feel comfortably superior; but does it ever really accomplish its end?

As a matter of fact, people will inevitably respond to the wants that seem to them the most important. The problem of the political progressive is to build up wants that are now felt only indifferently into wants that are vivid and clamorous.

### But What of the Appeal to Reason?

But the defender of reason now objects. We ought not to demean ourselves by appealing to people's wants. What people want may be stupid or childish or positively mischievous. What we ought to appeal to is their reason.

Thus many parents say, "My boy, I am telling you this for your own good. You may not believe me now—you may go your own gait; but some day, some day, my boy"—etc. So teachers solemnly proclaim: "I know you don't like all this; but you've got to learn it anyway. It's for your good." This is the high "intellectual discipline" way. And so, again, political purists say: "You're not interested in your city's politics? My dear man, it's your *duty* to be interested." The political purist seems never to think that perhaps it is somebody's duty—his own, no doubt —to make politics worth being interested in; to give them such vitality and pertinence that citizens will *want* to attend to them as enthusiastically as they attend to golf or bridge.

What is there in this contention that we ought to appeal to the reason of people rather than to their wants? As a matter of fact there is a great deal in it; only it is unfortunately expressed. It seems to oppose the "reason" of people to their "wants." But no appeal to reason *that is not also an appeal to a want* can ever be effective.

What is really meant is this: we all have our narrower, more immediate wants, the wants which may seem, at the moment, to have the most pressing claim upon us, but which, in reality, are far less important to us than other, more vaguely felt wants. The trouble with many of us is that the more immediate, really less important wants absorb our attention and get our instant reaction; while the less immediate, but really more important wants are scarcely attended to. Thus it is really far more important that a man's country be secure than that he should have a particular automobile. Usually, however, it is the automobile that gets his most absorbed attention.

An appeal to a man's reason, then, means making vivid to him one of his wider, really more fundamental but less insistent wants. That happened, of course, during the last war. Men were swept out of their more immediate concerns into a concern that ordinarily did not concern them—the relation between their nation and certain other nations of the world. So, in like manner, when the economic revolutionist appeals to people's reason, he tries to get them to feel vividly that their deepest concern—their most important want—is for an economic system which will bring to them far more than they now can receive.

The phrase, appeal to reason, is a misleading one when it

is taken to mean—as it often is—that "giving reasons for things" is enough—giving reasons to a child, or to a student or to a voter.   Our chief task, really, is to arouse the more important but slumbering wants into action.

### Some Fundamental Wants

What, now, are some of the fundamental wants to which effective appeal can be made?   It is most instructive in this connection, to watch the appeals that advertisers make. The advertiser wishes to influence human behavior.   He wishes people, in short, to change their habits to the extent of purchasing what he has for sale.   If he is a skilled advertiser, he does not *tell* people that they *ought* to buy his article—as a father tells his children that they ought to do thus and so, etc.   What he does is to induce them to want to buy his article—as a father ought to induce his children to want to do what he wishes them to do.   The advertiser knows that if he can make the person who sees his advertisement feel a particular want with sufficient strength the sale is made.   He does not have to argue.   If only parents could be clever enough to arouse wants and so avoid the necessity for arguing!

In this respect, the advertiser, despite all the hard things we have to say of him, is a pioneer in psychological technique.

### Comfort, Appetites and Sex

Note how the advertiser does it.   Here is the picture of a man leaning back in a comfortable chair, one elbow on the arm of the chair, the other resting on his crossed knee.   A cigarette is between his fingers, a smile of satisfaction on his face. Above him is the caption: "What a whale of a difference just a few cents make!" It is the picture of solid comfort, solid enjoyment! Now, what we all want—other things being equal—is just that. Hence the power of such appeals to comfort and appetite. It is not the highest type of appeal, no doubt; but it has its place.

Another obvious want which we all have, when we are old enough, is sex satisfaction, in any of its multitude of forms. Here is an advertisement: "No More Wall-flowers!" and the picture of a dancing couple, with the indication that a four-lesson course will make one a popular dancer for almost nothing! We may deplore the exaggeration of such an advertisement. Let us, however, note its appeal to a fundamental want. We want to be popular in social gatherings. Another advertisement is headed: "Irresistible!" and shows the picture of a young man playing a saxophone with an admiring young lady standing by his side, her hand upon his shoulder. "You can be expected, anticipated, welcomed with open arms. You can be a favorite at parties, dances and other social affairs." Do you want to be a favorite? Of course you do! And so if you are the young man you are tempted to buy the saxophone and take the lessons.

Again, "Pebeco not only makes your smile lovelier, it keeps your teeth strong and safe." The important thing to the young lady looking up into the face of the Arrow Collar young man is that Pebeco is making her smile lovelier. Do we want to be lovely—at least those of us who are women? We do. And so the sale of dentifrices increases.

Now we need not be cynical. These are all perfectly

wholesome human wants. A young lady who did not care
to be lovely might stubbornly refuse to brush her teeth.
A young bluestocking might prefer to dance like a stick just
to prove her high intellectuality; but the world would not
necessarily be the better for that. What makes us a bit
angry about advertisers is not that they appeal to meretricious wants, but that they often appeal to perfectly wholesome wants in meretricious ways. Compare for example
the advertising of lipsticks and rouge with the advertising
of a good soap under the caption: "Keep that schoolgirl
complexion." The difference between them is that, appealing to the same wholesome want—the possession of a beautiful complexion—the first suggests a means of securing the
end which may easily be doubted; whereas the second suggests a means that is unquestionably wholesome.

It is to be noted, in the above cases listed under "sex
satisfaction" that the appeal is never to a single want.
Take the "No More Wallflower" advertisement. If you
do not wish to be a wallflower, it is not only because you
desire the subtle sex satisfaction of dancing. You desire
the sociability of the dance. You also desire the feeling
of being competent in a social undertaking. Furthermore,
you desire to be regarded as even a little more skilled than
the others. And besides all that you wish the sheer joy of
rhythmic bodily movement. Thus the appeal is powerful
because it is made not to one but to a group of fundamental
wants.

### Affectionate Devotion

Here, again, are two pictures that make an appeal to an
identical want. In the first, a boy stands in the forefront,
grinning the full grin of a delighted twelve-year-old. He

has a repeating rifle in his hands. The caption reads, "The Biggest Day in Your Boy's Life." The appeal of the advertisement is not to the boy but to the parent of the boy—affection, comradeship, the want to make one's child happy. "Sure," says the father, "I remember how it was when I was a boy. We'll get the kid one for Christmas." In a second picture, a young woman is seated at a table reading a document. She is sad of face; but not too sad. A little bobbed-haired daughter is standing near her. The caption reads: "Everything Depended on What She Found. Suddenly and Without Warning it Had Come." When the man has read through the story, he remembers with a clutch at his affections, that he has not yet taken out life insurance! Here is a fundamental want, to protect and bring happiness to those we love.

In no one of these cases, be it noted, have we referred to "instincts." There is much controversy among psychologists as to what precisely "instincts" are or whether they are at all. There can, however, be no doubt that, partly as a result of our inborn impulses—which we unquestionably have—partly as a result of our socially acquired habits and valuations, there are a multitude of wants which we feel deeply and persistently, the appeal to which is, as a matter of fact, the *only* successful way in which any of us can be induced to do anything at all.

### Surplus Energy, Play

Here is an advertisement of a well-known breakfast food. A father and his small son are running gaily down the snow-swept road. One can feel the crispness of the air; the pounding beat of the rich red blood. The caption

reads: "That Extra Energy! And precious Golden
Years!" The appeal is to what is almost as fundamental
as anything in us—the want for play and for the buoyant
health that makes play possible. No one wants illness,
depression, boredom. If work can be made into play, so
much the more powerful is its appeal.

## Security

Of quite a different and yet equally fundamental nature
is the appeal to one's fears. We are biologically as well
as psychologically conditioned to avoid danger. Where
the danger is not too great, we may seek it in the spirit of
adventure—which indicates another want, as in hunting,
exploration, gambling, etc. But normally danger is something to be avoided. So we advertise windshields for
automobiles: "He didn't see the danger in time to avoid
it. And so—a lifetime of regret!" A lock: "Foils the
Auto Thief." A correspondence course: "What Would
I Do if I Lost My Job?" An antiseptic toothpaste:
"Back of Beauty May Lurk Dread Disease!"

## To Own Something

Property is an extension of our personality. A carpenter with a kit of tools can do what a carpenter without a
kit of tools cannot do. An accountant with an adding
machine multiplies his power. A salesman with an automobile can double and treble his territory. A small boy
with a holiday and a dollar in his pocket has the world by
the tail.

The love of money may, indeed, be the root of all evil,
when the love is miserly; but the secure control of the tools

of life is the root of all our fine powers and satisfactions. Hence—despite our squeamishness about materialism—there is something fundamentally wholesome about the appeal: "Get Ready for a Big Pay Job!" "Be an Electrical Expert." If the big pay goes with a job well done, then the pay is simply tools added to tools well used. If the appeal had read: "Be Clever! Learn How to Make Easy Money by Doing the Other Fellow!" we might talk of materialism!

The wish then, to possess, when with the possession goes use, is fundamental and wholesome.

## To Be Efficient

Here is an advertisement with the caption: "Most Men Shave the Wrong Way." The appeal is instant. No one, if he knows it, wishes to do a thing in an inefficient manner. If inefficiency means the expenditure of more effort for smaller returns, it goes counter to the quite fundamental factor of "least effort." No man deliberately tries to put more effort into the accomplishment of a thing than is necessary—unless he is enjoying the effort itself; and then the pleasurable effort is the end sought. Hence the strength of all appeals to the saving of time and energy—filing systems, washing machines, kitchen cabinets, vacuum cleaners, adding machines.

## Social Esteem

Then there is social pride. We live among our fellows. A great part of the satisfaction which we derive comes from the attitude of our fellows towards ourselves. To be looked down upon or pitied or scorned gives us intense pain.

We wish to be looked up to—by somebody; preferably by as many as possible. There is a good deal of sentimental talk about the sin of pride. As a matter of fact the wish to be thought well of, particularly by those of whom we think well, is quite fundamental; and, one might say, it is as civilizing an attitude as we possess. It may take extravagant forms—as in conspicuous display, boasting, extravagant, useless expenditure—but normally it is the stimulus which keeps us up to the mark.

Advertisers, of course, constantly appeal to our feeling for social esteem. Here is the picture of an elegant mansion, with elegant ladies and gentlemen issuing from the door, an automobile awaiting them. The male who precedes the party is quite obviously well satisfied. The reason why? "The Human Desire to Own the Best Suggests the Cadillac."

To be sure there is something about this kind of appeal that makes many of us feel a little dubious—perhaps even furious. Men and women make such fools of themselves, waste so many of the precious energies of life— especially the life of others—in the effort to achieve social distinction! No doubt the process of becoming more civilized is the process of discarding vulgar and wasteful display for the display of qualities that are of fine human value. Nevertheless, even when we have discarded vulgar display, the fundamental wish for social esteem remains. Only, then, we take more pride in our brains than in our Cadillacs.

### Pride in Appearance

Then there is pride in our personal appearance. It can take exaggerated forms; but, fundamentally, it is a worthwhile pride.  To be sure it puts the emphasis upon externals.  And yet it has in it a certain spirit of social good will.  No one loves to see a slattern.  No one rejoices in a pimply face.  There is a satisfaction in a well-groomed figure; a delight in a beautiful skin.  A social group in which no one cares how he or she looks will doubtless be found lacking in many of the social qualities—of courtesy, consideration, ordinary kindliness.  Hence there is a certain wholesomeness as well as power in the appeal to personal appearance.  "Individuality—How Often it Depends on Appropriate Spectacles and Eyeglasses!"  "The Most Beautiful Ankles are Enhanced by Beautifully Fitting Real Silk Hosiery."  "Here's Positive Proof that I Can Grow New Hair."  (There is no virtue in wishing to be bald—although in this case we may well doubt the "positive proof.")  "It's a Fownes—That's All You Need to Know!" (Shapely gloved hands.)

### Cleanliness

Closely allied is the appeal to cleanliness.  Here is the picture of a mother standing before her kitchen stove. The children have burst in from school and have tracked a lot of snow upon the floor.  The mother is quite unperturbed—unusual condition!  Why?  "Brush the snow off, children; it can't hurt mother's new Congoleum Rug!" What an appeal to the housewifely heart!

And so with the thousand and one advertisements of soap and cleansers and spot removers and the rest.  Not a highly intellectual want, indeed; but a powerfully wholesome one!

## In Briefer Mention

We might run on at great length; for the powerful human wants are legion.   Let us simply list a few of the more important.   We want:

Adventure (hunting; exploration; excitement; games);

Travel;

Leadership (emulation; triumph; "being looked up to;" "being an authority");

Novelty (curiosity about the unknown);

Propriety (modesty; good taste; being in style; good form; good manners);

Constructive Achievement (planting a garden; making a radio set; hammering out copper; organizing a company; making an invention; playing the piano);

Conquest (power to overcome—sometimes our fellows; sometimes Nature; sometimes a problem);

Sympathy;

Help for the Weaker;

Humor;

Harmony with our Fellows (Social Ethics);

Harmony with the Universe (Religion).

## Our Subtler Motivation

"Man, forsooth," writes Samuel Butler,[1] "prides himself on his consciousness!  We boast that we differ from the winds and waves and falling stones and plants, which grow they know not why, and from the wandering creatures which go up and down after their prey, as we are pleased to say without the help of reason.   We know so well what

[1] *The Way of All Flesh,* Chap. III.

we are doing ourselves and why we do it, do we not? I fancy that there is some truth in the view being put forward now-a-days, that it is our less conscious thoughts and our less conscious actions, which mainly mould our lives and the lives of those who spring from us."

And, writes Pascal: "The heart has its reasons of which the reason knows nothing."

The student of human nature who thoroughly learns the lesson of our subtler motivation has a fair chance of escaping the arid ineffectiveness of the abstract intellectualist.

In every situation, in short, the human individual is moved by a multitude of wants, of most of which he is not even conscious. The effective teacher, for example, is the one who is sensitively and sympathetically aware of this. But how often the teacher goes to her daily task simply with her head full of "the work for the day." She will teach so much geography; so much arithmetic; so much grammar. She has it all neatly planned out; she is a veritable marvel of pedagogical efficiency! Her object is to cover exactly so much ground. It is seldom that she asks herself whether her young charges really want to cover that ground, or whether, indeed, they can be induced to want it. What are their wants anyway? It does not matter. The curriculum calls for two pages of grammar on Monday morning; and so two pages it must be!

But children do have wants. For example, they have conversation wants. They like to talk to each other. Cannot grammar be taught by appealing to the conversation want? They have superiority wants. Cannot the slips in grammar be detected by members of the class themselves, instead of marked in red ink by the teacher? They have dramatic wants.    Cannot they write plays of their own and mutually correct their errors in speech?

The more progressive trends in education are all in this direction.    "Never teach anything unless you tie it up with a real want in the child's life."

The rule is equally applicable in the home.    The usual situation is that we parents want something done and tell our children to go and do it.    But it is not our wants that should motivate, but theirs.    *We* want them to brush their teeth; *we* want them to take baths; *we* want them to be less noisy; *we* want them to pick up their things; *we* want them —heaven knows how many things *we* want of them.    No wonder the main indoor sport of parenthood is "telling them what to do."

Of course, obedience is a comfortable quality to develope in our children—comfortable for us.    But obviously if we get it by subduing the child—by shouting him down, scolding him into submission, threatening him into quietude— we are hardly laying up treasures for his later social life. We are probably shaping him into timid subservience or into suppressed rebelliousness.

Can we tie up what we want with what our children want?    Let me illustrate the point from one of my own parental experiences.    It was at our summer camp in the mountains.    Being without a maid, we were doing our own work; and we were consequently anxious to induce the three boys to lend a hand in the daily routine.    But, with woods around us and a lake at our door, the hands refused to be loaned.    With breakfast inside them, the boys would be out of the house and away; and father and mother had re- sentfully to straighten out the morning chaos of beds and breakfast dishes, kitchen floor and the melancholy rest.

Besides, teeth were left unpolished, ears in an uncivilized condition. We found ourselves engaged mainly in violent shouting after fleeing youngsters, in angry scolding, and in direful remindings of things to be done and left undone. Here was a beautiful vacation surely going to wreckage! And of course mother and father shook their heads: "Boys are such selfish creatures!" "What they need is a good thrashing."

Then it suddenly occurred to us that perhaps it was we who were at fault. Why should healthy boys be interested in brushing their teeth; in wiping dishes; in sweeping up a kitchen floor? Heaven knows that we ourselves, grown up as we were, were only mildly interested in the first and not at all in the second and third. Quite the contrary!

So the problem suddenly took shape. How could we tie up these uninteresting tasks with something that really gripped the boys? That change of attitude on our part was nine-tenths of the victory. The rest was easy. It took only a little thinking for us to devise for each boy a schedule on which was set down the various morning tasks. Perpendicular lines were drawn and spaces left for checking up the daily performance of each task. A generous bonus was allowed for a week's perfect schedule; graduated payments for lesser degrees of perfection, and so on.

The simple little device worked like a miracle. Next morning, the boys were up and at the checking. There were no more yellings, no more remindings. The vacation was saved; and character building was in full swing!

What was it that did it? Obviously we had appealed to a number of their real wants. Every child wants to earn money and ought to be given the opportunity. Note that in this case they earned it. Every child likes to compete, even with himself (later in life he competes with bogy). But, above all, every child, without knowing it really, wants to be clear about his life's business. Hitherto we had given their immature minds no clear grasp of their morning's program. We had forgotten that a child's mind does not organize itself as easily as does an adult's. Now, at last, on a small sheet of paper, they could see all that was expected of them; see it in due order; and grasp it as a whole.

I know of no point of view more effectively transforming, both for parents and children, than this one of trying to appeal to real and legitimate wants. It marks the difference between intelligent experimentation, intelligent devising of effective means, and a stupid adherence to old ways, with a whining despair at the difficulties of parenthood.

### The Older Technique of Duty

The chief problem, of course, in the training of children is to get them to want what is really worth the wanting. Children want many things which are of quite inferior value. In this, no doubt, they are not altogether unlike their elders. The problem of child training is to give opportunity for the more worthwhile wants to grow strong and multiply.

In the past generation, the concept of duty was the whip that was applied to us. As children, we had no love for duty. Often, we hated it with all the bitterness of our souls. "Now, Jane, you know it is your duty to take care of your little brother;" or, "Now, Thomas, don't whine. It's your duty to go to Sunday School." "It's your duty to practice;" "Your duty to be kind." We hated it at first; but as we gradually became conditioned to it, there often

grew up a kind of grim love for duty.  We sacrificed ourselves with a bitter pleasure; we did what we did not like to
do for the sake of what we felt we ought to do.

There was something severely strong about this.  Many
of us feel that the present generation, brought up without
the stern sense of duty, is weak and willful.  Perhaps.  But
the older training was not without its dangers.  It tended,
often, to develope a kind of  bigoted self congratulation.
"Look at me!  I don't like to do this.  But I'm strong—
strong enough to make myself miserable for duty's sake!"
It was, therefore, in large measure, a breeder of moral
egotism.  Also, it easily led to intolerance.  "This is your
duty, young man.  Do it!"  And that was the last word.
The stern eye and the unrelenting heart!  Worse than all
this, it too often made for hypocrisy.  "I know it is hard
on you and the children, my dear, but my duty calls me,"
and the man went off to his adventure with a sorrowful face
and a glad heart.

Morally as well as psychologically, the training of children by emphasis upon their duty was bad because it was a
training by compulsion rather than by free inner development.  The duty, in the first instance, was never something
willed by the child; it was something imposed from without.
The child might, indeed, be battered into acceptance; it might
even, in the end, become so habituated to the duty as to feel
it as its own.   But in the process, it tended to lose that fine
strength of personality which comes from a free choosing
and a self-determined carrying out of one's chosen end.

If many of our present generation of young people are,
indeed, weak and willful, it is doubtless because we of the
older generation have not substituted for the severe, external discipline of duty the subtler, but far more powerful

discipline of an inner choice of that which is really worth the choosing. We have not yet learned, in short, how to help our children organize their wants; how to estimate their relative values. Brought up ourselves on the easy duty technique—"Do this and do that"—we are altogether at a loss in this new situation. How, as a matter of fact, does one get a child to want to do the right, the fine thing? That is a most difficult problem. It is infinitely easier to say, "Do it." Most of us, therefore, adopt the easier way.

The appeal to wants, then, presupposes, first of all, an understanding of the fine, worthwhile wants that *can* be aroused in children; and secondly, an intelligence capable of opening up opportunities and devising situations which will arouse those wants. The parent, in short, is to be, in the main, not a giver-of-commands but an opener-up-of-opportunities. In a later chapter, we shall discuss more in detail how this task is to be accomplished. At this point we wish simply to emphasize the basic difference between the duty technique, which operates by compulsion and from without, and the appeal-to-wants technique, which operates by intelligent suggestion and from within. The latter, although far more difficult of application, is without any question, psychologically and morally the superior.

## Summary

"No appeal to a reason that is not also an appeal to a want is ever effective." That ought to dispose of a good deal of futile arguing. It ought to put an end to most of the angry denunciation and bitter sarcasm wherewith we infuriate each other. It ought to mend the ways of the preaching parent, the expostulating, scolding parent. It ought to indicate to the arid pedagogue a way of escape from his aridity.    And finally, it ought to suggest to the earnest political reformer more effective techniques for capturing and holding that difficult, but psychologically quite normal entity called "the people."

Thought (reason) is, at bottom, an instrument of action; and action, whatever it may be, springs out of what we fundamentally desire.    There is, indeed, a place in life—a most important place—for pure thought—thought, that is, which has no interest in immediate action.    But for the most part, thought (reason) is, for us, an instrument of exploration; it enables us to see more clearly where we are going, and how we may best go.    But where do we actually wish to go?    If we are sure of that, then we gladly enough busy ourselves to find ideas which point the path and clear the way.

Hence, as we have seen, the arguer must first arouse in his respondent a real want to know what is being argued about, a real wish to understand, or his argumentation is only words.    The trouble with most arguers is that they are too much in a hurry to unload *themselves*.    They quite forget that, preliminary to the unloading, there must be awakened in the respondent an eagerness to want.

That perhaps is the best piece of advice which can be given to would-be persuaders, whether in business, in the home, in the school, in politics, etc.: first arouse in the other person an eager want.

He who can do this has the world with him.    He who cannot walks a lonely way!

# CHAPTER III

## THE PROBLEM OF VIVIDNESS

Let the reader try to recall the smell of a peach. He will no doubt find it a little vague. Let him try, now, to recall its taste. Still vague; but perhaps less so. Now let him try to recall what a peach looks like. Not vague at all. The image of the peach leaps to the mind.

Most of us are visual minded. This means that anything that can be presented to the eye has a far greater chance of being retained and recalled than something which is presented only to the organs of taste and smell.

To put an idea into visual form, then, is to increase its power. For the power of an idea depends upon two things: (1) the swiftness and clarity with which it is received: (2) the ease with which it is recalled.

We have all suffered under the colorless speaker (note the visual condemnation in the word colorless). We have all groaned under too great abstractness of presentation. We have all had the baffling experience of trying to recall what a certain chapter was about. And we have all gratefully had the opposite experience, of a speaker who gave us a vivid sense of the reality of what he was talking about; of a writer who so "pointed up" his material with visual illustration that he left us with a clear sense of his essential meanings.

*Picturizing With Words*

Note the picture value of the following advertisement:[1]

*A $12,000 Advertisement*

It was only a small advertisement; but some freak of fortune brought it into the hands of a Chinese firm in Hongkong.

A few weeks later a Cleveland concern received an order from Hongkong, for $12,000 worth of merchandise.

It was a sizeable order. They needed it badly. Yet they could find no credit data relating to the new customer.

They 'phoned to the Foreign Department of this organization. Within ninety minutes, they had four closely typewritten pages concerning their customer and his financial status.

Yet this is only a sample of the service at the command . . .

The power of that advertisement lies in the picture-phrases of which it is so largely made up: "Only a small advertisement;" "some freak of fortune brought it into the hands;" "Chinese firm in Hongkong;" "a Cleveland concern;" "an order from Hongkong;" "$12,000 worth of merchandise;" "they needed it badly;" "they 'phoned the Foreign Department;" "within ninety minutes;" "four closely typewritten pages."

Let us reconstruct that advertisement along the lines of abstract dignity:

*Credit Information*

The Foreign Department of the Union Trust Company is prepared to give reliable credit information at short notice concerning business houses throughout the world.

[1] The Fine Art of Picturizing; by Arthur T. Corbett. *Advertising and Selling Fortnightly,* Nov. 19, 1924, p. 18.

No pictures whatever there, except, perhaps, a whiff of one in the phrase "at short notice!" "Throughout the world" is far less arresting than "Hongkong," because it is too general, too diffused to form a picture. "Credit information" is an understandable phrase; but it leaves us cold beside the vivid picture of an actual instance, in a specific place, of credit confirmation.

Notice the picture value of the following names: Camp Fire Girls; Boy Scouts; Pioneer Youth; Children's Bureau; International Community Center; Day Nursery; The Road of Anthracite; New York Central. Suppose the Camp Fire Girls had been called: Association for the Promotion of Friendship and Outdoor Life Among Girls!

Notice the fuzzy abstractness of the following names: The Joint Committee on Methods of Preventing Juvenile Delinquency; The American Public Health Association; New York State Committee on Mental Hygiene; New York, Westchester and Boston Railway.[1]

## Be Creators of Images

Most of us, as we have said, are naturally "visual minded;" but comparatively few of us are "visual worded." There is no need, therefore, that we train ourselves in the power to receive visual images; there is every need, however, that we make some deliberate effort to train ourselves in the power to create and transmit visual images.

[1] I have just tested the recall value of the latter name by looking it up in the telephone directory. First, I discovered I could not recall the order of the three localities. So I started with Boston;—Boston, New York, Westchester; Boston, Westchester, New York; no luck! Then Westchester, Boston, New York; Westchester, New York, Boston; no luck again! Then New York, Boston, Westchester. Finally, after ten minutes or so of irritated turning of pages, the absurd combination!

We can do this, first, by taking passages from the great writers—men like Tolstoy; Anatole France; Shaw; Huxley; Emerson; Carlyle—noting the picture words used. To build up a fairly adequate vocabulary of such words is itself of value. Of greater value, however, is the habit which thereby develops of being aware of the power which such words give to the writing. As we begin to note the presence of visual words in the great writers, we note, the more easily, their absence from our own efforts. Another excellent procedure is to examine writing which is obviously dull and ineffective and note in how far the weakness of the writing arises out of the poverty of picture-building words. The same procedure may be followed in the case of effective speakers and dull speakers.

Then we shall be ready to take ourselves severely and successfully in hand. We can stand over our own dull paragraphs, or keep an ear upon our own colorless speeches, and point them up by substituting "eye" words for the commonplace, foggy symbols which help to hold us within the ranks of mediocrity.

## The Anti-Picturizers

We now go a step further, and as writers or speakers put our material into visual form by the use of pictures. There is, among many so-called intellectuals, an instant and ominous "thumbs down." Pictures are lowbrow. No really intelligent person is supposed to look at pictures—unless they are framed and hung in a gallery!

This is a curious attitude, since a picture, very often, is obviously the clearest and simplest means for transmitting ideas. Take, for example, a printed verbal description of a house or a landscape.   We all know how difficult it is to follow the verbal process.  Is there any particular advantage in having to grope through a wordy description, achieving, at the end, only a vague and inaccurate visual image, when a picture would give us instantly all the characteristic details?   Or take a description of how to swing one's golf club properly, or how to do a crawl stroke?   The objection to the use of pictures seems to be a curious left-over from the ascetic philosophy that life must be made as difficult as possible, never as easy.   Pictures make things too easy for us.

There is, of course, a degree of truth in this.   A generation brought up exclusively on pictures would doubtless become lazy and passive-minded (unless the pictures were stimulative of ideas).   But no one in his senses, surely, would advocate such a wholesale use of pictures, particularly of pictures which in no wise roused the mind to active response.

In life we apply tools to the material of our environment. One kind of tool is applied to physical things.  Now it would be a curious carpenter who would insist that it was demoralizing to use a modern set of steel tools on the ground that it made carpentering too easy.   It is true that a stone hammer would cause the carpenter far more trouble; would tax his patience and his ingenuity to the utmost. But would that additional effort be worthwhile?   Even at the best, he could never accomplish with his ascetic stone hammer what he could easily coax out of a full kit of modern tools.

The point is that the modern "easier" tools do not make the carpenter lazy; do not weaken his craftsman ability.

They simply release his energies for work impossible with the cruder tool.

Now words and pictures are tools. They are tools for communicating ideas, stimulating interests, arousing feelings and emotions. The sole question we have to ask about these tools is, which of them does the tool-work most effectively?

When we state the issue in this way there can be no doubt about the answer. "A picture, with a few words of explanation, will make it possible to get over an idea in one minute that would require two minutes without the picture." If that is true, then the picture is the more effective tool of communication. We need not worry about the fact that the receiving mind has, in this case, worked less hard (a minute less) in getting the idea by picture than by word. That simply means that it has more time left to get other ideas.

And therein, after all, lies the secret of what we, as human beings, are after. We make our life increasingly successful as we are able to minimize the time spent upon certain tasks, in order that our energies may be released for other worthwhile tasks and opportunities.

## The Imitative Picture

There are two types of pictures which are of interest to us in this connection: (1) the imitative; (2) the selective. Obviously, the imitative picture serves many time-saving, idea-clarifying purposes. A photograph, or photographic drawing, of a dress, or gun, or bicycle, or building is so far more effective than a verbal description that business men have long since abandoned the letter, save as supplementary to the picturization. The eye grasps instantly a hundred details, gets the "wholeness" of a thing in picture form, where it would crawl along slowly from word to word of a description and in the end have no clear image. Books on anatomy, physiology, biology, botany, horticulture, agriculture, etc., are largely effective in proportion to the clear and precise illustrations contained in their text. That pictures are not more generously used in such texts is due to the relatively large cost of their reproduction.

### The Selective Picture: Diagrams, Graphs, Curves

The most significant type of picture, however, is the selective picture. At the farthest remove from imitative representation are those skeleton-like picturizings which we call diagrams, graphs, curves. "When large groups of figures are to be presented it is often useful to employ diagrams which enable the eye to grasp at once the series as a whole. There are many varieties. Popular discussions of comparative populations, wealth, navies, and so on often represent the various figures by lines or surfaces which are so juxtaposed as to show at once to the eye the relations of the several quantities. . . . Or we might employ rectangles with equal bases, or points on a curve." [1]

Often skeleton maps with shaded areas show most effectively diminutions or increases in numbers.

Such selective picturizing is a comparatively recent device. It is a form of "conceptual shorthand" which very greatly increases the clarity and the power of the ideas.

It is significant that the making of such selective pictures

[1] Jones, A. L.; *Logic;* p. 226. Holt, New York.

is only slowly being introduced into the schools. Here verbal technique is still in the ascendant, although verbal technique is, in these cases, immeasurably inferior. But so, likewise, students are still required solemnly to add and subtract, multiply and divide, extract roots, etc. (long after they have attained skill in these), despite the adding machine and the slide rule!

## The Cartoon

Is there a more effective, idea-clarifying and emotion-arousing device than the modern cartoon? The cartoon is in a preëminent way a form of selective picture which conveys an idea. Through conveying an idea with simple clarity, it often arouses powerful emotion. It frequently does what words cannot do. It crowds the salient details of a situation into a few square inches of space; places them there with such selective clarity that the eye and the mind catch them instantly.

The power of the cartoon is the power of all art, the power of selective emphasis. The cartoonist knows that most of us go about with only a hazy kind of attention. We see people indeed; but we recognize them only by a few conventional marks. The cartoonist wants us to see the vulgarity in that fat woman's face; or the pathos in that girl's thin arms. A bit of accentuation; and the trick is done. We now *see*. He has extended our human insight. He has given a new direction to our thought and feelings.

Or he wants us to be aware of the danger in a certain political situation. A few accentuated characters thrown together within his small area; and the whole story is told!

The cartoon is still one of the step-children of the arts. Some day it will be lifted to the place of honor which is its due. An artist who has genuine ideas about human life, genuine insight into human situations, might well be proud of the power to sweep his thoughts and feelings into the swift compass of pictures that grip us with their clear pertinence.

Here, again, we are the victims of our own early conditioning. Practically none of us, in our childhood days, were taught to "say it with pictures." And as for the pictures that we were taught to admire, they were the paintings on gallery walls.

But why should our children not be taught to "say it with pictures?" Why should we confine our children to copying leaves and plaster casts—a wholly imitative, idealess enterprise; when they ought, from their youngest years, to be learning how to give graphic expression to their ideas? When we find Thackeray, Clarence Day, Hugh Lofting, Willem Van Loon and others, telling their stories in pictures, we exclaim with delight. We seldom think that this is what all of us ought to be able to do; that it is a power which our word-dominated education has failed to develop in us, but which ought to become part of our everyday human equipment.

### The Gallery Picture

Nor do we mean by this to detract in any degree from the high form of art which hangs on our gallery walls. The trouble with our gallery walls is—that they are gallery walls. The pictures on them are seldom seen; and when seen, they are looked upon as something rare and quite apart from ourselves. Usually, we do not even know how to look at them. We drag through wearily, giving a glance here at a mother slicing bread for her children or there at a generallissimo on a snorting horse.

What do these pictures on our gallery walls really intend to convey? What good do they do? What use are they to our human enterprise?

The usual thought is that artists are queer folk who like to paint. Sometimes the pictures tickle our fancy; and we stand for a moment and look at them. Then we pass on.

But, of course, there is much more to it than this. A picture, if it is worth anything, is a more or less powerful means of communication. The artist has seen something. You and I have been in the same place, perhaps; have looked at the same object; but we have not seen just that peculiar, rare thing which the artist sees. Why? Because, as we said above, we usually see only the ordinary, conventional marks whereby we identify the objects and creatures of our world. But in this particular commonplace object—say it is a tree—the artist sees something which we have passed over. He sees a sturdiness, a stubbornness in the windswept branches. When he paints his picture, it is sturdiness, stubbornness that he paints into his canvas. He accentuates. He brings these out so that even our attention-dulled eyes can see.

What a picture does, then, is to fasten our attention upon aspects of our own world which ordinarily escape us. It is for that reason that galleries are usually psychological monstrosities. No one of us can have our attention whipped alive a hundred times in every few hundred feet; a thousand, several thousand times in the course of an hour. Every picture that is worth seeing is a stimulus to an unusual act of attention on our part. Each picture must, therefore, be given its full opportunity. We should hardly expect a person to listen with a peculiar joy to a single musical note, if a hundred discordant whistles were blowing. No more can we expect these selective bits of experience which we call pictures to arouse us to their peculiar new way of seeing things, if a hundred of them are claiming our distracted attention.

In one of our women's colleges there is a wise art director. One room is set apart; and in that room is hung one picture—usually for an entire week. Also in front of that one picture, at a great enough distance, is a bench with a back. The director knows that if we are to incorporate the new and rare experience, we must be given time; and that if we take time, the rest of our bodily organism must not be crying out for attention. He knows that we ordinarily see galleries not with our eyes but with our protesting feet.

Pictures seen in a real way add new feelings, new insights to our life. Architecture and sculpture also influence human behavior by picturization of ideas and feelings. There can be little doubt that to the Athenian the Parthenon was a very important, though doubtless quite unconscious, influence. There it reposed, a white jewel of beauty, on the top of the Acropolis. No hundred other "objects of art" to compete with it. The Athenian passed it scores of times; could look up at it from any part of the city. Suppose that instead of the gleaming white Parthenon, there had been a huge illuminated sign, with dancing silly-billies, advertising *Woggly's Chewing Gum: It Sticks!*

The Parthenon was a work of art, not only because it was beautiful, but because it was selective. It accentuated

beauty of line in the human body; beauty of movement; beauty of proportion.  We could easily imagine a
gargoyled temple crowded with hooded figures.  Such a
temple would be selective of other features of experience
and would have had an influence notably different from that
of the Parthenon.  The Parthenon taught the Greeks to
see human life in one of its major aspects; it influenced
them unconsciously towards the development of a taste for
beauty of line, movement and proportion.

## Two Necessary Projects

There are two things which, apparently, we must learn to
do if the full value of picturizing is to be realized in our
modern civilization.  First, we must unlearn most of our
habits of thought about art.  We must learn what pictures,
sculptures, and works of architecture really have to say.
Once we see that what they communicate is something
selective; something taken out of the vague and helter-
skelter mass of our experience and made to stand out as
beautiful and worthy of our attention—once we see this,
every picture or other work of art becomes for us a means
to arouse our attention to something unique, something ordinarily unnoticed.  A work of art, then, becomes for us
a key to unlock a rarity.  It is not simply something to look
at and exclaim:  "Why it's an exact copy!"; something to
give the date of and the author; something to hunt up in a
catalogue.  It becomes in itself a new, enlightening experience.

But, in the second place, we must ourselves learn to speak
the language of pictures.  We must begin by noting the
unusual, the rare.  We must begin by trying somehow,

even though with the greatest awkwardness, to set down our own experience of what most people do not see. Technique can follow in due course after the artist eye is opened.

And so, if we are adults and have not yet learned to speak the language of pictures, our best plan will be not to copy plaster casts but simply to try to note what is characteristic about the objects around us—the saucy tilt of a nose; the expressive solemnity of huge ears; the pathos of knuckled fingers; the self-reliant stubbiness of a small dog's tail; the lordly droop of a chrysanthemum. We can try, in our awkward ways, to set down in simple black lines these things we see. We may never become skilled technicians; our drawings may be ridiculously crude; but one thing, we may be assured, they will not be—if they are drawn out of our actual seeing of what is rare and characteristic, they will never be dull. And they will do this for us: they will enable us to respond with a more instant sensitiveness to what the master artists are trying to convey.

But, of course, all this training ought to be begun early in life. It is a pity that our children spend years in learning the art of speaking with words, but, for the most part, no time at all in learning the art of speaking with visual images. There are signs, however, that a new understanding of the value of this art is being reached. In the more progressive schools, children begin to draw freely from the kindergarten on. They are never asked to copy anything —in the pedantic way demanded of old. They are given generous spaces of paper, a goodly equipment of paints and brushes and allowed to go ahead as they wish. And the wise teacher does not say: "Ah, Jennie, but don't you see that human arms don't hang that way? Let me show you how." No, she lets the arms hang in whatever way they wish to hang, being fully assured that the spirit is more than arms and legs, and that while arms and legs will eventually find their proper placing, the spirit must blow where it listeth.

It is not in order that children may paint that we do this, or that they may bring home their pictures to fond papa and mamma. It is that they may learn to see and to express what they see. It is, in short, that their eyes may learn a sensitiveness to the rarer aspects of experience, instead of becoming dulled to all except the most conventional utilitarian marks whereby we identify the objects around us.

There is much loveliness in our world which quite escapes us. Looking out upon a landscape, let the reader bend down until his head is horizontal instead of perpendicular and let him look at the landscape from that angle. A subtle change comes over the scene. Colors not before detected now stand out, contours hitherto unnoticed are now in sharp relief. By a slight change in the angle of our perception, we have brought out new qualities in the scene before us. Art does that for us—when we really see art. All the more reason, then, that we should all, in some degree, become artists.

Thus we enrich our own experience. And thus, if we can really learn the art of selective expression, we enrich the experience of others. A civilization is drab, Main-Streetish, when it sees only the utilitarian values. It escapes drabness, it beautifies its Main Streets, when it develops in its members new and more subtle sensitiveness of vision.

The effort to picturize, in brief, is valuable in many different ways. If we can cast aside the colorless, abstract words of ordinary currency, and substitute words which suggest images; if we can create what people shall see—

whether we be writers, or advertisers, or teachers, or artists —we add not only to the clarity of our thought, but also to the power of our influence over human behavior.

### Inducing an Imagined Experience

Picturization, then, lends a vividness such as is not usually experienced through the imaginative use of the other senses.  To see with the eye of the mind concretely, is to apprehend more of the object, and more vividly, than to hear with the ears abstractly.

But there is something more effective even than seeing with the imaginative eye.  It is the condition in which we imaginatively feel a situation with more or less of our whole personalities.

Let us suppose that I wish to interest some one in the starving children of Russia.  I can tell the person that it is his duty to help these children in distress.  Such admonition will probably not move him very greatly.  Or I can ask him whether he will be so good as to help these poor, suffering children.  He may be slightly moved by my appeal to his pity; more particularly, perhaps, by my flattery of his humanity; and he may give me a contribution.  Suppose, however, I could take him over with me to Russia and let him see starving children; talk with them; help them individually.  I should no longer have to argue or to plead.  He himself, of his own free will, out of the intensity of his own feeling, would give the maximum of his help.

Obviously, the best technique we can ever use is to put the person completely into the situation.  But in most cases in life this rather expensive technique can hardly be applied.    Hence we are called upon to use a second-best, namely, the technique of putting a person *imaginatively* into the situation.

We sometimes call this the power of suggestion.    That word, however, has so mysterious a sound; it has become so associated with curious psychological procedures like hypnotism, auto-suggestion, etc., and with erotic "suggestiveness," that I prefer not to use it, but to use a phrase which quite clearly indicates precisely what we do.

We induce an imagined experience.    Not all of us, of course do.    When we do not, our speech or our writing is abstract, unarousing, "pale."    We talk "about it and about."    When, however, we do successfully induce an imagined experience, we have a power which, for effectively influencing human behavior, is almost, if not quite, the greatest that a writer or speaker can have.

Let me illustrate.    The power of a person like Billy Sunday lies in the effective use of this technique.    We may not be particularly interested in the kind of imagined experience which the Reverend Billy induces.    As psychologists, however, it is important that we note the source of his power.    *The New York Times* recently reported one of the characteristic feats of the preacher.    "BILLY SUNDAY TALK ENDS LONG LOOTING."    "WOMAN MOVED BY SERMON ON THE 'WAGES OF SIN,' REVEALS ALL TO THE ELMIRA POLICE."    "Before an audience of 7,000 in the Sunday Tabernacle, the famous evangelist declared that 'no person in whose heart reposes guilty knowledge need expect to make peace with God until confession is first made,' and the statement struck terror to one woman's heart, for she had been concealing the knowledge of extensive robberies for nearly ten years and yet devoutly wished to make her

peace with her Creator.    Leaving the tabernacle she sought
the seclusion of her room and remained upon her knees
in agonized prayer until the first flush of dawn, when her
decision was made."    Here was a case of inducing an imagined experience, that of standing before God with a guilty
secret in one's heart.    The preacher doubtless portrayed
the situation with such vividness that the guilty woman was
terror-stricken.

The colored minister often has this power.    The following amusing yet psychologically most significant story is told
by Professor F. M. Davenport (quoted by Allport, *Social
Psychology*, p. 247):

"In a little town between Cleveland, Tennessee, and Chattanooga,
it was the purpose to give a donation to the colored minister.    One
of the brethren in the church volunteered to make a collection from
the various homes, and an old woman loaned this brother her cart
and a pair of steers for the purpose.    After he had been throughout
the neighborhood and had secured a load of provisions and clothing,
he drove off to Chattanooga and sold everything, including the cart
and the steers, pocketed the proceeds and departed on a visit to
Atlanta.    Consternation and indignation reigned in the community
when the affair became known.    After some time the culprit drifted
back, in deep contrition, but having spent all.    Indignation once
more arose to a white heat, and it was determined to give him a
church trial at once.    The meeting was crowded; and the preacher,
after stating the charges, announced that the accused would be given
a chance to be heard.    He went forward and took the place of the
preacher on the platform.

" 'I ain't got nuffin to say fo' myse'f,' he began in a penitent voice,
'I'se a po' mis'able sinner.    But, bredren, so is we all mis'able
sinners.    An' de good book says we must fergib.    How many times,
bredren?    Till seven times?    No, till seventy times seven.    An' I
ain't sinned no seventy times seven, and I'm jes' go' to sugges' dat

we turn dis into a fergibness meetin', and eberybody in dis great comp'ny dat is willin' to fergib me, come up now, while we sing one of our deah ole hymns, and shake ma hand.'

"He started one of the powerful revival tunes, and they began to come, first those who hadn't given anything to the donation and were not much interested in the matter, then those who hadn't lost much, and then the others. Finally all had passed before him except one, and she stuck to her seat. 'Dar's one po' mis'able sinner lef',' said he, 'dat won't fergib.' (She was the old lady who had lost the steers.) 'Now I sugges' dat we hab a season ob prayer, an' gib dis po' ole sinner one mo' chance.' And after they had prayed and sung a hymn, the old lady came up, too!"

## Imagining It Does It

Note the difference in effect between the following two statements made to a person: "I would advise you to have a regular examination by a physician;" and "By Jove, man, you're looking positively ill. You ought to have a doctor look you over!" In the one case we present a perfectly impeccable bit of abstract statement, with the result that nothing happens! In the second case, we "induce an imagined experience." The friend sees himself looking sick; he feels himself getting sicker. And because it is he who does the feeling, no argument is needed. He goes to the doctor!

Amusing and yet instructive psychological experiments have been made along this line. A number of young men are subjects. They are told that experiments are to be made upon them to try out the effect of stimulating and of depressing drugs upon their heart-beat. They are accordingly given a few pills, which, they are told, contain strychnine; and it is explained to them that strychnine has the effect of whipping up the heart to more rapid action. After a certain lapse of time, the heart beats are counted; and in the majority of cases the beat is faster. The pills, however, as the reader may have guessed, were only milk sugar pills! And so with the other experiments.[1]

In these cases, "inducing an imagined experience" actually succeeds in so enlisting the entire organism that even movements ordinarily beyond conscious control are noticeably affected!

### The "Forward Looking" Mind

There is at present in America, among forward looking minds, a large amount of dissatisfaction with reactionary tendencies. This dissatisfaction takes itself out in bitter negative argumentation. The American public are roundly scolded for taking no interest in the European situation; for being smugly concerned only with their own affairs; for being intolerant of liberals; for curbing free speech. Apparently, nothing very noticeable comes of all this. The American public go on their way supremely indifferent, because they do not even read or hear these scoldings! And even if they did, they would doubtless only be annoyed into a more stubborn pursuit of their ways.

The failure, one may suppose, lies in the fact that no glowing, imagined experience is portrayed for the American people. Suppose that the critics should face about, should accept the idea of 100 per cent Americanism but go it one better. Suppose they should build up, in every possible way, the picture of America the pioneer, America the adventurous, the red-blooded, the unafraid; America always on

[1] Dearborn, G. V.; *Influence of Joy;* p. 90. Little Brown & Co., Boston.

the firing-line of social and political advance. Suppose they could make the average citizen feel that kind of America, feel the thrill of pride in belonging to such a country. I doubt whether the indifference and reactionism would remain quite unaffected. As a matter of fact, "100 per cent American" is a powerful slogan, precisely because it does induce an imagined experience; does give a thrill of proud feeling.

Instead of arguing *against* keeping political refugees out, the more successful way, apparently, would be to build up the picture of America as the Haven of the Persecuted. Instead of arguing *against* standpattism, the more effective way would doubtless be to build up the picture of America as open minded, as indeed the very America it is, because of its eagerness for new ideas. Instead of inveighing against the timid reactionaries who are constantly harking back to the signers of the Constitution, the really powerful thing to do would be to build up the picture of America as forward looking.

Each of these phrases we have used, it will be noted, is a picture phrase, a phrase which puts one into a situation, and which consequently arouses the feeling of being in that situation.

The secret of all true persuasion is to induce the person to persuade himself. The chief task of the persuader, therefore is to induce the experience. The rest will take care of itself.

## For the Reader

The reader will find it a most valuable undertaking to examine the extent to which the technique of inducing-an-imagined-experience is used in various forms of print and speech. Advertising is a rich field of research. Almost every really effective advertisement gives one a sense of actually experiencing the delightful situation: travel advertisements, food, sport, clothing, health advertisements. He will soon be able to detect the difference between an advertisement which makes one's mouth water, so to speak, and the type of advertisement, which, couched only in abstract terms, leaves one cold.

He will find that the power of a great novel is that it is able to induce in one the feeling of the actual experiences through which the characters pass; whereas a mediocre novel keeps one always in the condition of looking on. So, too, he will find that the speaker who moves people, achieves this through his power to make his audience experience what he is portraying. Enthusiasm is contagious to the extent and only to the extent that it does this. If it is unable to induce the imagined experience, it only seems rather silly.

He will find that the really successful parent is not the one who preaches or advises or explains or commands, but the one who can induce in his children vivid imagined experiences.

The secret of it all, of course, is that a person is led to *do* what he overwhelmingly *feels*. Practice in getting people to feel themselves in situations is therefore the surest road to persuasiveness.

# CHAPTER IV

# THE PSYCHOLOGY OF EFFECTIVE SPEAKING

We proceed now, in this and the following chapter, to the two techniques of speech and writing. Speech, when it has an object, is always an effort to arrest the attention and in some measure to affect the behavior of other human beings. To be sure, there is the kind of aimless speech of conversation which seems to have no particular end in view save to keep going. But even in the speech of conversation there is the effort to say things in such a way that the other party listens. No conversationalist delights in seeing his respondent fall asleep before his eyes. Where, however, speech has a more definite object—as in an admonition to a child, an exposition of a point, the discussion of a motion in a committee meeting,—the object is quite clearly that of influencing the listener to some kind of behavior. It may be simply the intra-organic behavior of mental assent; or it may be the extra-organic behavior of doing something. In any event, speech is used as a means of getting some kind of favorable response.

The problem of effective speaking, therefore, is essentially psychological. A good deal of training in public speaking seems to miss this point. It is a training rather in the literary, logical and physical mechanics of speaking—the arrangement of ideas, sentence structure, beginning, middle and end, gestures, enunciation. All these, of course, are quite essential matters. Nevertheless a speaker can be aware of them and even use his knowledge of them and be practically a failure. One finds particularly among young college speakers that they are often wooden, unconvincing. Even their finely prepared efforts have the effect of something not really meant. One listens, with half amusement, as to a child reciting something it has committed to memory, which it only half understands and in which it really has little interest.

It would seem important, then, that we approach the technique of speaking not from the side of its mechanics but from the side, so to say, of its "humanics." Our primary question in that case is not what kind of speech is best arranged, best enunciated, best gestured; but what kind of speech gets the most effective response. As a matter of fact, we can quite safely forget the lengthy "speech" altogether. If we can learn the fundamental psychology involved even in the slightest speech situation, we shall probably be far on the way to becoming successful speakers.

## The First Rule

The first simple rule of all good speaking, in any situation whatever, is: think of your audience. This may perhaps seem altogether too trivial a matter to need mention; but let the reader make a special point of observing the speech habits of people. He will note that a great many speakers are apparently not thinking of their audience at all. They are apparently speaking to relieve themselves. That is the reason why a bore is a bore. That is the explanation of the woman who endlessly and remorsely pours out the tale of her latest troubles. That is the clue to the lecturer who can go on and on and never seem to notice while people yawn and fidget and leave the room. Such speakers might be called unloaders. Their primary object apparently is to get rid of something. Their interest is not in their audience but in themselves—scholarly unloaders, scientific unloaders, family-troubles unloaders, business-grouch unloaders, etc.

Suppose, however, that we keep the idea constantly to the front that our speech should be for the sake of getting a desirable response. Then the first question we shall ask ourselves is: Is this manner of speech getting for me the kind of response I desire?

The scolding of children is mainly an unloading process. It is chiefly a relief to our exasperated feelings. As a matter of fact it often does more harm than good and so does not secure the response that is really desired. Hence, in so far, it is ineffective speech. The irate citizen is frequently found "rowing" the car conductor. The other passengers look amused; and the conductor simply grows obviously sulky. His "rowing" does no good—not even to himself. He has therefore failed in his speech technique.

If, on the contrary, we aim at desirable response, we shall try first of all to get the favorable attention of our audience. We shall not scowl at him or them; we shall not look lofty; we shall not mumble; we shall not appear frightened; we shall not seem to be evading his or their eyes by looking out of the window or at a fixed spot on the wall. We shall look and act as if we rather liked to be with our audience.

## Look At Your Audience

One of the first rules for all public speaking should be: look *at* your audience. There is something finely subtle about this which is very often missed by speakers. Quite often a speaker's face is conventionally turned towards his audience; but if one is in the audience oneself, one has the feeling that the speaker is not really looking *at* him. The speaker is only looking *towards* him. Therein lies a world of difference. For it is only when the speaker looks directly *at* his audience that the invisible wall between him and his audience falls away. Until that wall falls away, the speaker is relatively ineffective.

What do we mean by the difference between "looking at" and "looking towards?" It was implied in what we said a moment ago. He who thinks of his audience inevitably looks *at* them. He who thinks solely of himself or of his own subject-matter, inevitably has the focus of his attention turned away from his audience. We, in the audience, may not be able to express it; but what we subtly feel is that the speaker is distant, apart, aloof. Or we express it by referring to the invisible wall.

Let us recall again the technique mentioned in the first chapter—the *homeogenic* technique. Like begets like. If we are interested in our audience there is a likelihood that our audience will be interested in us. If we scowl at our audience, there is every likelihood that inwardly or outwardly they will scowl at us. If we are timid and rather flustered, they likewise will lack confidence in us. If we are brazen and boastful, they will react with their own self-protective egoism. Even before we speak, very often, we are condemned or approved. There is every reason therefore that we should make certain that our attitude is such as to elicit warm response.

## Finding the Audience's Interest

If, now, we are interested in our audience, we shall take our first step in the right direction: we shall say something, or suggest something that interests *them*. The tendency of a great many speakers is to say something that interests themselves, with the hope, perhaps, that what interests themselves will interest their audience. Parents and teachers are star performers at this. Science lecturers often display this trait to perfection. Now it is true that unless we are thoroughly absorbed in what we wish to say, unless we can convey to our audience the feeling that we really intend it all and believe in it, we shall not get far. Nevertheless, complete absorption in one's subject and complete belief in its value, while indispensable, are not always sufficient. We recall here the psychological rule that there must always be an element of the familiar in the unfamiliar or the latter makes no appeal. Translated into terms of what we are now considering, we may say that unless the speaker in some way ties up the thing that interests him with what interests his audience he fails to secure alert and fruitful attention.

Hence the speaker might well ask himself: is there anything in what I wish to say that is of interest to this particular audience? If, before launching out, he asks himself that question, and seeks for a specific answer, he is far likelier to discover the successful point of first approach to his audience than if he simply goes ahead unloading his ideas.

## *Never Make the Audience Feel Inferior*

But now having thought of the audience, let the speaker treat his audience as if he really had respect for them. Often, indeed, he has respect for them but unfortunately does not know how to show it. He feels that he must make an impression; so he tries to show them all he knows. He displays his knowledge with a flourish—and the audience feels subtly depressed. For when the speaker "tells" his audience, he implies that of course he knows and they do not. So he induces an inferiority feeling in them which is a little resentful.[1]

Let the speaker, therefore, never try to "show how much he knows." If he is conceited, let him keep it safely hidden. If he thinks well of himself and his knowledge, let him not make an offensive show of his self-congratulation.

Rather, the speaker should regard his audience as co-operating in the pursuit of the subject. He should talk, not down to them, but as with his equals. He should ask them questions, sincerely, and assume that they can give the answers.

In short (another rule), he should talk *with* his audience not *at* them.

## *Circular Response*

This implies something psychologically quite important. It implies that something is to be set going in the minds of one's audience (their response). But it also

---

[1] Recall the discussion of the Expository and the Putting-it-up-to-you techniques in Chapter I.

implies that something is to be set going in the mind of the speaker as a result of what is going on in the minds of the audience. This is why read papers are usually so unsatisfactory. The audience subtly feels that the speaker is not responding to their thought, not adjusting himself to what is happening in them. In fact, nothing is happening in the speaker's mind. It all happened long ago when the paper was being written.

Thus again the process is only in one direction—from the speaker to the audience; not back again from audience to speaker. This movement in two directions has been aptly named "circular response." It is fundamental to all effective mental intercourse.[1]

Thus the subtle, sensitive speaker is he who is so mindful of what is happening in his audience—he gets it from their facial expression, their nods, their blankness, their scowls, their interrupting questions—that his own thought and expression are influenced.

Hence the two important rules: (1) Keep your audience thinking with you. (2) Keep thinking with your audience.

The first rule is perhaps the most important, for if we deliberately try to keep our audience thinking along with us, we shall inevitably so adjust our speaking as to make such active thinking possible. We shall not leave our audience hopelessly panting in the rear.

Here again, one notes the weakness of immature speakers. Their minds are turned inwards—upon themselves. They

---

[1] See *Creative Experience,* by M. P. Follett. Longmans. The reader is strongly advised to study the process in all its applications. Miss Follett's book presents a brilliant and comprehensive analysis.

are not trying to get the audience to think along with them. Hence their speech lacks vitality. The audience simply hears words.

### Use Humor Humorously

Humor, of course, as we shall later show, is one of our greatest assets. He who has it has a golden way ahead of him. But humor is a dangerous gift. It can be used in such a way as to wreck the whole speaking enterprise. Hence the admonition: Use humor humorously.

This means, use it in proportion. Many speakers in the effort to be humorous, drag in long stories. The speaker might make the following question the test of his powers: Can I be humorous without telling a story? Particularly let him ask that question if he is to be an after-dinner speaker; for nothing has so lowered the art of speaking as the well-nigh universal convention that the after-dinner speaker must offer a goulash of irrelevant, side-splitting stories. Such a performance should not be called a speech but a vaudeville act.

Humor should be an attitude—of playfulness, of not too great seriousness; the sudden twist of a word, the flash of a grotesque idea. Humor is invaluable to the speaker because (1) it enlists the audience. It gives them a feeling of good fellowship with the speaker. Hence it evokes the opposite of the inferiority feeling. And it breaks down the "wall." (2) It gives to the audience exhilarating bodily reactions. It stimulates the nerves and circulatory system; it raises the emotional tone of the audience. Hence it makes them better listeners. A laugh is the best sleep dispeller. (3) It keeps the sense of proportion, both in speaker and audience.

### A Word About the Angry Speaker

The yelling, scolding speaker is pitiable. He is chiefly pitiable because he accomplishes nothing by his anger—save the discomfort and resentment of his audience. Ill-feeling, unless it leads to action, is a depressant. The audience which hear themselves being lashed by the sarcasm or the anger of a speaker can do nothing. They must simply sit. Hence they store up bitterness. As we said in Chapter I, the speaker can be angry, provided he carries the audience with him in his anger against something or somebody. Here, again, we note that the aim of the speaker must be to get the psychological processes of the audience moving along with him.

### The Voice as an Instrument

The voice is so powerful a factor in its effect upon an audience that one wonders why speakers pay so little attention to its cultivation and effective use. There is, in the first place, the quality of the voice. Is one's voice raspy, or nasal, or squeaky or otherwise a nuisance? Why inflict it upon a suffering public? Raspy, nasal and squeaky voices can be corrected. Why not bring to one's audience a beautiful voice instrument?

In the second place, there is the important matter of voice modulation. The ordinary American speech-habit is to play one's entire melody on one note—or at best two,—the dominant note sustained throughout the sentence and the drop-note at the end. Such speech can become intolerably monotonous. The American speaker in particular needs to increase the up and down range of his voice and not be afraid to use that range in his speaking.   He tends too often to think that flexibility and range of voice sound affected, and so he drones along in his Main-Streetish monotone.   Few things, however, add more to the pleasure of a speech than a musical voice of a fairly wide range and flexible use.   Note this quality in the competent actor.

### And Then One's Appearance

The speaker must remember that however fine his ideas, he himself is in the foreground.   If his appearance is distressing or humorous or bizarre, so much the less attention remains for his ideas.   If he wishes his ideas to be in the foreground, his appearance must be relegated to the background.   This means, of course, that it must not be intrusive, like the new spring millinery on the heads of choir singers, or a too tight dress on the body of a fat woman chairman.

Very often a fairly agreeable but non-intrusive appearance is quite spoiled by annoying mannerisms.   Eyeglasses are jerked on and off till the audience writhes in nervous desperation.   The hair is given successive and quite unnecessary brushings; a finger continually caresses the cheek; a watch chain is twisted and untwisted; sometimes even legs are screwed and unscrewed until the nervous members of the audience are ready to shriek.   The speaker must remember that whatever muscular feats he performs, the audience tends, intra-organically, to perform with him. Thus a speaker who strides up and down a platform can tire out his audience; a speaker who stutters and stumbles over his words has the audience likewise in a state of verbal prostration.   On the other hand, a speaker who holds himself perfectly still throughout a long speech also tires the audience, since the gestures of the speaker are a muscular release not only for him but for his audience as well.

If, in short, the speaker constantly remembers that what he does the audience will also tend to do, he will doubtless have sufficient mercy upon the long suffering folk in front of him to keep his disagreeable mannerisms well out of sight.

One cannot, in this connection, refrain from making especial mention of what is perhaps the most universal and also one of the most exasperating mannerisms of speakers. I mean the hesitating "er." Hesitation in speech is not a bad thing. In fact, in a speech, he who never hesitates is lost. Rattling on without a stop gives the effect of something learned by heart. But when the speaker pauses between his words or sentences as if to formulate more clearly his idea, let him, in the name of all that is artistically wholesome, not slip in the distressing "er." Practically every speaker does slip it in at times; so there is no hope of our getting completely rid of this tonal nuisance. But if one is addicted to its use, a little awareness of the mannerism and a constant self control at the precarious moment when the "er" begins to take shape, will tend to clear this noxious thing out of one's speech.

The difficulty, in this matter of disagreeable mannerisms, is that, as the advertisement has it, "even your best friends won't tell you." And so we go on accumulating bad habits without knowing that they are bad. Ergo, find a friend who is willing to risk his friendship by telling you just how disagreeable or nonsensical or pathetic you are!

### Let Your Speech March

Often a speaker will suddenly discover that he has lost grip on his audience.   Attention relaxes; heads begin to move; there are whisperings, shufflings, twistings of the body.   If he will watch his speech at such a moment he will often find that he has been saying over and over again what he has already made clear.   This is a curious tendency which is present in most of us without our being aware of it.   We make a perfectly clear statement.   Then, a few sentences later on we make that same statement again.   A few sentences later and out comes the statement again. The writer came upon an amusing example the other morning in an elevated train.   At 116th Street, two girls were talking about their rising time.   "I get up at six thirty," said one.   "I like to get up early.   Gives me more time." "Well, I don't get up till seven," said the other.   "Guess I'm lazy; but seven's early enough for me."   At Christopher Street, twenty minutes later, they were still saying the same sentences!

When the speaker finds himself marking time, or going around in a circle, or saying what he has already said, then is the moment when he should remember the kinetic technique and set his speech marching ahead.   Nor should it just march aimlessly—up the hill and down again; it should give one a sense of one thing leading out of another and toward another, and all toward a climax partly revealed and partly concealed.   Each step, in short, should have the flavor of novelty.   In a later chapter we shall discuss in some detail how dramatic quality is achieved.   Here we content ourselves with noting the fact that a speech which does not march, and march with dramatic effect towards something is a speech precariously calculated to induce somnolence.

## Avoid the Commonplace and the Bizarre

Speech, to be distinguished, must have not only distinction of idea but distinction of phrasing. As a matter of fact, the two interact; for, as we shall presently show, attention to accuracy of phrasing develops accuracy of mind. The effective speaker, however, is one who learns not only accuracy but power of phrasing. He uses words that stick; he formulates sentences which the audience do not easily forget.

In this connection, the speaker will find writing his most trusty aid. In the act of writing one has the time to ponder and invent; while in the rush of speaking, one tends to use what one has become most accustomed to use. Thus the ready speaker who does little writing is apt to fall into commonplace habits of speech. He constantly resorts to the least common denominator of his speech-habits.

However, one should also avoid the bizarre, for a bizarre word or phrase instantly attracts attention to itself and in so far diverts attention from the flow of the ideas.

## The Flat-Land Mind

We have spoken of the one-tone voice. There is also the one-tone mind. All facts to it apparently are of equal value. There are no emphases; there is no hurrying over unimportant details; no slowing-up at the greater significances; only one steady drone, which places everything said in the same category of importance or unimportance. A speech should be like mountains and valleys, not like a monotonous flat-land.

Another type is the string-of-beads mind. One fact is strung along after another, no relationship being shown between them. A speech, however, should advance not fact by fact but by groups of facts. These groups should themselves point to a larger grouping and to an encompassing idea which ties all the groups together.

The powerful mind is the organic mind. Just as the body is not simply an aggregate of single cells, but is made up of differentiated cells united into organs, which themselves are united into the entire integrated being called the organism, so a speech should be a grouping of groups of individual units.

The effective speaker is able to keep his audience aware of the particular grouping of unit-facts that is being discussed and the relation of this group to other groups. Such a speaker does not permit his audience to lose themselves in the multitude of details, but by constant, effective recall of the main idea and the related sub-ideas, gives them a sense as of moving easily and understandingly through what would otherwise be a bewildering maze of details.

The one-tone or flat-land mind is an unrhythmic mind. Rhythm depends essentially upon contrast. The iambic beat is a short and a long; the dactylic, a long and two shorts. The rhythm of waves is a swing of up and down. Joy in rhythm is, for a number of unexplained reasons, basic in life. Hence our pleasure in rhythmic speech.

## Close With a Snap

Finally let the speaker, having "respected the attention limits," learn the delightful art of closing with a snap. Let him not keep promising to close. If he is reading a paper let the audience have the joy of seeing the sheets diminish in number. Some readers have the bad habit of placing the sheets under each other as they read, so that the audience is cheated of the delightful feeling that the speech is really coming to an end. If he is simply speaking, let him indicate quite clearly that the blessed end is near at hand, and then without further ado let him make an end. Such a speaker, if he has the other graces, will be beloved of his hearers!

## Summary

The foregoing may be most effectively summarized in the following score of admonitions:

1. Do not be an unloader.
2. Think of your audience.
3. Look *at* your audience.
4. Find what interests *them*.
5. Never make an audience feel inferior.
6. Keep your audience thinking along with you.
7. Think along with your audience.
8. Use humor humorously.
9. Never be angry at the audience, only with them.
10. Cultivate a voice that can be endured.
11. Keep off the monotone.
12. Do not let your appearance occupy the foreground.
13. Eliminate distressing mannerisms.

14. Let your speech march.
15. Avoid the commonplace and the bizarre.
16. Do not be a flat-land mind.
17. Nor a string-of-beads mind.
18. Organize your speech into groups and larger groups.
19. Give an effect of rhythmic movement.
20. Close with a snap!

# CHAPTER V

## THE PSYCHOLOGY OF EFFECTIVE WRITING

There are many excellent books on the art of writing; but they approach their subject chiefly from a literary point of view. One finds among them scarcely any consideration—certainly no systematic one— of the psychological aspect of writing. Grammar, sentence and paragraph structure, logical sequence, proportion, metaphors, similes, etc. All of these are important; nay, the knowledge of them is quite indispensable. Writing, however, like speaking, is something more than a mechanics of word-combination. It is essentially a psychological enterprise. It has the aim of arousing the attention and holding the interest of readers. It is, in short, a form of stimulus which seeks to win favorable response. Now it is obvious, of course, that if one uses unclear words, confused sentences, and drearily long paragraphs, no favorable response is likely to be evoked. Hence there is indispensable value in training along these lines. But it is a question whether expertness in these literary matters is enough. Must one not go farther and understand the psychological factors involved in good and in poor writing?

Writing, we have said, is a form of stimulus which seeks a response. Good writing does something to the reader. Poor writing does something else. What is it that good writing does, and that poor writing fails to do? Most of us who write at all, simply write, without any thought of how certain quite fundamental matters affect our reader

As a matter of fact, most of us have been poorly condi
tioned with regard to writing.  In our childhood years we
had laboriously to learn to write long before we were
interested in writing.  Or, perhaps more accurately, we
were taught to write in ways that made 'he process most
uninteresting to ourselves.  Who does not remember the
irritated pencil-chewing over the compositions that the
teacher demanded of us?  We had no more wish to write
compositions than to take castor oil.  But the teacher had
ordered the prescription; and there was no escape.  The
result was that most of us were launched into life with the
feeling that writing was a bore.  If one were to make careful investigation, one would probably find among the large
majority of adults a fixed aversion to the effort of putting
their thoughts into written form.

A good part of this aversion, no doubt, is also due to
the impression usually given in our school days that there
were a great many complicated principles which had to be
learned about writing before one could dream of being
expert.  The false pedagogical technique was employed of
starting to teach the principles first.  It was the same
pedagogical error, in short, which is even today commonly
committed in the case of music, where lessons in the
technique of music are given to the protesting child before it
has learned to enjoy and use music in ways natural to its
child life.

Hence most of us, as adults, regard writing as a necessary
evil.  If we have fair facility, we can write good, commonplace, uninspired prose.  Or, if we are still verbally clumsy,
we write, laboriously and under inward protest, cumbersome, loose-jointed prose.  Or we dictate to our stenog-

raphers, who mercifully, for a consideration, carefully reconstruct our worst ineptitudes.

## *Writing Our Most Precious Art*

As a matter of fact, writing is perhaps our most precious
art. Without it man and his works would be as passing
as a dream. To use Korzybski's phrase, writing is the
great "time-binder." It holds the past for us in such a way
that the past functions in the present. It enables us, in
short, to inherit the experience of the race and to pass it on
with such additions as we ourselves may make.

Writing, then, because it has enabled us to preserve and
contemplate what in itself is transient and unretainable, has
been the profoundest and most wide-reaching of all the
humanly devised factors influencing our behavior. Homer
and Hesiod invested a few events and a few ideas with
permanence and became thereafter the continuous shapers
of Greek civilization. The Hebrew Bible, for the same
reason, placed its characteristic stamp upon Christian
civilization. The writings of Confucius and of Lao Tze,
which grew out of relatively transient individual experiences, gave permanent direction to two contrasted streams
of Chinese culture. The Koran became the rallying point
and the code of life for millions of human beings. Darwin's "Origin of Species" literally created a new civilization.

These are some of the master works of writing. Today
books, articles and stories multiply by the hundreds of
thousands. Every one of them is in some measure a point
of influence. The aggregate of these points of influence is
simply incalculable.

There is something so thrilling about this that one would suppose the art of writing would be cultivated as the most splendidly human of our accomplishments. A curious dualism of view has tended to inhibit this. It is the view that after all the real thing is the idea; that writing is only a kind of tool, an external conveyance for the "inner" idea. But let us note this: an idea is always a verbal form. Let the reader try to discover an idea in himself which is utterly wordless. He will not succeed. To be sure, we make statements like, "It is quite inexpressible!" "There are no words for it!" What we really mean by these expressions is that the type of experience which we vaguely feel has not yet clarified itself sufficiently to be put into words. Philologists have a way of exploring the mind-systems of ancient peoples. They note the absence of words expressive of certain ideas from the vocabularies of these peoples; and they are quite correct in inferring that the absence of the words presupposes the absence of the corresponding clearly defined ideas. In a later chapter, we shall note how the attempt to clarify our expressions leads to the clarification of our ideas. Hence it is a most unfortunate conception that attention to the verbal vehicle is after all quite unimportant; that the only real importance attaches to the "inner" idea. There is every reason to believe that the clumsy, unclear, unprecise writer is a clumsy, unclear, unprecise thinker. Also there is every reason to believe that such a writer becomes a more effective thinker through the very attempt to overcome the awkwardness and the vagueness of his written expression.

But, again, ideas are not simply delectable morsels to retain in the inner sanctuaries of our consciousness—whatever that may mean! They are potential instrumentalities of our social life. The power which they exert depends upon the way in which they enter the social life. One does not easily forget the Bible phrases. Hence the ideas conveyed by those phrases have for centuries been powerful. The Greek was gripped by the thunderous roll of Homer's lines. It was the lucidity, the logical and dramatic "march" of Darwin's writings that helped to make his ideas the storm center of an age.

There is another unfortunate factor which has inhibited the enthusiastic pursuit of the art of writing. Students in the schools and colleges get the erroneous idea that writing is only a literary art, indulged in by literary people. By literary they more or less vaguely mean something having to do with the (narrowly conceived) æsthetic and imaginative life. Thus one takes courses in writing if he intends to be a poet or story-writer; if, on the contrary, he intends to be a scientist or engineer or man of business, writing is one of the literary frills inflicted upon him by a faculty of "cultured" professors. English departments are to an extent to blame for this, because the chief emphasis of their work—a much needed emphasis, to be sure—is almost invariably upon poetry and imaginative prose. Even in the attempt to teach the art of good writing it is these types of writing which are used as patterns. The harm done is really considerable; and it would seem to behoove the traditional English department to split itself into two: into a department of Written Expression and a department of Literary Appreciation. An excellent beginning of this is to be noted in the rather widespread establishment of independent departments of Oral Expression.

Writing, then, as the great—our greatest—art of putting ideas more or less permanently into the world, should be one of our chief concerns. If we cannot now write with power, we should set about to learn. There is nothing mysterious about writing, any more than there is about cabinet making. There are tools to use and objectives to attain. Neither are beyond our power.

### Art and Artisanship

But to compare writing to cabinet making will set many heads to shaking. Particularly to say that there is nothing mysterious about writing! "All real art, my friend, is a mystery. We can, indeed, make good ordinary artisans in writing, but to make artists! Art is a gift of the gods!"

In apparent support of this let me quote a well-known passage from Tolstoy's "What is Art:" "I have else-where quoted the profound remark of the Russian artist Bruloff on art, but I cannot here refrain from repeating it, because nothing better illustrates what can and cannot be taught in the schools. Once, when correcting a pupil's study, Bruloff just touched it in a few places, and the poor dead study immediately became animated. 'Why you only touched it a *wee bit,* and it is quite another thing!' said one of the pupils. 'Art begins where the *wee bit* begins,' replied Bruloff, indicating by these words what is most characteristic of art. . . . The teaching of the schools stops where the *wee bit* begins—consequently where art begins."

The Bruloff expression is perfect. What is questionable is the mystical Tolstoyan inference. It gives too much aid and comfort to pedantic professors. If art cannot be taught, then of course professors need not be artists. But cannot we analyze the "wee bits" that transform good artisanship into art? To declare at the outset that we cannot would hardly seem to be the height of intelligence. Perhaps art is indeed something inaccessible—dark and mysterious. But perhaps it is not.

## What Makes Writing Dull?

Let us begin at the extreme opposite, with writing which, by no stretch of the imagination could be called literary art, in short, with incontestably dull writing. What makes writing dull? Apparently one or more of the following:

1. *Stodginess.* No "unfamiliar in the familiar." No phrases that hit off the ideas in ways that are different. *Clichés,* platitudes, "standard verbal equipment."

2. *Verbosity.* Too many verbal stimuli for the required effect, inducing weariness, tempting us to skip.

3. *Circumlocution.* The stimulus always coming; never arriving; hence the reader always uncertain, impatient, irritated. "Do, in heaven's name, get to the point!"

4. *Lack of clearness.* Involved phrases, long sentences, ideas badly arranged. The stimulus never quite clear. The reader makes no swift favorable response, because he does not know what it is all about.

5. *Lack of dramatic quality.* No "luring" quality. No awakening of the reader's curiosity. Hence the reader nods.

6. *Abstractness.* No vivid pictures. Pale. Slips out of the mind. Leaves no impression.

7. *Absence of Rhythm.* Nothing that "carries on." Jerky, disordered, clumsy.

8. *Monotony of Rhythm.* Movement all the same. No variety.

Now if we are suffering from any or all of the above there is no reason whatever why we should not take our particular malady in hand and go far toward curing it. There is every reason to believe that if we can achieve *distinction of expression; brevity and directness; lucidity; dramatic quality; concreteness; beauty of rhythm; daring; flash; adventurousness of phrase and idea,* we need not wonder timidly whether we have achieved that mystery called "art." We may, I think, confidently assert, that in the process of achieving these, we become artists in writing, whether we write stories, poems or scientific treatises. In short, in the above we have some of the clues to the "wee bits" that change artisanship into art.

### The Psychological Instead of the Literary Approach

It should be clear that in the above we have been considering matters which are fundamentally psychological. When is writing dull, we asked—and of course we replied, when it is dull to the reader. When is it fascinating to the reader? Apparently, so the answers ran, it is dull or fascinating when the writing-stimulus does or does not evoke certain fundamental responses in the reader. Commonplace phrasing, for example, is not just a literary quality. It is a psychological one inasmuch as it implies no effective response to the "novelty wish" of the reader. Verbosity, circumlocution, lack of clearness are psychological in that they "fog" the stimulus. Abstractness is psychological in that it places too great a tax upon our essentially concrete minds. Lack of dramatic quality is psychological in that it fails to arouse the reader's basic interest in the "chase." And so on. Once we note this, that the qualities which have been found to be requisite in good writing are requisite because they are kinds of stimuli which evoke kinds of responses, most of the mystery which resides in the "principles" of the art of writing disappear. The reason, in short, why every one of the above excellent qualities is excellent is that the reader likes them. There are, in other words no canons of literary art which prescribe them. They are prescribed, simply and solely, by the likes and dislikes of the reader.

One who wishes to write well, therefore, will make his most effective approach to the art, not by asking "What does the art of writing require of me?" but rather, "What does my reader require of me?" A great deal of the teaching of writing, one suspects, is deadly dull and ineffective, because there is in the minds of the teachers no inkling of the second question.

By this, of course, we do not mean to imply that every literary artist asks himself these psychological questions. But there can be no doubt that what he does—consciously or unconsciously—has, in preëminent degree, these psychological effects. Is there, we may ask, any advantage in becoming conscious of what many great ones do unconsciously? To say no would be to cast all teaching whatever into the discard. Let us assume then that if we know what makes writing psychologically effective we will have a measurable chance to achieve some of these effects ourselves.

Keeping in mind the above psychological points of view, let us consider, in order, the two fundamental factors in written expression: (1) words; (2) the movements of words.

## The Psychology of Words

We must develop a sensitiveness to words and word combinations. In the first place, we must learn, wherever possible, to prefer the concrete, pictureful word. The abstract word is often the lazy word. It is so much easier to say "she wore a new hat" than "she wore a perky spring hat" or "a sombre, drooping hat" or "a pot for a head-covering," or "a saucy tam-o-shanter." These descriptive terms require effort of observation. They accent the significant characteristics. They are selective. Consequently—because art is essentially an act of selective emphasis—they are art. "She wore a new hat" is just a good, utilitarian statement conveying enough information to pass muster, but no more.

In the second place we must learn to use words that have nuances. A nuance is a subtle shade of meaning conveyed with the minimum of external means. Take, for example, the sentence, "He had a quizzical lift of the eyebrow." Suppose we had said instead: "He was a person who always seemed to be saying something without actually saying it. What he always seemed to be saying was something a little humorous, a little ironic, a little sceptical. One felt that inwardly he was laughing at people, having his little joke, a joke too subtle to be put into the form of words, a joke between himself and—well, the understanding angels." The latter is fairly good prose. But it is all said, really, in the brief sentence: "He had a quizzical lift of the eyebrow." The word "quizzical" in short—or perhaps the phrase "quizzical lift of the eyebrow"—has just the whiff of nuance that makes it more than—a "wee bit" more than—an ordinary, honest-to-goodness statement.

We first wrote the concluding words in the foregoing paragraph: "an ordinary statement." Then the nuance-word "honest-to-goodness" popped into our mind, perhaps because the phrase "an ordinary statement" did not seem to say quite enough. The reconstructed phrase "an ordinary, honest-to-goodness statement" has a superiority that is at once apparent. It has an atmosphere, a suggestion of hard-headed, practical, unimaginative men which the phrase as fashioned first did not have.

So, again, such sentences as, "he walked uplifted"; "his manner was suave"; "his eye shifted, the veriest trifle" say so very much more than they actually say that they have the quality which all art has of building out of the meager-est materials a world of fascinating suggestion. To learn the art of saying more than one actually says—this is to escape the dullness of literalism. In all its numberless forms, this is what we mean by nuance in writing.

In the third place we must develop a sensitiveness to shades of meaning. In music the difference between a phrase of distinction and a banal phrase is often so slight as to be ludicrously simple, the difference, let us say, between using the dominant or the subdominant, between flatting or sharping a single note. "Anybody could have thought of that!" Verbal discrimination is often as subtle and as apparently trifling. Shall we use the word "home" or "house?" The insensitive writer will use either indiscriminately. The sensitive writer will be aware of a connotative suggestiveness in the one which the other does not have. Shall we use "country" or "nation?" Shall we use "government" or "state?" Shall we use "marriage" or "wedlock?"

In the fourth place we must learn to use "affect" words.

The most powerful approach to the reader is always through that which stirs his emotions. Every word therefore which has an "emotion" quality has power as over against the word which is emotionally neutral. The emotion quality of the word may be slight, but wherever it exists at all, it is so much to the good. Note such "affect" words as "cocky;" "mooning;" "tears;" "sighed;" etc. There are words that chuckle; words that laugh right out; words that weep; words that droop and falter. These are the words that grip the reader.

In the fifth place, we must be sensitive to the way words fit together. In the next to the last paragraph, we first wrote the sentence thus: "The sensitive writer will note a connotative suggestiveness." On reading the paragraph over, the incompatible tone quality of the two words "note" and "connotative" was at once apparent. What is it that makes some words fit and some words fight? Doubtless there is no more reason to be given than there is in the case of the harmony or the clash of certain colors. We know, however, that we can learn what colors do and what colors do not clash for most of us. In word-clashes the matter is not so simple. There are no rules; chiefly, perhaps, because the matter has never been thoroughly investigated from a psychological point of view. One has therefore to trust to his ear. But it is doubtless true that as one goes on writing and applying one's intelligence to one's writing, a sensitiveness to the harmonious fitting together of words develops. It is significant that children for the most part are insensitive to the fitting together of words in their compositions. Practice in writing (and in reading one's writing aloud) apparently develops this sensitiveness.

Here again, the factor is psychological. The great writer is one who never or seldom offends his reader's ears.

Finally, one should avoid verbal pretentiousness—long words, stilted, unusual words. They are only an annoyance to the reader and reveal to him all too surely the pretentious conceit of the writer. One of the really great poems in our language—Edna St. Vincent Millay's *Renascence*—is made up of such simple words—almost words of one syllable—that one would suppose it written either for or by a child. There is in the poem the lucid simplicity of genius (another mystical word which sadly needs analysis):

> "All I could see from where I stood
> Was three long mountains and a wood.
> I turned and looked the other way
> And saw three islands in a bay.
> So with my eyes I traced the line
> Of the horizon, thin and fine,
> Straight around till I was come
> Back to where I started from."

One does not need big words for big effects.

## Phrases of Distinction

And now we come to a difficult question: when does a phrase have distinction? Here, again, we are troubled by the "wee bit" which seems so difficult to explain. Perhaps not much can be said that is helpful. Let us, however, make a few analyses. Take Tolstoy's sentence above quoted: "The teaching of the schools stops where the *wee bit* begins." Suppose we change the Tolstoy sentence: "The schools are unable to teach the *wee bit* which constitutes art." Does that sentence have the distinction of the first? Of course not. It is dull, prosaic. What gives the flash of distinction to Tolstoy's sentence? Note in the first place an effect of balance and of contrast: "stops"—"begins." Note in the second place that these are both picture and action words. Note in the third place, the rise and fall of the rhythm. None of these qualities are found in the second sentence. Just a plain statement of fact; no picture words and only very vague action words; and no pleasurable rise and fall of rhythm.

Take, again, this sentence of Emerson: "Through every clause and part of speech of a right book, I meet the eyes of the most determined of men: his force and terror inundate every word: the commas and dashes are alive; so that the writing is athletic and nimble—can go far and live long." Let us turn that into undistinguished prose. "Whenever I read a great book, I feel the strong personality of the author; I feel the force behind his words. They seem quite living." Everything here is commonplace. It is as anyone else might have said it. But "I meet the eyes of the most determined of men;" "his force and terror inundate my soul." Note the picture words throughout; also the action words; also the surge and sweep of the rhythm.

Can we say briefly what makes a phrase distinguished? I doubt it, save perhaps that whatever else a phrase of distinction is, it is not as others would say it. There are doubtless innumerable qualities which makes phrases distinguished —a brilliant picture, an unexpected turn, a new combination of old words, a suggestion of contrast, a surge of rhythm. One who would gain effectiveness in writing could scarcely do better than to find phrases of distinction and analyze them to find out precisely why they have distinction. Such analysis would go far towards developing sensitiveness to what is rare and an aversion for what is commonplace.

### Rhythm

We come now to one of the most interesting and yet most neglected of the psychological aspects of writing—rhythm. Rhythm is fundamental in all the great arts. Rhythmless music is simply scattered tones; a rhythmless picture is a hodge-podge; a rhythmless mansion is a monstrosity. Rhythmless writing gives us the same vague discomfort that absence of rhythm in these other arts gives us.

Rhythm is a fundamental quality in human life. It might be called the "carrying on" quality. Note the rhythm of one's stride in walking. The "swing" of it already predicts the steps to come. Each step, in short, has a tempo and a space function which "carries over" into the next step. Suppose one should be asked to take a stride like this and to keep it up for several miles (no combination of steps to be repeated) :

. .      . .      . .    . . . . .     .      . .     .     . . , etc.

Obviously, one would be exhausted in a few hundred yards.

What gives us our delight in rhythmic poetry but its "carrying on" quality?

"I had a little sorrow
   Born of a little sin
I found a room all damp with gloom,
   And, locking the door tightly, for safety's sake, I shut us within."

What a monstrosity! We were expecting the fourth line to swing on triumphantly. We already felt it in our bones. Then all those unexpected squeaks and jerks. But when Miss Millay writes the fourth line: "And shut us all within," we swing along delightedly with her in her exhilarating stride.

Now many a prose writer who otherwise has excellent qualities fails for some unknown reason. His writing vaguely distresses us. Taken separately his phrases are clear, his sentences not too involved, his paragraphs unified. His ideas are sound and interesting. He is sincere. We feel that he is trying very hard to tell us something. We respect him. But we do not like to read him.

Take as an example the following passage by a distinguished sociologist, Leonard Hobhouse. Mr. Hobhouse is so notable a scholar that I dislike to use him as a horrible example, but his case illustrates so clearly one of the major weaknesses of many scientific writers that I cannot refrain:

"Into the family thus constituted a wife passed on her marriage. The marriage might be accomplished by either of two forms, and it might also be made valid apparently without any form at all. The first form was *confarreatio*, in which the essential feature was the eating by both bride and bridegroom of a cake—an act of the kind which we call symbolic, but which to primitive man is rather magical, actually efficacious in establishing a unity of the man and woman. The second form was called *coemptio*, and was of the nature of a formal sale, almost certainly, in the light of what we know of other peoples, preserving the memory of a real purchase of the wife by the husband, which as anything but a form had already fallen into disuse when history begins."

Now if the reader has read with care, he will doubtless agree that the following was his experience with that passage: For the first two sentences he swung along with a good, even stride; also through half the third sentence. Then he began to trip, to falter, to take a long step and then a short. In the fourth sentence he found himself going ahead, then being pulled back, making a dash for it, tripping and falling, getting up again, taking a running jump, and so on. At the end, the passage left him exhausted.

Now it is this—poor rhythm, not the profundity of ideas —which usually makes a book hard reading.

I know of few things to which a writer can more profitably direct his attention. Practically all of the books which are anathema to the general mind could be made readable by the simple device of changing their jerky, leg-breaking, nerve-irritating rhythms into rhythms that "swing." It is small wonder that people love to read Anatole France. Note the "carrying on" quality of the following first lines from the "Majesty of Justice." Every movement is forward—big and little movements, swift and slow, like the surge of billows.

"In every sentence pronounced by a judge in the name of the sovereign people dwells the whole majesty of justice. The august character of that justice was brought home to Jerome Crainquebille, costermonger, when, accused of having insulted a policeman, he appeared in the police court. Having taken his place on the dock, he beheld in the imposing sombre hall, magistrates, clerks, lawyers in their robes, the usher wearing his chains, *gendarmes,* and, behind a rail, the bare heads of the silent spectators. He himself occupied a raised seat, as if some sinister honor were conferred on the accused by his appearance before the magistrate. At the end of the hall, between two assessors, sat the President Bourriche. The palm leaves of an officer of the academy decorated his breast. Over the tribune were a bust representing the Republic and a crucifix, as if to indicate that all laws divine and human were suspended over Crainquebille's head."

Let the reader follow the rises and falls in the foregoing. *Rise:* "In every sentence pronounced by a judge in the name of a sovereign people (we are now on the crest of the wave); *fall:* dwells the whole majesty of justice. (Note the powerful down-sweep of that!) *Rise:* The august character of that justice was brought home to Jerome Crainquebille; *Pause:* costermonger; *further rise:* when accused of having insulted a policeman; *fall:* he appeared in the police court. *Rise:* Having taken his place in the dock; *further rise:* he beheld in the imposing sombre hall; *further rise:* magistrates, clerks (note how the wave sweeps up to its high crest), lawyers in their robes, the usher wearing his chains, *gendarmes,* and behind a rail: *fall:* the bare heads of the silent spectators. And so on.

Compare, in short, the successive surges of rise and fall—never a back eddy, never a rock in the way—with the turgid lashings back and forth of the foregoing illustration.

Recently in reading Galsworthy's *"Forsyte Saga,"* a really great book, I had the strange feeling of the drag of it in many places. Being at the time interested in this matter of prose rhythm I turned to the opening lines of the book and examined their movement. Let the reader decide why I felt a drag.

"Those privileged to be present at a family festival of
the Forsytes have seen that charming and instructive sight—
an upper middle class family in full plumage.  But who-
ever of these favored persons has possessed the gift of
psychological analysis (a talent without monetary value and
properly ignored by the Forsytes), has witnessed a specta-
cle, not only delightful in itself, but illustrative of an obscure human problem.  In plainer words, he has gleaned
from a gathering of this family—no branch of which had
a liking for the other, between no two members of whom
existed anything worthy of the name of sympathy—evidence
of that mysterious, concrete tenacity which renders a family
so formidable a unit of society, so clear a reproduction of
society in miniature."

My own feeling as I follow those lines is that, as I
stride along, I am constantly being plucked by the shoulder
and bidden to wait just a minute.  A parenthesis is slipped
into the second sentence—"just a minute please!"   A dash
is introduced into the third sentence—again comes that
arresting hand!  I must stop and listen for a number of
clauses before I can swing on again to the sentence's end.
I think we have here the secret of a certain "slow movement" quality in Galsworthy's writings.  His ideas are
perfectly clear; his pictures finely drawn; but his rhythm
constantly hesitates, holds back, then goes on, only to be
again at its irritating trick of plucking the reader by the
shoulder.

Compare the hesitating rhythm of the foregoing with
the straight-ahead rhythm of the following first lines from
Margaret Kennedy's "Constant Nymph":

"At the time of his death the name of Albert Sanger
was barely known to the musical public of Great Britain.

Among the very few who had heard him, there were even some who called him Sanje in the French manner, being disinclined to suppose that great men are occasionally born in Hammersmith.

"That, however, is where he was born, of lower middle-class parents, in the latter half of the nineteenth century. The whole world knew of it as soon as he was dead and buried. Englishmen, discovering a new belonging became excited; it appeared that Sanger had been very much heard of everywhere else."

Even this has its jerks and is consequently far less resistless in its sweep than the lines quoted from Anatole France.

Note now an example of breath-exhausting rhythm:

"The quarrel between the President and the Senate over the latter's refusal to confirm the nomination of Charles B. Warren for the office of Attorney General has revealed in the first days of the administration the anarchy which prevails in American party organization and the inability of the Republican party to agree upon any important positive policy. Considering the recent record and the public attitude of official Republicanism, there was no reason why the Republican majority in the Senate should not have confirmed him. It is true, he was more of a business man than a lawyer, and it is true that he had been responsibly associated with business interests which have apparently been engaged in defeating the purposes of the anti-trust law; but his record, while it justified the opposition to him of the Democrats and the outlawed Progressives, did not furnish any sufficient excuse for the parade of similar scruples by regular Republicans."

Does not a merciless rhythm of this kind exhaust the reader?

It is curious that so powerful a factor as rhythm in prose receives so little attention. Nevertheless from the point of view of the effect of prose writing upon the reader it is of fundamental importance. The person who would write effectively should study the movement of his lines as closely as he studies their phrasing.

## The Man Behind the Words

There is another factor which is perhaps not so easily within the control of the writer. "The personality of the speaker runs through all the sentences of real literature. That personality may not be the personality of a great poet; it may be only the personality of a penetrative seer. It may not have the atmosphere in which visions are seen, but only that in which men of affairs look keenly cut in outline, boldly massed in bulk, consummately grouped in detail, to the reader as to the writer.[1]

It is an enlightening task to note how far this is true. Personalities reveal themselves in practically all writing, not only, as Mr. Wilson would seem to believe, in "real literature." Of late, the cock-sure Smart-Aleck type of personality has been revealing itself, particularly in reviews of books and plays, in newspaper "Columns," in "snappy" essays. One needs but to read a number of these, comparing them, for example, with Lincoln's Gettysburg address to note how inevitably personality shines through the printed words.

What is the writer to do about it? Apparently only this: if he wishes his writing to be powerful, the personality revealed must be powerful. But if one's personality is

[1] Woodrow Wilson: *Mere Literature,* p. 19

weak, timid, irritable, unlovely? There is nothing to do about it but to change the personality. Is that hard doctrine? One wishes that it were more seriously considered by those who take their short-cuts to story writing and flood our magazines with literary piffle!

And so, with this idea, that, whether we will it or not, it is the personality back of the writing which gives the writing such power or lack of power as it possesses, we come once more to the conviction that the problem of effective writing is most deeply of all psychological.

## Summary

In the foregoing, we have made no effort to give an exhaustive account of the psychology of effective writing. That would take a volume. We have tried simply to suggest, quite briefly, some of the chief psychological matters to which attention may well be paid if one is to secure the effects which all good writing achieves. We have noted in the first place that dullness of writing follows from the fact that the writing falls short in a number of respects of being an adequately arousing stimulus:—it is vague, rambling; it stirs no curiosity, awakens no delighted anticipation. We found that the aim of the effective writer is to sharpen the stimulus at his command,—to have phrases that are arresting, that are clear and concise, that possess dramatic quality.

We noted, furthermore, that with reference to the words used, the effective writer aims at concrete (picture) words, at nuance words (which intrigue the imagination), and at "affect" words. Further, he is apt at discriminating shades of meaning and at sensing the auditory fitting together of words.   Finally he is chary of pretentiousness of words and phrasing.

Above, all the writer who would be effective will be as careful of his rhythms as the symphonic composer.   For his rhythms are what give his writing the "sweep" and "carry" that hold the reader to the end.

Finally, he will remember that somehow or other his personality—drab or brilliant, smart-Aleck or greatly humble—will shine through his writing; so that in very truth he will discover that "the style is the man."

If the person who is interested in writing will deliberately hold himself to this psychological point of view, he will in all probability learn secrets of effectiveness that too often are missed by those for whom writing is merely a matter of rhetorical or literary construction.

## CHAPTER VI

## CROSSING THE INTEREST DEAD-LINE

There is, in all communication—written or spoken—a certain dead-line of interest. If we can cross that dead-line we have the world with us—temporarily at least. If we cannot cross it, we may as well retire. The world will have none of us.

Note the following initial paragraph of an advertisement:

"People's Popular Monthly has grown in power and influence with its subscribers because of its outstanding editorial strength."

Am I lured on to read more? Five paragraphs follow. I may be hard to please, but I have still to read them. Why? Because there is nothing of particular interest in that initial paragraph. The statements made are quite general and commonplace. Even the phrases are *clichés*: "in power and influence"; "outstanding editorial strength." Thus, there is nothing in the paragraph that arouses my curiosity; nor does the paragraph point ahead to something which promises to be of interest.

The paragraph has hit the interest dead-line!

Note by contrast, the following initial paragraph of another advertisement:

"There are always those who question whether two and two always make four, whether a bird in the hand is actually worth two in the bush, and if a straight line is the shortest distance between two points."

Aha! here is something that has flavor and zest!  Do I read on?  I do.

"The Missouri-minded we have always with us."

Better still!  For I feel that I am being referred to as the Missouri-minded, and that I am being complimented. And so I read on to find out what is being said about the Missouri-minded.

That advertisement, in short, deftly leaps over the dead-line of interest; pulls us along into the second paragraph and has us following inquiringly to the end! [1]

Note the lure of this initial paragraph:

"It's a huge organization employing thousands of workers.  And yet it is controlled by a handful of executives."

Or these two unusual paragraphs:

"I am not interested in making up finished drawings, though I can handle this part of the work if you so desire.

"I am interested in giving you a new slant that will help you sell your goods."

Then note this dull initial paragraph:

"If in doubt about the expansion activities of the Gas Industry look for 'Construction Items' in any current issue of Gas Age-Record."

Compare it with

"Until recently it took an expert operator in our plant a day to turn out 300 inside mortises.  This was his maximum production."

[1] I am indebted for the central idea of this chapter to an article by B. Franklin Joy, entitled, "The Danger Line in Copy"; *Advertising Fortnightly*, March 26, 1924.

What happened after that? I ask myself. And I read on to find out.

Note, now, how a writer of a semi-technical paper can begin an article with a running jump. "Every now and then out of the laboratories of the psychologists comes"— what? The reader inevitably asks himself that question. And so he goes on to read—(he's over the dead-line!)— "comes an indication of a new interest on the part of scientists"—in what? "In the business of advertising."

Well, well, that sounds like something, says the business reader. "They are beginning to take the mechanism of selling apart and look with inquisitive eyes"—at what? "At the springs that make it work." Good! "To be sure, one notes in their findings a certain condescension"— of course, says the business reader, a little set up, college professors; don't we know 'em? But then, what are these scientific chaps discovering about business advertising anyway?

Does not the business reader wish to know? Of course he does; and so he proceeds to find out.

Note in the above introductory sentences how "movement" (recall the kinetic technique) is the major note. "Every now and then;" "out of the laboratories;" "comes" (a mighty word to keep us going!); "they are beginning to take the mechanism of selling apart;" "look with inquisitive eyes;" "at the springs that make it work." Every phrase gives us a sense of moving on to something else.[1]

Note, now, how a dramatist does it. In Ibsen's *John Gabriel Borkman* the scene opens in Mrs. Borkman's drawing-room. Mrs. Borkman sits on the sofa, crocheting.

[1] The article is by McAlistor Coleman—The Behavior of Crowds and Its Effect on Markets; *Advertising Fortnightly,* March 26, 1924.

She sits for a time erect and immovable at her crochet. (A dramatic vacuum that cries out to be filled!) Then the bells of a passing sledge are heard.

*Mrs. Borkman* (*Listens; her eyes sparkle with gladness and she involuntarily whispers*). Erhart! At last!

(She rises and draws the curtain a little aside to look out. Appears disappointed, and sits down to her work again, on the sofa. Presently the maid enters from the hall with a visiting card on a small tray.)

*Mrs. Borkman* (*quickly*). Has Mr. Erhart come after all?

*The Maid.* No, madam. But there's a lady——

*Mrs. Borkman* (*laying aside her crochet*). Oh, Mrs. Wilton, I suppose——

*Maid* (*approaching*). No, it's a strange lady——

Not only are we carried along with expectancy from movement to movement and from word to word (no word is useless), but almost instantly the dramatist gives us the feeling that there is something back of all this. The play is not just beginning. Much of it, we feel, has already been played. What has happened? What is going to happen? Here is the consummate art of the dramatist.

Note how a novelist does it. The first paragraph of Marcel Proust's, *Swann's Way* begins as follows. It is a long first paragraph—shudderingly long! But we do not grow tired. And for quite obvious reasons.

"For a long time I used to go to bed early. Sometimes, when I had put out my candle, my eyes would close so quickly that I had not even time to say 'I'm going to sleep.' And half an hour later the thought that it was time to go to sleep would awaken me and I would try to put away the book which, I imagined, was still in my hands, and to blow out the light; I had been thinking all the time, while I was asleep, of what I had just been reading, but my thoughts had run into a channel of their own, until I myself seemed actually to have become the subject of my book. . . ."

Compare that with some of the dull opening descriptions in the novels you have read—and liberally skipped in the reading!

Or, finally, note how an essayist does it. The following are the first sentences in H. L. Mencken's *On Being An American*:

"Apparently there are those who begin to find it disagreeable— nay, impossible. Their anguish fills the liberal weeklies, and every ship that puts out from New York carries a groaning cargo of them, bound for Paris, London, Munich, Rome and way points— anywhere to escape the great curses and atrocities that make life intolerable for them at home."

How do these advertisers, novelists, dramatists, essayists do it? Unquestionably, they have a way of luring us on. "Luring" perhaps is not the happiest word to use; but no other seems quite so appropriate. They have the art of stirring us out of our mental sluggishness and carrying us along with them wherever they will.

Obviously, no writer without something of this art can hope to be widely successful. No teacher without it can hope to be anything but dull; no speaker whether on the platform or in the drawing-room, anything but a bore.

In what, precisely, does this art of crossing the interest dead-line consist?

### Start With Situations

The first thing we note is that in each of the above "luring" paragraphs, we have not just words, abstract ideas, but a *situation*. A man questioning whether two plus two equals four! Whether a bird in the hand is worth two in the bush! A huge organization, thousands of workers, and only a few executives! A man telling you outright that he does not wish to do your finished drawings but will give you ideas.

Note by contrast the dull paragraph about the "power and influence" and "outstanding editorial strength" of the *People's Popular Monthly*. No situation, there: only words about something general and quite uninteresting.

Note again, how the skilled dramatist, instantly, at the rise of curtain creates a situation. Note how one situation passes swiftly into another and another. The outstanding weakness of amateur dramatists—particularly those who write "dramas of ideas"—is that they are wordy. They let their characters make long speeches or engage in supposedly witty dialogues while the action halts precariously at the dead-line. Words, to have dramatic quality in a drama, should serve one of two purposes: either to carry the play from situation to situation—always, in brief, pointing forward (unless a backward reference is necessary in order to carry the action forward); or to bring out essential traits of character. In both cases, words must be in the service of what is concrete—an action situation or a character situation.

Note again that our novelist starts, not with general observations, but with a concrete, easily visualized, and interesting situation. Nor is the situation a static one. Each sentence is a situation, which is part of the larger one; and each moves us on to the next.

By a situation we do not necessarily mean something taking place in the outer world. Note the following mental

situation portrayed in an opening sentence by John A.
Hobson, the British economist: "Nobody really loves the
state or its government." There is something arresting
about that. Suppose, however, Mr. Hobson had begun
his article: "The question whether, in the present day,
industry is to be more and more governmentalized, or
whether governmental activities are to be increasingly re-
stricted in scope and potency, is one which needs rather
profound consideration." Should we not be mildly dozing
at the dead-line?

### Start With Something That Makes a Difference

Scientists and philosophers have the reputation of being
the most wretched writers in the world. All honor is due
them for the keen and rigorous use of their intelligence.
One wishes, often, however, that a bit of the artist could
be mingled with their scientific and philosophic souls. No
doubt science and philosophy would have a less difficult
time making their effective entrance into our common life
if all scientists had something of the artistic genius of a
Huxley, a Pasteur, a Bergson, a William James.

Now the chief literary and dramatic vice of the scientists
and philosophers is that they seldom begin at the point of
the reader's or hearer's interest. Here, for example, is a
book on botany. It begins—heaven save the mark!—with
a long account of the history of botany! But what do you
or I (poor laymen we!) want to know about the feeble be-
ginnings of botany? We want to know—provided, of
course, that we want to be something more than the lady-
like botanists who only know the names of flowers—we
want to know what the border-land problems of botany are;

in what direction botanical research is tending; what difference all this botanical research makes anyway; why it is
worth studying.

An introductory chapter in any book on science should
begin, then, not by looking backward, but forward.   What
is in process of happening now?   And what difference does
it make if it is happening?   Therein lay the strength of the
article about what was coming out of the laboratories.

We who teach philosophy have much to answer for on
this score.   We usually begin—holding ourselves rigorously
to the logic of the calendar—by first studying the philosophy of years and years ago: the naïve thoughts that
Thales thought, and Anaximander and Anaximenes.   Not
that it makes much difference to us what they thought.
But since it is logical to begin at the beginning—and philosophers worship logic!—we go through the whole chrono-
logical agony.

As a result, most of the students—all except those who
have a pathological passion for picking up every possible
scrap of useless information about anything—very soon
hit the interest dead-line.   Later, at class reunions these
students talk in a kindly way about Professor XYZ and his
philosophy lectures and admit that about all they remember
is that Thales fell into a well and that Socrates had a wife
named Xantippe.   The other students, the pathological
ones, go on and take Ph.D.'s.

If philosophy is indeed to be a recondite study for a
curious few, this mode of approach is, of course, justified.
But if philosophy is something that needs to function in the
lives of all students, the approach is, dramatically, about
as poor as can be.

The first task of a philosophy teacher or writer, then, is

to start at the point where philosophy makes a difference.

If one watches carefully, one notes that the usual dullness of a dull scientific lecture arises out of the fact that the lecturer describes one small fact after another. *He* knows that he is building up a structure of facts; *he* knows that if the audience will only manage to keep alive throughout the preliminaries, they will be in at the killing. But the audience, knowing not whither it is all tending; seeing no wider significance in the meticulously elaborated details, soon lose all hope, and sink, with a despairing gurgle, into the tides of slumber.

A newspaper writer is wiser. First he tells the essential story—in a sentence or two. Then carefully, he rehearses it detail after detail. Every detail, now, is significant, because the reader knows what it is all about.

## Begin With an Effect Needing a Cause

If a savage hears a leaf rustle, he is all alert. "What did that?" If we find a large box in our room which was previously not there, we are suddenly aroused. "Who put that there?" "Who was in the room?"

We are essentially causal-minded creatures. Not that we think much of causes and effects in our ordinary life; but let something new enter the range of our experience and our mind leaps instantly to the causal question: "What or who did it?"

A something new, which is at the same time unexplained, acts as an instant whip to our attention. Therein lies the attention-arousing power of the paragraph quoted above about the expert operator who, until recently, turned out only 300 inside mortises a day. It is implied that now he turns out more.    As a matter of fact, we find, in the second paragraph, that now he turns out 17,200 a day!    Instantly the causal question leaps to our mind: "How does he do it?"

Therein, too, lies the power of Mencken's introductory sentences about the anguished Americans leaving their country for London, Munich, Rome, etc.    Why are they leaving?    What makes them leave?

Therein lies much of the power of Ibsen's opening.    The maid brings the card.    Oh, the usual thing, Mrs. Wilton. No, says the maid, a strange lady. . . .    Why, the strange lady?    What brought her here?

We have already spoken of situations that are like vacuums which demand filling.    Wherever, as in the above cases, an effect is presented without its adequate cause, we have what might be called a dynamic form of vacuum.    If we can induce such a dynamic vacuum, the mind of the reader or hearer is at once alert to fill the causal emptiness with adequate explanation.

## Or Begin With a Cause Implying an Effect

In the previous section we have noted how the mind, given an unexplained effect, inevitably proceeds backward to the cause.    In the same manner, a mind presented with an uncompleted cause inevitably tends to proceed forward to its effect.    Therein lay something of the interest of the paragraph quoted about those who are always questioning whether two and two make four, whether a bird in the hand is worth two in the bush.    Unusual individuals, aren't they?    What comes of it?    And therein lay something of the luring power in the assertion "I am not interested in making up finished drawings." Well, then, being such an unusual creature, what do you do?

The following are the two opening sentences of a section of an article: "The lady descended upon me after my lecture like a locomotive spurting steam. I edged back from the spray of her words." Here is a cause in full action, implying an effect to follow. Instantly, we want to know what happened. "So *you* are the man who wrote that nasty article about Americans in Mexico?" We have leaped on to the moving platform of cause-effect and we are not satisfied until we have reached the ultimate conclusion of it all.

So the rule is a good one: Present a cause in action. The mind will demand the outcome.

### The Shock Technique

Sometimes we are altogether too polite. I do not wish to make a plea for rudeness; but sometimes it takes a shock to awaken people out of their indifferences. In the play "The Goose Hangs High" the father has to lose his job before the children are shocked out of their unthinking selfishness. That seems a bit hard on father; but if the shock works . . .

"Dr. Wiley tells a story of a member of a certain Middle West legislature who sought an appropriation of $100,000 for the protection of public health; but could secure only $5,000. One morning he put upon the desk of each legislator before the opening of the session, a fable which ran something like this: A sick mother with a baby is told by a physician that she has tuberculosis and that she should seek a higher altitude. Lack of means prevents her going. She applies to the government and is told that not a dollar is available to save the mother and her child from death. At the same time a farmer observes that one of his hogs has cholera symptoms. He sends a telegram, collect, to the government. An inspector comes next day, treats the hog with serum and cures it. Moral: Be a hog! The $100,000 appropriation was promptly granted." [1]

Now suppose this legislator had been sentimentally inclined as well as polite, and instead of saying, quite brusquely, "Be a hog!" had written: "Shall we place the life of a hog above that of a mother and her baby?" would not most of the effectiveness have been lost? "Be a hog!" The legislators were not apt to forget that phrase!

The peculiar power of Bernard Shaw is that he delights in shocking us wide awake. For the shock is always a challenge to what we have accepted as right and respectable. Instantly, then, we are up in arms, perhaps, in the end, to agree with the shocker. At any rate, a good shock makes us fairly leap over the interest dead-line.

## Present a Conflict

Fundamental, of course, to all dramatic movement is the presence of conflict. A situation arouses us when two forces are at grips; and when we are unsure of the outcome. That was why, some time ago, we followed the dash to Nome with breathless interest. It was human grit and dog grit against wild Nature. Most dullness is dull because we are not precipitated into the midst of a fight. We need not be squeamish about this. All life that is at all significant is in some measure at grips with something—science

[1] Quoted from *Public Speaking;* by James A. Winans. The Century Company.

at grips with a disease; a movement at grips with a social evil; progressives at grips with conservatives; enlightenment at grips with ignorance.

To dramatize anything at all means to present it in the form of a conflict.

May the writer refer once again to his own subject of philosophy? Suppose one wishes to make so apparently undramatic a subject dramatic; what must one do? One most successful way is to find the points of sharp conflict, not the conflicts that meant something to people thousands of years ago or that are of a purely theoretical interest, but the conflicts that are real to people now, the outcome of which makes a vital difference to them. Are there any such living conflicts? Certainly to start out with a discussion of Monism *versus* Pluralism means little if anything to most of us. Suppose the world is one, or is many, what of it? In either case we shall go about our human concerns in quite the same way. But suppose we describe a real conflict between two types of mind today: Mind A, eager to improve the human situation; profoundly believing in our power to achieve progress; Mind B, aloof, amused, a little cynical, coolly declaring that we human beings, from our limited point of view, cannot have the faintest notion of what progress means; and that, even if we did have it, we should be unable to achieve anything ourselves, since it is not the human mind that governs but vast impersonal forces beyond our control. The activist and the quietist; the ardent worker and the disillusioned looker-on.

In France, Auguste Comte writes an essay with the title: "A Prospectus of The Scientific Works Required for the Reconstruction Of Society." In America, William Graham Sumner writes an essay with the title: "The Absurd Attempt to Make The World Over." A clash of viewpoints! Here, then, is a conflict that has profound significance for all of us, for if the impersonal view of world change is to be taken, there is little need for determined effort on our part; whereas if the contrasted view is held, it may be precisely the determined effort which will turn the trick for human progress.

Philosophy presented from such a point of view leaps over the interest dead-line.

## Summary

We get our readers or our hearers over the interest dead-line, then, first of all, by placing before them situations rather than abstract ideas; second, by giving them at the outset the feeling that here is something which really makes a difference. In the third place, we do it by presenting a situation which calls for explanation or from which something is bound to follow. Again, we may shock our hearers or readers by a phrase or an event which interrupts the calm flow of their ordinary consciousness. Finally, dramatic effect is attained through the presentation of conflict.

Most of us, as writers or speakers, have died many deaths at the fatal dead-line of interest. Doubtless many of us have never sought out the causes of our various demises. A very slight analysis should show us, however, that "holding people's interest," "carrying them along with us," "keeping up their expectancy" is not the result of some vague and mystical "dramatic" power possessed by a few fortunate individuals. It is the result of doing one or more of a few very simple things. When we state these simple things they seem to be so obvious as not to bear mentioning. And yet it is precisely because we do not do these very simple things that the interest-quality of what we say or write so often expires even before our audience have had time to settle comfortably into their seats.

These deaths we have died, therefore, are by no means necessary. It is altogether probable that attention to such matters as we have mentioned may quite measurably reduce our mortality average.

## CHAPTER VII

## MAKING IDEAS STICK

In the chapters on speaking and writing, we mentioned in passing the importance of the right use of words and phrases. There are two points of particular psychological significance, however, which we did not there develop. The first is with regard to the attention-holding power of certain words and phrases. Obviously, if we are really to influence persons, it is not enough simply to capture their attention. We must hold it. If what we have to say "goes in one ear and comes out the other" nothing very profound can be expected to happen. If, on the contrary, what we say "sticks in the mind," we may be sure that our words have a power to affect behavior.

### The Name That Sticks

Words are of two kinds, those of common currency, and those of special mintage. The ordinary mind uses the former almost entirely—horse, chair, house, train, river, paper. That is why the ordinary mind, in the effort to express itself, is usually dull. The out-of-the-ordinary mind, on the other hand, has a way of giving a new twist to the old words, or of arrestingly inventing new words.

"A new twist to old words" is a simple but effective formula for getting a purchase on the memory. We are not likely to forget the term, "passive resistance." Both "passive" and "resistance" are words of common currency. The combination of them, however, is of special mintage. The power of that newly constructed word-combination lies in the fact that it brings to swift, crystal-clear expression a number of ideas hitherto vaguely felt or surmised and only expressed with cumbersome circumlocution. Now that this combination of ideas is named, it becomes, for multitudes of people, an actual plan of action.

A striking example of the attention-holding power of a verbal invention is the word pragmatism. The author of pragmatism, Charles Peirce, expounded the pragmatic philosophy, but failed to realize the value of the name. William James, with his brilliant sense of literary and dramatic values, and his delight, too, in being somewhat of an *enfant terrible,* snapped up the name and gave it currency. Thereupon pragmatism began to have a vogue quite unprecedented in this supposedly unphilosophic land. So far as the American public is now concerned, William James is the author of pragmatism, although James repeatedly and more than generously referred to Peirce as the one and only original.

It is quite obvious, in this case, that it is the suggestive name that has captured and held attention for this philosophy. It is a name easily remembered. It is short and crisp. It suggests something already familiar and highly valued. It can be carried about in one's mental vest pocket and slipped in and out with easy grace.

In fact, it may be fairly ventured that the mere name, pragmatism, has secured its thousands of adherents where the full exposition of the philosophy has claimed barely its hundreds. This, perhaps, is not particularly complimentary to the race of thinkers on the American side of the Atlantic; for it seems to suggest a quite undue readiness to strain at a philosophy and swallow a title. Nevertheless, since we are psychologizing, the fact must be noted. The historic flower that was born to blush unseen probably was unlucky enough to have been unnamed. Had William James called his philosophy, "Metaphysics of Instrumental Values and Anticipated Outcomes," he would doubtless have had the scholar's profound satisfaction of seeing his *magnum opus* still-born.

We might give a long list of the names that are not easily forgotten: materialism, mechanism, vitalism, atomism, imperialism, nationalism, militarism, fundamentalism, radicalism, modernism, Marxianism, Bolshevism, behaviorism. Some of these are already passing into common currency; and yet, as names that have had attention-holding values, they have all been rallying cries; they have all profoundly influenced human behavior.

Note the attention-holding power of the following—also the delightful gaiety of some of them: jazz, flapper, robots, bootlegger, lounge-lizard, pussy-foot, pee-wee politician, fascist, Rotarian.

## *Regarding Reformers*

"The frequent failure of the reformer," writes Professor William Bennett Munro, in his *Personality in Politics,* ". . . is due to his deficient understanding of group-psychology as well as to his intolerance, his antipathy to discipline, and his lack of team play. The success of any new cause depends not only upon its merits but upon the way in which it is brought to the public attention. Truth is mighty, of course, and will prevail; but it does not always prevail immediately. To get the truth accepted is sometimes a long and difficult fight. . . . Those who have merchandise to sell are well aware of the fact that successful marketing is largely a matter of making the right sort of appeal to prospective purchasers. So they give heed to the psychology of advertising. They find that it pays to give their wares an attractive name; the name, indeed, is so important that great care is taken to find the best one.

"Now the selection of a good designation, or symbol, or slogan, is equally important when it comes to placing *ideas* on the market, for you can sell an idea to the country, just as you sell a brand of soap or a breakfast cereal—by the effective and reiterated stamping of an impression upon the public mind. But . . . when (reformers) have a meritorious idea to plant in the minds of the people they have usually designated it by whatever makeshift of a name happened to be at hand. Civil service reform, for example, is an appellation borrowed from England, where the whole body of permanent governmental employees is known as the 'Civil Service.' But in America the employees of the government have never been generally known by that name, and hence the term civil service reform has proved to be neither appropriate nor self-explanatory. It has been a dead-weight upon a worthy cause. Of late, the attempt has been made to substitute 'merit system,' which is a far better term and one that ought to have been adopted forty years ago; but usage has now hardened the old terminology. So with the clumsy 'initiative and referendum.' Reformers who stand sponsor for this device now prefer to call it direct legislation or direct lawmaking. Why did they not project it into public discussion under one of these better names at the outset? The Populists, thirty years ago, began a movement for 'the imperative mandate.' But no reform could ever make headway among the American people with that appellation hitched to it. So the name was presently changed to 'the recall.' Many other illustrations might be given. Terms like proportional representation, segregated budget, and excess condemnation are a handicap to the reforms that they embody. Compare them, for example, with such terms as short ballot, open shop, woman suffrage, and city manager. . . .

"Reform ought to be sold to a people in their own language. When Theodore Roosevelt spoke of giving everybody a 'square deal' he said something that the wayfaring man could get hold of. In two words he wrote a whole program. But when reformers go to the factory gates and discourse about the reduction of maximum surtaxes, standardization of salaries, unit-costs and personnel administration, they might better save the strain upon their throats."

## Phrases That Stick

We are all getting to be a little ashamed of slogans. They belong, many of us feel, to "Babbittry and boost." Social workers, in their efforts to galvanize a lethargic public into response, have been compelled to sloganize so much that most of them are sick to death of slogans. A recent satirical novelist has invented the phrase: "The son of a sloganeer."

Perhaps it is because the slogan, as used in our strenuous campaigns, is too obviously intrusive. It is like the eager person who plucks you by the coat; pulls you toward him, and talks forcibly into your face. Lest we find ourselves in too bad company, therefore, we prefer to use the expression: "phrases that stick."

Phrases that stick are powerful as attention-holders and as influencers of behavior. The kinds that are really effective, of course, are those that delight us; those that awaken a strong emotional response; those that express for us swiftly, powerfully what we feel and think. They may convey intensity of feeling, as "My country right or wrong;" or "No entangling alliances;" or "Deutschland über alles;" or "God save the King;" or "Equal rights to all and special privileges to none." Or they may be a call to action: "Workers of the world unite!"

Phrases and sentences like these are powerful because they are so brilliantly economical of our thought-power. They do not enter our minds by long, circuitous routes. No sooner are they spoken than they are part of us. And once part of us, they refuse to be forgotten.

In England one hears constantly the saying: "What Lancashire thinks today, England will think tomorrow." Whether that is actually true or not, I do not know. I question whether anyone knows. But I have no doubt that the very pithiness and confident assurance of that saying has had a powerful effect upon the English public. Even though derided by individuals, it must already have established an attitude towards Lancashire hard to deflect or reverse.

One wonders what effect upon human behavior the following old Yorkshire motto can have had:

> "Hear aw, see aw and say nowt;
> Eat aw, tek aw and pay nowt;
> And if thou does owt for nowt
> Do it for thysen."

Here is cynicism immortalized! Pity that we have no way of measuring what it actually did to old Yorkshire character!

"Say it with flowers" is a phrase that has come to be part of our everyday life. When we are in doubt, we need no book of etiquette. The phrase leaps to mind; and we "say it with flowers." The same may be said of the phrase "Safety first," which has helped to bring about a new era in the safeguarding of life against preventable accidents. "Unhooking the hookworm"—used by the Rockefeller Foundation to describe their work—is doubtless more

effective than a whole volume of reports.    "A salesman is
known by the customers he keeps"—a prize-winning slogan
of a New York company—might well be destined to produce a most desirable type of salesman.

In the attempt to teach safety habits, competitions in
the making of "safety slogans" have been held in numbers
of schools.    The following are part of an ABC alliterative
list made by the children of the Abbot Street School, Wor-
cester, Mass:

> Avoid All Accidents
> Beware Before Bumping
> Carelessness Causes Casualties
> Don't Do Daring Deeds
> Eye Every Exit
> Fire Finds Filth
> Gasoline Gathers Gloom
> Health Has Happiness
> Ignorance Invites Injury
> Joy Riding Justifies Jail.

The Bible has been powerful because it is so easily quot-
able.    "Blessed are the merciful;" "I am the vine and my
Father is the husbandman;" "Father forgive them, for
they know not what they do;" "The Sabbath was made for
man, not man for the Sabbath;" "I will lift up mine eyes
to the hills whence cometh my help;" "My help cometh
from the Lord;" "The Lord is my Shepherd, I shall not
want."    Translate the last into good literal English and
see what happens:    "In matters that concern my bodily
and spiritual welfare, I am convinced that God is a
thoroughly dependable caretaker!"

Our attitudes towards influencing behavior have been

so predominantly moralistic that we have, for the most part, failed to realize the power that lies in the creation and the use of words and phrases that stick. Even now the reader may be shuddering at this chapter. "How trifling! How purely external!" And yet, if the reader will explore his own mind and recall what has really been of profound and continuing influence in his life, he will no doubt find that it is, in large measure, the words and phrases that have sunk so deeply into his consciousness that they have become part of himself. Hence, if we would be powerful in influencing our day and generation, we must not scorn verbal facility as something too external to be bothered about. We may indeed be great enough to be mentally powerful and verbally clumsy. But there is no virtue in verbal clumsiness. Nor do we abdicate our profundity, if we seek, with the spirit of the artist, to sharpen and intensify our verbal expressions.

### Toning Up the Cliché Mind

This brings us to our second point: attention paid to the sharpening of our verbal expressions is attention paid to the sharpening of our minds. Only as our minds are sharpened are we able to fashion the "phrases that stick." Let us, for a moment, discuss that rather frequent phenomenon, the mind that constantly uses commonplace expressions or *clichés*. Of course we all use *clichés*. We use them by the dozens and the scores. We cannot help doing so. The very phrase that we used in the former sentence is a *cliché*. We might, in an attempt to be brilliantly different, have said: "We use them by the fives, the sevens, the thirteens and the twenty-ones." That

would at least have been arresting.   But what would have
been the good?   We should only have succeeded in arousing arithmetical annoyances and in diverting attention from
what we were going on to say.   One can, in short, be altogether too brilliant.   In one's attempt to be different,
one can (to use another *cliché*) lean over backward so
far that one risks being taken for a vaudeville tumbler.

And yet there comes a time in the speech of men when
we sometimes pray that we may be delivered.   Listening
to a number of addresses a few days ago, we collected the
following literary—heavens! we were just going to write
"gems"!   Another radiant *cliché!*  Let us call them
"literary prunes"!   "I feel it a great honor to be present
on this occasion;" "extend a most hearty and cordial welcome;" "in paying my humble tribute;" "let us express a
hope;" "it is but fair to say;" "of whom we are proud"!

Can not the reader catch the orotund solemnity of those
phrases that surely hark back to Hammurabi and the Pyra-
mids!   Particularly of that grand old wheel-horse of a
phrase: "of whom we are proud!"

But these were not all by any means; for in due order
came: "it is a rare privilege;" "in the chosen field of his
endeavors;" "we are honored by the presence;" "who
drank at the fountain of learning;" "on this occasion we are
gathered to pay tribute."

Then the inevitable stock-in-trade of reminiscence!
"That summon up the memories of one's youth;" "in my
mind's eye this splendid auditorium fades into perspective;"
"the dear old chapel;" "those who have passed into the
Great Beyond;" "my heart is filled with gratitude;" "that
respect for age and tradition;" "lessons of the past;" "in
this my native city;" "this beloved institution of ours."

And finally, in one grand rapture of ecstatic eloquence: "that stimulus to high ideals of character and citizenship which . . . !"

There is a point, in short, at which the use of *clichés* becomes a symptom. We may all use a goodly number of them and do no harm; but one more, another and still another; and the proverbial camel's hump breaks beneath the final straw! A physician will often make a profound diagnosis from what is apparently a most trifling aberration. Take the knee jerk, for example. Most of us have knee jerks, but are quite unaware of it. But let the physician discover in us an absence of this useful little kick; and he pulls a grave face. There is, then, something deeply the matter with us. So, in like manner, the absence of those slight qualities of difference in one's phrases, of nuance, suggestiveness, should cause the expert reader of minds to regard us a little closely; to inquire solicitously about our mental processes; to doubt whether the vitality of our intellectual life was quite up to par.

A *cliché,* of course, is, by definition, a "stereotype plate." Printers, in America, have a less elegant name: "boiler plate." "Boiler plate stuff" is a short trade name which speaks volumes. There is in it a fine, airy contempt for the kind of literary "junk" that is bought by the ton—particularly by the small country newspapers. No brains required of the editor. Just so much per pound, delivered; and the trick is turned!

Some day we shall cease attempting to read character by the face. Our faces are born with us; and there is not much that we can do about it. But our phrases! "Well what do you know about that!" There are at least seventy million back fences over which that phrase is being tossed with open-eyed wonder. "Did you ever!" "You don't say so!" "Well I never!" "And so I sez to him, sez I; and he sez to me!"

"Out of their mouths shall my people be judged." That is good psychological doctrine; for our verbal habits are in large measure the reflex of our thinking habits. The inveterate cliché-ist is apt to be the inveterate platitudinarian. He is animated boiler plate. He is—particularly if he is earnest and eloquent—resounding literary junk.

## What Can Be Done About It?

How does one get that way? Political stump speakers are apt to be the star performers with *clichés*. Is it because they have grown so used to appealing to the least common denominator of the crowd intelligence that their own intelligence has ceased to function? We know that a subtle thought, an unusual proposal, a new idea has a poor chance to "get across" in a large political meeting. For the most part, only platitudes win applause. Only the accustomed clap-trap appeals. Does a political speaker deliberately suppress his subtler intelligence; keep it assiduously hidden; does his intelligence grow flabby from disuse; or is he perhaps a successful political speaker precisely because he has no truly searching intelligence?

There is of course a value in accustomed phrases. They represent verbal habits which, in the aggregate, save a prodigious amount of one's energy. It would be as foolish to ask a person to frame a novel phrase for each meaning expressed as to bid him tie his necktie in a new way every morning. Habits are formed for the sake of releasing other worthwhile energies. And so it is with these mental habits called commonplace phrases. One need therefore not be ashamed of using a good many commonplace phrases provided that in some region of one's speech, one's phrases wear that mark of precision and of distinction which announces a living, functioning mind behind the words.

The *cliché* mind is the mind which never shows these marks of distinction, which on all occasions and in every way, uses the words and the phrases that everybody is using. One would suppose that this kind of mind rarely exists. As a matter of fact it exists in droves. Most persons, in short, show in their speech precisely that absence of subtle distinction and uniqueness of phrasing which is the sign of the commonplace, the nondiscriminating mind.

But if this is so, what is to be done about it? If the mind is commonplace, the speech will be commonplace, will it not? and there's an end of it! Are we contending here that by attempting to polish up one's phrasing, one can change one's commonplace mind into a mind more distinguished?

Precisely. And for this reason. The mind is no mystical entity, existing in aloof, metaphysical changelessness as either commonplace or distinguished. *The mind is what it does*. Or better still, *the mind becomes what it does*. Give a mind something new to feed upon; give it something new to do; and it becomes a different mind. Let us suppose, for example, that a person, convicted of the rather inordinate use of *cliché* phrases, set about to overhaul his speech. Suppose he deliberately noted down all the quite commonplace phrases he used; and then, when no one was attending, tried out all the possible modifications and improvements of which he could think.

That would be an exercise in sharpening his own mind! In short, in the very effort to halt a *cliché* on its banal way; in the very effort to make it say more precisely, or more colorfully, or more subtly what he wished to say or what he might have wished to say had he known better, he would be emerging from the *cliché* class.

It is not sufficiently understood, perhaps, that the power of a mind is directly conditioned by its verbal equipment. A person with a very small vocabulary inevitably has a small range of thought. A person with a larger range of vocabulary has a larger range of thought. The reason for this is fairly clear. Suppose a person has never heard of the word "ethnology." He consequently does not possess the clearly defined idea-system suggested by that word. Suppose now he learns the meaning of the word, so that he can use it freely. A new idea-system has been added to his stock. Thus, as our effective vocabulary increases, our thought-systems increase.

Even by the simple process of increasing our verbal tools, therefore, it is within our power to increase our thought-systems. Now the same result occurs when we attempt to substitute for phrases that are vague, colorless, and commonplace, phrases that express our meanings with greater vividness, subtlety and precision.

To clarify a phrase, therefore, is to do more than engage in a mere bit of literary brightening. It is to clarify one's mind. Thus by becoming thoughtful about our commonplace phrases we become thoughtful about our commonplace ideas. We begin to probe them; to modify them;

and sometimes to discard them altogether.    And so we begin to shape ideas of our own that are less commonplace
—which signifies the quite noteworthy fact that we have
passed out of the stage of easy acceptance of phrase and
idea into the stage of individual creation.

Adults often complain that they have no opportunities
for continuing their education.    But here is a laboratory
constantly at our command.    We can place the microscope
over our words and phrases; we can apply the scalpel of
our analytic intelligence; we can experiment with our expressions, trying them out until they hit off exactly what
we think we mean.    We are curiously inhibited from doing
all this by the quite misleading idea that words are only
external after all and do not really count; that only our
"inner thoughts" count.    If we could clearly grasp the
idea that the words are our thought-responses, that vague
words and phrases indicate vague thoughts, precisely as a
carpenter is known by his tools, we should realize that we
sharpen our thoughts not by some esoteric process of turning inward, but by deliberately working away at the symbols which we use to convey to others what we mean.
When we do that we begin to be able to say things in ways
that are not easily forgotten.

## Summary

Words and phrases, then, are far more than mere symbols about which we can be relatively indifferent.    They
are perhaps the most powerful instrumentalities we possess
for effectively and permanently lodging ideas in the mind.
To be able to devise a name or a phrase that will stick,

is to have a way of entry into the mind that is swift and sure.

Again, to pay careful attention to the "pointing up" of one's words and phrases; in other words, to try to be less commonplace in one's verbal expression, is not simply to engage in a kind of literary polishing. It is to engage in a process of sharpening and clarifying one's mind.

Hence, attention to words and phrases has profound psychological significance. He who would influence human behavior can hardly do better than to proceed quite seriously and persistently to overhaul his verbal equipment.

# PART TWO

# FUNDAMENTAL TECHNIQUES

## CHAPTER VIII

## HOW TO CHANGE PERSONS: THE ENTERING WEDGE

Our influencing of persons is of two types. The first may be called incidental influencing. Thus, for example, by a proper approach, we induce·a person to buy our products; to vote for our candidate; to study what we suggest; to listen to our speech; to read our article. A great deal of this incidental, more or less impermanent kind of influencing goes on in the world and must go on. In the ordinary acceptation of the phrase, a person "makes good" to the extent that he is able, in general, thus to be persuasive with people. Therefore it is important that we know how such persuasiveness is most effectively accomplished.

Many of us, however, find ourselves with a more difficult problem on our hands. We find it necessary to influence certain persons in a profounder and more lasting way; to change them, in short. They may be our children, our husbands or wives, our pupils, our fellow workers, our employees. This problem takes us into regions far more difficult than any that the foregoing techniques have explored; although, as we analyze the deeper issues involved, we shall discover that much of what we have learned about the incidental techniques will apply.

How may we most effectively solve this profounder

problem of changing individuals? We wish, for example, to build up a stronger character in our child; to alter what is disagreeable in this or that individual's personality; to make this or that person more responsible; or this or that person less sexually irregular. This is no child's play. It means, at the least, that we must understand rather thoroughly what people are and how they can be induced to alter the accustomed, ofttimes "ingrained" manner of their lives.

At the outset we are stopped by the vagueness—one might better say, the mysteriousness—of such terms as the following: "character;" "personality;" "the individual;" "human nature." What, as a matter of fact, is the "character" of a person? If we wish to set about changing his "character," at what point do we start? Again, what is the individual's "personality?" Is it, in the main, something born in him; something hereditary, innate; something not really subject to alteration? What is "the individual?" A mysterious ego? A metaphysical entity? What does one do with an individual if one wishes to change his individuality? And finally, what is one's human nature? Most often, when we try rather profoundly to change people, we are told that human nature cannot be changed.

With all these mysterious terms confronting us, the task of making any really striking and permanent alteration in the character or personality or human nature of an individual seems more than difficult.

Let us begin first with human nature, since it is in its name that most sins are committed. When we are asked what we mean by human nature, most of us are probably at a loss. It is one of those terms which is more easily used than understood. This man, for example, is an industrious worker. Is industriousness part of his un-changeable human nature? This man refuses to give his seat to a lady. Was he born that way; and is it quite impossible to make him otherwise? This man dislikes artichokes. Certainly that is not part of his irrevocable human nature. This girl prefers jazz to Beethoven. Can nothing be done about it?

We know, of course, that it is of the permanent nature of human beings to have two legs, two ears, a pair of eyes, and so on. Is it likewise of the permanent nature of any human being to be a liar, or a thief, or a movie fan or a college professor? Perhaps the lying propensity is just as inborn as two-leggedness; perhaps a poor infant, even in its cradle, is already doomed to be a college professor.

Much of this, of course, is obvious nonsense. And yet it is not always easy to say precisely where the human nature that is unchangeable leaves off and the human nature that is changeable begins. What our modern psychology seems to teach us is that there is a certain raw material of human nature which is practically unchangeable. For example, we all have the impulse to avoid danger; to seek food and warmth; to unite with the opposite sex; and so on. In these respects we are all precisely the same; and there is no more hope of changing us than there is of transforming an oak tree into an armadillo.

But we are far more than raw material. We do not live long in the world before we are raw material shaped into particular forms. Thus, while we all are born with the impulse to avoid danger, an Amazonian learns to avoid danger from jungle animals and fever; while a New Yorker learns to avoid danger from automobiles and subway jams. While we are all born with the impulse to unite with the opposite sex, the cave-man goes out for his mate with a club; while the young civilian of Paterson, New Jersey, goes out with a box of candy. And even in Paterson, New Jersey, techniques differ. One youth has learned to prefer flowers to candy; another a dashing motor car; another a volume of Carl Sandburg's poetry.

It is in the manner in which the raw material of our human nature is shaped that each individual differs from every other. Is the shaping within our power? It would be an extreme hereditarian, indeed, who would maintain that one youth is born to "say it with flowers" and another to "say it with a motor car!" These youths, for a number of reasons—home influence, the novels they have read, the money at their command—have developed different courting habits.

Now habits, apparently, can be shaped and changed. There is no mystery about them; for we have all watched habits grow in ourselves; and have all, with more or less success, discontinued certain of our habits. It is only when we think of changing "character" or "personality" that the mystery begins. But what, now, is one's "personality" or "character?" If one thinks of one's personality *as a whole,* one gets nowhere. But if one analyzes it, a very significant fact begins to emerge.

Let the reader consider himself, for example. He is doubtless proudly aware that he has a far more delightful personality than that of his brother, let us say. Just what is the difference? Well, for one thing, his brother is never up on time in the morning. That is most annoying to the family and leads to much expostulation and the characterizing of him as lazy. The reader himself is always up on time. Now what this means is that he has one system of rising habits, while his brother has another. Again, his brother never finishes a job. Therefore the family call him a slacker. The reader himself always finishes a job. So the family call him reliable, trustworthy, a pusher-through-of-things. Here also, the difference between the reader and his brother is that the former has one system of work habits, and the latter has another. Again, the reader's brother is rather inconsiderate of other people. He never offers to clear up a room or wash the dishes when the maid is away. The reader himself is always offering to clear up rooms and wash dishes; and so he always gets the job. This means, in other words, that the reader has one kind of social habits; his brother has another.

And so on. If the reader will examine carefully what he calls his "traits" of character, he will find that they are nothing very mysterious; they are only his predominant habit systems. The reader's kindliness, for example, is his habit of thinking of other people; of doing them a service; his thoroughness is a habit he has, in every task he undertakes, of seeing that each detail is attended to; his lack of irritability is his habit of controlling himself under trying circumstances.

Everyone, in short, has a large number of habit-systems. Let us enumerate a few of them. Everyone has a system of work habits (thoroughness; accuracy; slovenliness; passing-the-buck; watching-the-clock); consumer habits (paying cash; running up accounts; keeping a budget; living beyond one's means); bodily habits (clean face and hands; daily bath; neat clothes; or the opposite of these); play habits (fair play; sticking-it-through in play; generosity to opponents; cheerful losing); moral habits (truthfulness;

lying; dependability; loyalty); emotional habits (irritability; meanness; interest-in-others; sympathy; comradeship), etc.

A person, in short, is what he is by reason of the more or less unified aggregate of his habit-systems.[1]

## The Habit-System as the Point of Approach

Now it is obvious that when we think of changing a person *as a whole,* the task seems quite hopeless. And usually when we talk of changing an individual's character or personality, we are thinking of him *as a whole.* When we note, however, that a person is not just one mysterious entity, but is a complex of many systems of habits—literally dozens and scores of them—the task of changing him reduces itself to the not so difficult task of changing this or that particular system of habits. [2]

It should be clear, then, that whether we are interested in changing persons into the kind of beings we should like them to be, or in changing them from the kind of beings they are, the successful way to "get at" them is through

[1] This same view "that our personality is but the outgrowth of the habits we form" is presented in brilliant fashion by Dr. John B. Watson in Chapter XII of his *Behaviorism.* The People's Institute Publishing Company. New York.

[2] One of my friends, listening to the above account of personality, felt sorely troubled about the "ego." What had become of it? Were we simply "bundles of habits?" He was respectfully referred to metaphysics. In this practical, work-a-day world, admitting to the full all the mystery that still surrounds the processes of human life, an individual *is* the more or less unified system of his habits. What these habits depend upon is, of course, a further question. They may depend upon dozens of conditions: a normally or abnormally functioning thyroid gland; shortness or tallness of stature; birth in a minister's home, or a physician's; an invalid mother, and so on.

their habit systems.   These give us the entering wedge to personality.

Let us note how this may be done in child life.   The following is a case of profoundly changing a personality.[1]

### "Waking Up"

"Alice Gould at fourteen had not yet . . . got beyond the point where reading was a painful exercise. . . . In other school subjects she was somewhat retarded, partly because of a general intelligence level which fell slightly below average, largely because of a succession of severe illnesses.   She had, however, been pulled up noticeably toward the normal standard for her age during her last year in an opportunity class.   Her hand work was especially good and she showed artistic ability.   But all the efforts of her teacher had not availed to inspire her with the faintest glow of enthusiasm for the printed page.

". . . She was listless and indifferent.   She took little interest in what was going on about her, was shut-in and unsocial.   Her teacher felt that she needed to be 'waked up.' . . .

"Alice was an orphan and an only child.   She had been taken at the age of five by her father's brother and his wife, who were childless.   Dr. Gould, the uncle, was a successful physician.   Both he and the aunt had been pleased to have her come to them—she was dainty and attractive, very quiet and well behaved.   But as she grew tall and ungainly, and as she failed to make normal progress in school, Mrs. Gould in particular began to show marked sensitiveness over the child's backwardness.   This sensitiveness was rendered more acute as time went on by the growing contrast between Alice's failures and the successes of two girl cousins who lived next door.   The older at sixteen was preparing for college, the younger

---

[1] *The Problem Child in School;* by Mary B. Sayles; p. 93.   *Joint Committee on Methods of Preventing Delinquency.*   New York.   This book is rich with material for the study of techniques.

at twelve was already in the seventh grade. . . . The pride displayed by Mrs. Gould's sister-in-law in these two daughters . . . grew more and more painful to the childless woman who had hoped to find compensation in the small person she had been mothering. This much of Alice's story was known to her teacher and was passed on by her to Miss Jones, the visiting teacher.

"In her first talk with her new charge Miss Jones employed certain devices suggested by her experience in the effort to find out where Alice's interests lay. Some simple tests revealed good powers of observation; Alice gave an excellent description of a farm scene which had been worked out by the first grade in their sand table, and became interested in solving problems of practical life put to her in connection with the farm. She took this as a game and her attitude, which at first had been a bit stand-offish and suspicious, grew friendlier. It presently appeared that she enjoyed housework and sewing. She associated very little with the girls in her room, many of whom came from poor homes. She had dropped out of Sunday school because she read so poorly that she was ashamed to go. . . .

"The Gould home proved to be a charming new colonial cottage on a hillside overlooking a recently developed park. Mrs. Gould, an attractive, intelligent-appearing woman, received the visiting teacher with marked coldness. Her manner suggested that a visit from anyone connected with the school could only mean added disgrace, and that she would much prefer not to discuss her niece's shortcomings.

"Miss Jones, however, . . . began by talking of Alice's practical accomplishments, her skill in sewing and household tasks, with a manner that assumed the aunt's pride in such talents. Mrs. Gould was manifestly pleased; her whole manner changed as she eagerly agreed that Alice had real gifts in these directions. It appeared that the girl was doing well with her music.

"At Miss Jones's request, Mrs. Gould brought out a volume of Longfellow belonging to Alice. From this the girl read, haltingly,

'The Children's Hour.' Then, asked to retell it, she condensed it into two short literal sentences. 'You see what a practical mind she has,' commented Miss Jones. 'Not everyone could tell the story in so few words.' Mrs. Gould beamed with pleasure. What Alice needed, it was pointed out, was practice in reading and encouragement. After considerable discussion of the situation, Mrs. Gould agreed to spend half an hour every afternoon in listening to Alice read aloud. Apparently it had never occurred to her that she herself could thus help in the solution of her niece's problem. She had been a competent business woman before her marriage; teaching and child psychology had been quite outside her realm.

"Another topic touched upon in this conversation was that of Alice's possible future career. The child had never pictured herself as anything but a business woman like her aunt. . . . Miss Jones suggested the possibility of work with small children—Alice was devoted to youngsters of the kindergarten age; or specialization in domestic science. These new ideas fairly startled the girl out of her habitual lethargy. . . .[1]

"After this home visit Alice reported every week to the visiting teacher. She practised reading regularly with her aunt, and in an astonishingly short time showed such marked improvement that she began to do her share of reading in the general school exercises, even taking part in a play at the Christmas celebration, much to the surprise of her classmates.

"Beginning with the new term Miss Jones had Alice report at the same hour with a number of other girls, who also needed waking up, and welded them into a little weekly class in world events. Each girl was responsible for bringing in one story a week of some important happening or phase of living in a foreign country. Miss Jones herself stimulated them by telling tales of high adventure in distant lands, figuring such heroes as Livingstone and Dr. Grenfell. The girls were to get their material from books or magazines, or from conversation with their elders.

[1] Note the technique of inducing an imagined experience.

"After some weeks of this exercise, Alice one day brought in : story about the stamping out of malaria and yellow fever in th Panama Canal Zone. Her uncle, it appeared, had become intei ested in the mental awakening of his niece. He had set her the task of doing a certain amount of newspaper reading every day and reporting on it to him at dinner time. Alice was made to feel that this was of value to him, and her pride and pleasure in her task were evident.[1]

"No less encouraging were the signs of social awakening in this shut-in listless child. Her manner took on a new liveliness and her relations with her classmates became friendlier. She began to take an interest in her appearance, and asked her aunt if she might have her hair bobbed.

.    .    .    .    .    .    .    .    .    .

"The new phase of Alice's existence which opened thus propitiously has continued to unfold itself. She has been making a good record in the domestic science department of junior high school. The future now holds many possibilities for this girl who less than two years ago could see nothing before her but a struggle to fit herself for work in which she felt doomed to failure."

## Entering Wedges

Now if the visiting teacher had thought of Alice Gould simply as a personality gone wrong, she doubtless would not have proceeded very far. What she saw was that Alice Gould was deficient in one rather important habit-system, the reading habit-system. Deficiency in that habit-system, she realized at once, might quite easily be the cause for deficiency in another important habit-system, the social. As a matter of fact, the little girl was listless and indifferent, was shut-in and unsocial. Wisely enough the teacher

[1] Note the putting-it-up-to-you technique.

took as her point of approach the deficient reading habit-system. In her investigations she soon discovered that the deficiency both in the reading and the social habit-systems was accentuated by a certain habit-system in the child's foster parent, namely, the criticism-and-expression-of-disappointment habit.

The problem, then was to modify these two habit-systems, the one in the child, the other in the foster parent. By a clever emphasis upon some of the strong habit-systems of the child, the criticism-and-disappointment habit of the foster parent was changed and incentive was given the child for the improvement of her reading.

An analysis of this kind shows that the crucial problem of personality was reducible to habit-systems. The little girl lacked the one type of habit which gave her the golden key to life. No wonder, then, that she was listless, shut-in, unsocial. A visitor to the school no doubt would have called her a dull child, without magnetism, and would have pitied her for not having been born with better endowments. An improvement in a single habit-system was effected; and the dullness disappeared!

May it not be true of many a person of whom we say that he lacks personality, that the lack lies not in some mysterious entity called the ego, but only in some as yet undiscovered habit deficiency? All that is needed, apparently, is to analyze the habit-systems of such a person to discover the one which is deficient and which has an inhibiting influence upon a whole group of habit-systems. If only that could be done, the drab and ineffective personality might easily flower into effectiveness and charm.

Such is the technique employed in a very amusing play by Rachel Crothers, "Expressing Willie." The heroine has one inhibiting habit, the habit of self-depreciation. That self-depreciation habit influences her other habits, makes her timid and awkward, hesitating in speech, subservient in her ideas, uninteresting. She is taken hold of by a clever artist at a house party and induced to "let herself go," to "express herself." Instantly her character is transformed. Her other habit-systems fall into line; and she becomes the fascinating center of the group.

No doubt Miss Crothers has, in this case, used dramatic liberties which go beyond the psychological probabilities; but taken as symbolic, the play presents a genuine case of the transformation of the whole personality through the correction of one deficient habit-system.

Let us take one other typical character problem from *Youth in Conflict,* by Miriam Van Waters,[1] a valuable discussion of juvenile court techniques for handling character conflicts.

"Four girls, fourteen, sixteen, fifteen and seventeen years of age are next on the calendar. They are high school students, healthy young Americans of 'good' families. They are involved in a 'school scandal.' One was discovered by her teacher to possess a notebook of dull obscenities, sex jokes and drawings, together with improper parodies of popular songs, and what would have been, if true, a casual, supposedly witty account of rape on a school girl. These she had obtained from another girl, the delicate daughter of a minister, who in turn had received them from a certain taxicab driver. This young fellow, on being brought to court, was discovered by psychological examination to be feeble-minded. The notebook had circulated among students, brilliant, dull, rich and poor.

"The four girls now before the court were the popular, well-dressed daughters of good families. They smoked, drank (when

[1] Republic Publishing Company. New York. Page 43.

they could get it), rode home from dances in taxicabs with young men, took all night joy-rides, used a great deal of paint and powder, swore at their parents. Each had a 'daddy,' although the tenure of office and length of service of these young lovers were precarious. The girls were sophisticated, tired; any exertion, besides dancing, wore them out. They detested athletics, books and housework. They stood about average in high school work.

"Three boys were also before the court, as witnesses, aged fifteen, seventeen and twenty. They were prominent students in scholarship and activities. They were not, it seems, 'daddies' of these girls, but there was some imperative, diplomatic reason why they should 'help' the girls who were in a 'scrape' or impending unpleasantness at home. So, the youngest boy obtained the parental automobile, the three boys and four girls 'eloped,' that is to say, went to the neighboring county-seat to procure marriage licenses. En route gasolene gave out. Thereupon the parental car was abandoned, and a strange one commandeered. In talking it over at leisure it was decided not to marry, the parents would probably 'fuss'; if one thing more than another was to be avoided it was 'fuss.' Now these girls were pretty and delicate, daintily reared, and the boys were 'manly,' 'regular fellows' in good society, yet in court they admit, not only sexual familiarity, but promiscuity and disregard of simplest requirements of decency and affection which would arouse honest contempt in the mind of a longshoreman. Early in the morning they had arrived at a road-house, and being without funds or gasolene, one of the boys telephoned to his parents. Now, charged with theft and immorality, they are before the court.

"They presented an amazing contrast to their parents. One would have thought it was the parents who were laboring under burden of guilt, while the children were calm and rather disinterested. Clearly the parents behaved as if the pillars of their family esteem had suddenly collapsed; dazed with surprise and humiliation they sat with bowed heads, utterly pitiable. On the other hand the young people were courteous, frank, submissive to questions of court, but there were frequent smiles and impatience at the futility of it all.

"Each had what is called a 'good home,' above average in comforts, and in good standing in public opinion. . . .

"It is now a question not of degree of guilt, or weight of punishment, but of understanding and helping young people. . . .

"Sex is not sacred to them, or terrifying; it is merely fun.  While their attitude may be less harmful than that of some of their critics, it is still dangerous, inadequate and abnormal, running swiftly into perversions.  The court will send each young person with his or her parents, if possible, to a socially-minded physician to be instructed in the elements of sex hygiene, for be it well understood all their glib, seeming information is spurious.  They do not know the body and its rules any more than they know the spirit of the creative force which they have been destroying.  The court, by probing, simple questions, tries to bring them a sense of birth, child-rearing, nursing, illness, love, courtship, self-sacrifice, discovery, struggle and happiness, parenthood and death.  Not fear, but understanding, and pity (where it is needed for helplessness, disease, blindness, suffering among the innocent, etc.) are sought, and since in race-history human situations have not changed much, these young people are often genuinely impressed after their visits to orphanages, children's hospitals and the like.  Their parents have shielded them and have veiled reality, but the court has never faced a 'flapper' who has not been somewhat touched by a true life-situation, squarely presented.  Funny parodies in the notebook become not quite so funny, if the mystery is removed, and biological sequences revealed.  The court, however, would be guilty of a wrong did it not see that in sex-instruction furnished these young people by doctor and probation officer, emphasis was on health and joy, rather than upon disease and pain.

"To parents the court must stress the need of studying their individual children, of not blaming other young people for their children's delinquencies; of the need of vigor in parenthood, not alone physically, but in ideals of family life which make child-rearing a genuine fulfillment.

"Surprising as it appears after hearing evidence, the largest proportion of these boys and girls from high schools and good neighborhoods, if taken to court early for first delinquencies, if there they are wisely handled, under adequate probation officers, if home, school, church and court coöperate, make good. They do not repeat delinquencies, they look on their former conduct as a fad they have dropped; they become rather sober-minded, critical young American citizens."

## Wholesale Condemnation

Many of us would have been inclined to regard the young people whose case we have just cited as abandoned women, degraded flappers, degenerate adolescents! As a matter of fact, these boys and girls were fundamentally sound. The root of their difficulty lay in a perverted habit-system. They had, through misinformation, as well as through the prudish silence of their parents, developed certain habitual ways of thinking and behaving about sex. In reality, they were profoundly ignorant of the basic significance of sex. Ignorance, in this case, however, meant, not innocence, but a system of habits built upon crude substitutes for information. It was this perverted habit-system which needed re-building. We have no report of the outcome in their particular cases; but it should be clear that in the intelligent re-forming of that one very powerful habit-system of sex-thinking lay the clue to the saving of these apparently degraded and abandoned young people.[1]

[1] Other valuable case records are to be found in *Three Problem Children*, published by the *Joint Committee for the Prevention of Juvenile Delinquency*, and in the case records published by the *Judge Baker Foundation*, Boston, Mass.

*Summary*

The personality or character of a person, we have said, is the more or less unified aggregate of his habit-systems. The reader will find this analytic way of regarding personality of utmost value. He might make an inventory of his own habit-systems, noting which of them predominate and the exact manner in which the predominating habit-systems control his other habit-systems. Then if he is interested in observing character, let him do the same thing with other people. Most of us do not know how to observe character; and for that reason we are poor at reforming it. We take people rather blindly as wholes, approving or condemning in a mystical kind of way. Once, however, we begin to observe our children or our friends in terms of their specific habit-systems, we obtain illuminating clues as to the causes of their strength or weakness, their charm or their absence of charm; and we learn how, most effectively, to take the initial steps towards the rebuilding of their character. Thus character training loses most of its mystery, and becomes a comparatively simple step-by-step process of redirecting and remoulding specific systems of habits.

# CHAPTER IX

## THE BUILDING OF HABITS: ASSOCIATIVE TECHNIQUES

How, now, do we proceed to build habits? When one considers the multitude of habits which need to be built up in a lifetime, the answer to this question might seem difficult. As a matter of fact, there is just one basic consideration in the building of habits. Every habit is built up by associating one specific type of stimulus or response with another specific type of response or stimulus.

Let us illustrate this, most simply, from animal behavior. We wish, for example, to train a dog to come for his food at the ringing of a bell. At the outset, of course, the bell has no food implications for the dog. Unlike the food, it is altogether an artificial stimulus. What we proceed to do, now, is to associate the artificial stimulus (bell) with the natural stimulus (food). At the same moment that we show the food, we ring the bell. We repeat this procedure a number of times. Finally, we ring the bell without showing the food; and the dog comes.

A habit has now been established. A certain specific type of response has become associated with a certain specific type of stimulus. We strengthen this habit of response if, every time the bell is rung, the food appears. We weaken the habit, if we continually break the association; i. e., if we ring the bell and do not produce the food.

Now all habit formation is of this quite simple pattern.

Psychologists call the above a conditioned reflex, for the reason that the response (to the bell) is not a natural one but is a response to a condition associated with the natural stimulus.

Let us note the process of habit formation in early childhood. Here is a child that is habitually crying. Granted that there are no physical distresses, how did this crying habit develop? The child was in distress; it cried; its mother came running to it; took it out of its crib; fondled it. Now the child, obviously, is not capable of reasoning that every time it cries, it will be taken up. But let us suppose that that is exactly what does happen. An association is built up between the two: crying . . . being taken up. The crying reflex is formed.

Let us suppose, however, that the mother has become aware of the unfortunate habit and seeks to break it. She will proceed, quite simply, by breaking the association. The child will cry and will not be taken up. Gradually it "learns" as we say, that crying does no good. With the breaking of the accustomed association, the habit is discontinued.

All of this seems almost too simple to need elaboration. We state it, however, because it is the clue to all the more complex types of habit formation. For example, we wish to develop the moral habit of truthfulness. Let us suppose that at one time a child, having broken a window, say, tells the truth and is severely punished. Obviously a strong association is established between telling the truth and physical punishment. Thereafter the child is well on the way to the formation of a truth-evasion habit. Let us suppose, on the contrary, that every time the child tells the truth, it is warmly praised. A different strong association is established. The child, consequently, is on the way to the formation of a truth-telling habit.

While, indeed, the psychological pattern of habit-formation is simplicity itself, the difficulty, in each specific case, lies in finding the effective associations. For example, with what type of stimulus should we associate the act of hand-washing-before-meals in order to develop it into a habit? We may adopt the inspection-at-the-table-and-scolding technique, which makes for a large amount of troublesome expostulation. We may adopt the inspection-and-reward technique, which has both advantages and disadvantages. We may adopt a warning-bell technique. In each case we attempt to build up a strong association between the act of hand-washing-before-meals and the scolding or reward or warning bell stimulus. We are psychologically intelligent in the exact degree to which we can select associative stimuli that are really effective.

## Two Contrasted Techniques

In the early life of children, disapproval and punishment are largely used as associative stimuli. We may call them pain techniques. The child, being taught to eat with a spoon, puts its fingers into its food. The mother cries: "No, No!" Perhaps she gives it a rap on the hand. The punishment or pain technique can, of course, easily be overdone; but at this stage of life when as yet so few of the rational associations have been formed, a bit of severity, restraint, even mild punishment helps in the formation of those elementary habits—particularly the bodily habits—without which no child can effectively develop.

But the punishment, or association-with-a-painful-experience technique soon outgrows its usefulness. Much of the wreckage we make of adolescent life lies in the fact that the more difficult technique—association-with-a-pleasurable-experience—is little understood and less applied.

Let us refer, for example, to the case of Clara. The elderly judge who examined her was so shocked by her past life that he called her an "abandoned woman." [1]

"But Clara is not a woman, abandoned or otherwise. She is fourteen years old, a frail American girl who comes before the courts in hundreds of girls' cases every year—aimless, drifting, unaware of waste or wreckage, wishing no evil, bearing no malice, their sole desire not to be 'picked at' by grown-ups. . . . Such girls long for easy approval. They do not get this at home, but on the street, well-dressed young men smile at them pleasantly. . . . At home a dull routine, not even a trapeze in the backyard, parents absorbed, and when aroused to attention, critical; when one is a little girl one must be lady-like,—there is an instantaneous suppression of the least outbreak in the daily schedule. There are no heightened moments, no adventures. There is talk about morals and 'being good,' but it is matter-of-fact, very dry. 'Honestly, mother and father seem sort of bored with life.' . . . Then the other world— smiling, gay, changing, no disapprovals, motion and rhythm in dance-halls and swift cars; unheard of intimacy, strange and stimulating food, vague awareness that though one may be 'bad' the adults who 'live this way' are contented and seemingly rewarded, at least in movies and magazines. More than all else there is a fascinating flood of knowledge about sex to be endlessly talked over. Experiences, whispered confidences, boastings and combats between men and women and rivals. Nothing else is so interesting as this information; it began in childhood with a persistent intensity that took the breath, shocking things that later became common-place, but amusing: in short a world of easy mastery."

[1] *Youth in Conflict;* p. 31.

A simple psychological pattern! Virtue associated with dullness, suppression, scolding. Being bad associated with gaiety, approval, excitement, mastery. A habit will form along the line of the most pleasurable association as inevitably as smoke will rise or water will run down hill.

Thus our problem in helping to shape the habits of adolescents is to associate the type of action which we should like to have become habitual in them with a pleasurable feeling.[1] This was what was done so effectively in the case, cited above, of Alice Gould. Reading had been strongly associated with unpleasurable feelings; namely, the nagging disappointment of the foster parent and the thought of entering upon an undesired vocation. By associating the reading with a pleasurable feeling—the sense of pride in being able to condense a long passage into a few sentences; by dissociating it from the pain of entering business; again, by associating it with the pleasurable feeling of being able to help her foster parent in his researches, the reading-habit was soon firmly established.

One reason, for example, why the learning-habit is so easily and swiftly put off by most of us is that in very many cases the habit is built up in the midst of a complex of strongly disagreeable associations: a censorious teacher, watchful-eyed, pouncing, bitter, sarcastic, angry; enforced silence and movelessness; the frights of examinations; demerits; staying-after-school. We said above that all this about habit-formation seemed too simple to require elaboration; yet when one realizes how the most elementary facts about building habits through pleasurable associations are completely disregarded in many of our classrooms, one doubts whether any elaboration can be too great. It is

[1] See Chapter II, "The Appeal to Wants."

wholly deplorable that one of the most precious habits which ought to be developed—the habit of intellectual curiosity—is blocked almost at the beginning of life by the psychological stupidity of a very great many teachers.

"The teacher herself should have made adequate adjustment to life, should not look to children to supply her with opportunities for outlet to anger, fear, wish to dominate or to be dominated. She should not use affections of children to gratify her need of love and approval; her own adult relationships should be established satisfactorily. The most important personality attribute of the successful teacher is ability to create and foster a sense of vitality and enthusiasm for life." [1]

### Association-Constants

It is important for the teacher to realize that she is a continuing stimulus in the child's life. The child is daily and hourly building up associations between her and what he is doing. If she is just, kind, enthusiastic, the reading, spelling, geography and the rest will be associated with her justice, kindness, enthusiasm. If she is unjust, cruel, a mere taskmistress, the child's mental activities will be associated with her disagreeable qualities.

Thus it is of profound importance that the teacher have the fine personality qualities—of courtesy, low voice, quiet manners, generosity, humor, and fair play. She, in her mere personality, quite apart from her teaching, is, for her pupils, a powerful habit-builder. We have an instance here of the homeogenic factor discussed in the first chapter. The same considerations, of course, apply to parents, and,

[1] *Ibid.*, p. 99.

in adult life, to employers, superintendents, foremen, etc.

Again, the environments we provide are habit builders. I remember, even as an adult, once beginning the habit of wandering about the streets at night.  I had rented a room on the East Side of New York in the neighborhood of a social settlement in which I was interested.  It was the only room I could secure at the time.  It had, however, the advantage of being so mean and dark and airless that I had no need to deceive myself into believing that I "belonged" to the poverty stricken neighborhood.  When the nights came, I found myself stifling; there was no pleasure in the thought of reading in that stuffy room; no pleasure in the thought of going to bed.  I found myself, night after night, picking up my hat and wandering out, to return at midnight or later.  Heaven only knows to what a disreputable end even so professorial a person as I might have come!

Obviously, if the home is crowded, dirty, noisy, we can hardly wonder if habits of vagrancy are developed.  Our juvenile case records are full of the amazement of respectable parents that their children should have gone astray.  But a single glance at a customary home—children sharing the same room; a dark kitchen with unwashed dishes; a mass of uninteresting furniture; father sleeping late on Sunday morning; stale air; mother padding about in torn kimono and unkempt hair; later father and mother wrangling; brothers and sisters wrangling; the voice of neighbors heard wrangling; clotheslines and garbage cans; —here are permanent association-factors which powerfully affect the social and domestic habits of young people.

So, in like manner, the school building and the school room are association-constants.  The schoolroom, with its glaring white wall; its stark blackboards; its mechanical precision of seats; its severe goddess enthroned, may be a terrifying thing to an incoming child. It is for that reason that the better types of schools wisely realize that the schoolroom should be a place of interest and beauty. One may fairly suspect that a large indictment for the intellectual aversions evident in our adult population is to be lodged against the dull, uninteresting school buildings and schoolrooms of our childhood.

A movement is taking shape now-a-days for adult education. This means that we are endeavoring to build up a new type of intellectual habits among adults. There are large handicaps to overcome:—the weariness of workers; the enervating evening comfort of the "bourgeois;" the general indifference to learning; the competing attractions of the theatre, film, and radio. It is noticeable, in most cases, however, that no effort is made to overcome these handicaps by establishing delightful association-constants. In Denmark, where the adult education movement has become powerful, every effort is made to link up the intellectual work with surroundings and activities that give pleasure. The same is true in some of the adult education centers in Switzerland. In America, however, the older connotation of education as something severe, even repellently severe, is maintained. Ugly lecture rooms; hard seats; absence of pictures, music, social life—it must be a hardy adult intellectualist who can flourish under such conditions!

## Devised Associations

Character is built up by the associations in which we take pleasure. Let us suppose that we wish to build up

what we might call a "tackle" quality in a youth's character—the quality of taking hold of difficult problems and
pushing them through. We are now at the point where
we see how ineffective mere admonition is; how less than ineffective mere sarcasm or scolding is—unless the person
who admonishes or scolds or is sarcastic is, despite his poor
technique, really admired—in which case the pleasurable
association is with him. We now see that if we are to
build up the particular habit-system which we call the
"tackle" quality, we must associate it with something which
is in itself pleasurable.

How shall we do this? One kind of answer is given by
a new type of school developing in Europe, the *Landerziehungsheime* of Germany and Switzerland (an outgrowth
of the Abbotsholme school in England). In these schools,
the students live a large measure of outdoor life, do carpentering and farm work, help build their school equipment,
sometimes even the buildings. The purpose is to achieve
the "tackle" quality through activities that are in themselves pleasurable.

The aim of the Boy and Girl Scouts, Campfire Girls, and
similar organizations, is much the same. Endurance, faith-
fulness, wish to help, coöperation, alertness—these are fine
moral qualities that can most readily be developed by associating them with activities which require no coaxing.

Most of the habit-systems which we wish to develop in
young people are not in themselves pleasurable. Take, for
example, the sense of responsibility. We can, however,
make it pleasurable by the simple device of giving young
people pleasurable responsibilities. Thus, for example, the
student safety patrols in our schools, who stand at the
street crossings and guard the younger children from traffic

dangers, are having the kind of experience which makes them the envy of every child. Because they are enjoying the responsibility so thoroughly, they are learning to enjoy being responsible.

Finally, we may establish associations through the imaginative life. The boy who thrills at the hardy adventurousness of Daniel Boone, establishes a powerful association which tends to build up a splendid moral quality in his life. We need hardly comment upon the boy who thrills at the exploits of the Deadwood Dicks, or who, in more modern fashion, follows on the silver screen the amours of the latest high-powered sheik.

## Summary

It is clear, then, that we build habits through associations. Our first task is to watch carefully the association-constants in our life—(1) persons:—parents, teachers, managers, foremen; (2) environments:—homes, school buildings, classrooms, churches, factories, offices. These, we find, are powerful in building up habits of aversion or of delight.

Our next task is to be intelligent in devising associations with situations and activities that are in themselves pleasurable.

Character, in short, is most effectively built by the associations in which we take pleasure. Once this is clearly understood, the punishment techniques which so largely prevail—because they are the easiest resort of our indolent human nature—will be reduced to a rational minimum.

# CHAPTER X

## OUR UNCONSCIOUS FABRICATION HABITS

Let us regard now some habits which grow up like rank weeds, and which are almost, if not entirely, neglected.

The normal mind is moved, among others, by two basic drives—self-regard and least effort. Out of self-regard spring most of the activities which tend to fit us into our human environment. For one to be wholly out of the environmental picture is to suffer the agonies of the isolated damned. But here is a curious thing about human life. Even when we cannot fit into the picture, our self-regard never permits us to remain wholly outcast. When the objective isolation is at its worst, we set about building for ourselves a world of fabrication into which we fit ourselves with more or less satisfaction. It is in this manner that the day-dream is born as the compensating state of mind for one who cannot fit himself into the objective situation. When the day-dream is so intensified and prolonged that it is the normal state, it becomes the hallucination of insanity.

Insanity is regarded as deplorable, not because the individual is unhappy; he is often the happiest of mortals. It is regarded as deplorable because the happiness is gained through an evasion of reality.

Between the sheer hallucination of insanity and the sheer objectivism of a harmony with one's environment, there are all degrees. Thus the day-dream may take the form of a relatively harmless playing with delightful possibilities. The dreaming may be but momentary and may in no way incapacitate one for serious attention to the realities. Or the day-dream may be a temporary compensation for certain inevitable weaknesses later to be outgrown. It is in this respect that the child is much given to dreaming. He is at a peculiarly helpless stage in his life's career. All sorts of fascinating possibilities present themselves which he is still powerless to realize. So he dreams of being a big man like his father; of eating all the pies he wants; of sailing off on a big ship; of being a general and leading an army to victory. Day-dreaming of this sort has at least the quasi-reality of anticipatory experience, and is outgrown as the child's power to master his environment develops. As he becomes adult, he substitutes for the pleasure of the dream the pleasure of objective achievement. Any postponement or balking of this normal development—this power to achieve—is deplorable. Any advance into adulthood which still preserves, as dominant, the day-dream habit of childhood is an indication of objective defeat. Such an individual, in short, has not been able to fit himself into his objective environment. He returns therefore to the easy, compensatory way of childhood and lives a life of infantile unreality.

In this day-dream habit we note the play of the other basic drive, that of least effort. Often the day-dream is a substitute for effort. It is a way of achieving exquisite satisfactions without going through the hard labor of subduing the recalcitrancies of nature. Many a man slips into this easier way, is too indolent to face the facts and grapple with the realities. Then, since the desire for maintaining one's self-respect is also basic, he unconsciously elaborates self-excuses which confirm him in the belief that the fabricated way is the better way. He regards himself as more sensitive than the common herd; he finds reality vulgar; he detects in himself a poetic strain; he glories in living apart, in being of finer stuff. In the end, as he becomes habituated to his evasion of reality, he builds up a delicately self-enhancing picture of himself; and he goes through his days delightfully unaware of the fact that he has regressed to or never grown beyond the stage of infancy.

This pattern of the compensatory day-dream is now familiar to most persons. What is not so familiar is the manner in which it plays its part in our ordinary social thinking and serves to hinder the types of thought and action which are necessary for social progress.

## Romantic Evasions

The great historic example of a day-dream so incorporated into everyday life that it became a hindrance to progressive social thinking was the heaven concept. The heaven concept was distinctly compensatory. It was born out of human helplessness. In the midst of a situation which seemed too difficult to control, it offered an escape, on the one hand from utter hopelessness, on the other, from grilling objective effort. It was the easiest way to secure achievement.

It is significant that the heaven concept (of some kind) is the more vividly held the more we go back into the childhood of the race. There objective controls scarcely existed, and the only escape was through a complete outflanking of objective reality. It is also significant that the heaven concept with which Christians are familiar was born out of a condition of social impotence. The early Christians could do nothing with their great brutal world of Roman domination. Their easiest way, therefore, was to build up the fabrication of a compensatory order, instituted and governed by a power friendly to themselves. It needs, of course, hardly to be said that this fabrication was not known as a fabrication. The peculiarity of our unconscious motives is that they fabricate without letting our conscious selves be aware that it is pure, self-easing and self-excusing fabrication.

What interests us in this heaven fabrication is that it went distinctly counter to what was socially wholesome. It excused and justified the slackening of men's efforts to straighten out their immediate objective world. It produced in them an effortless futurism, a Micawber-like willingness to let the great and glorious thing "turn up."

What is significant about our present civilization is that, as objective controls have increased, the willingness to engage in celestial day-dreaming has decreased. Many of the churches are distressed at this, much as a teller of children's stories might be distressed at the gradual diminution of the ranks as her little hearers grew up into youth and adulthood. Where, on the contrary, the churches have become alive to the significance of what is happening, they have come to see that, as historic elaborators and cultivators of the heaven-fabrication, they have played the part of hindrances to social effort and advance. Such churches discard the fabrication and shift their emphasis from an ideal future life to ideals that are to be striven for in this present state.

Progress in religion, in short, may be psychologically expressed as a progress from the infantilism of fabrication to the adulthood of objective achievement in the realm of ideals.

A hundred years or more ago the great source of easement for the ordinary person—particularly for the woman —was the reading of the Bible. Here was imaginative compensation. As the pious person read, the difficulties and the sorry defeats of everyday life fell away. A great Reality unrolled itself, which swept the reader up into its sublime joys.

Today the Bible has, in a large measure, ceased to be a source of easement. A critical age has pronounced it to be, in large measure, historically and scientifically untrue. Has the critical age therefore abandoned altogether the easement that lies in fabrication, and set out resolutely to obtain its exquisite joys only through objective achievement? Today the place formerly held by the Bible is held by the romance. And significantly enough it is the woman, in the main, who reads the romance—although as the delights of this means of evasive satisfaction are becoming known, Adam is a close second to Eve in the eating of the apple.

With the woman, apparently, it is again a case of compensatory fabrication. Although far advanced beyond her pious sisters in social emancipation, she is still the relatively helpless member of the community. She is still peculiarly tied to a single function and, in most cases, to a single personal association. Her sphere of objective achievement is still relatively stereotyped and limited. To be sure, her peculiar function of child training is, in view of our psychological illuminations, becoming far less stereotyped; her personal association is far less of the purely submissive kind; while, in turn, broader fields of objective achievement have been opened up to her. Nevertheless, compared with the man, she is still the creature largely bound. It is not at all surprising then that she should find her way of escape by the pathway of fabrication.

For the romance is a way of escape. It is a powerful means whereby we identify ourselves with imagined persons and situations that express our own unconscious wishes. It is a notorious fact that the novel-reading habit may become a kind of narcotic vice, making its victims insensitive to the difficult necessities of their environment, slackened in power to grapple effectively with objective realities.

Here again we note the socially hindering effect of this type of fabrication. It is an easement, an easement by evasion. The person who can live in the glowing ecstacies of romantic imagination has as little feeling of the stark inadequacies of his world as the alcoholic singing his joyous songs in the midst of squalor, or the infantile religionist babbling his happy hopes of heaven.

We must, of course, discriminate; for the novel is not all romance. There is the type of novel which, like the new type of church, discards as completely as it can this fantasy-breeding habit; the novel which seeks, with dramatic power as well as with psychological and social accuracy, to depict the situations in which we must take our part; and which by making us identify ourselves with personages and situations, awakens the habit of social analysis and effort. But such novels are few compared with the multitude of fantasy-breeding stories that give delusive easement from troublesome reality.

## Fabricated Superiorities

The object of all fabrication of this kind is to place one-self securely in a position of superiority. One of the most persistent ways in which this is done is through social fabrications. It seems almost essential to our self-respect that we find some group or class or set which we can consider inferior to our own. It is a well-known psychological fact that what we strongly wish to find we invariably do find, although in the finding, we may have subtly to dispense with some of the less convenient canons of truth. Thus, for example, is all ethnocentrism born, the conviction that one's own group is the superior one.

Ethnocentrism is very amusing when seen with the sophisticated eye in others, as for example when the Chinaman thinks his people superior to ours; or the Esquimo or the Hindoo. It is far less amusing when one is himself convicted of it. The curious thing indeed about this racial or group self-deception is that it can only be seen at a distance. Near by, it vanishes, and is supposed not to exist. But this, psychologically interpreted, simply means that it functions,—but for that reason, with greater effectiveness—only in the unconscious.

Thus the American gentile who holds his skirts aside at the approach of a Jew, does not realize that he has probably unconsciously fabricated a racial view which gives him prodigious satisfaction. Consciously, he may, with great earnestness, express his sympathy for the Jews—that they are outcast; he may even be intelligent enough to deplore the fact that two thousand years of persecution have put the Jews out of touch with the niceties of the Christian civilization that persecuted them. He may seem to be full of sympathy; but even that sympathy is a self-glorification which makes him walk with firmer step and more uplifted head. In fact, without some such creature as this to pity— and to exclude—he would miss some of the most exquisite joys of self-congratulation.

As is well known, the more insecure one's own social superiority the more one finds the need for buttressing his self respect by centering his attention upon the inferiority of the members of some other group. Thus in this case of antagonism to the Jews we find that the hatreds and intolerances are the fiercer and more uncontrolled the lower the scale of intelligence. It is the thoroughly ignorant upon whom one depends for the pogroms. As one rises in the scale to persons highly intelligent and finely discriminating, one discovers the anti-Jew feeling progressively diminishing, until in those whose refinement and intelligence are without question, one finds it, as a purely racial antagonism, altogether absent.

Ignorance, relative or absolute, is always the fertile soil for fabrication. Superstition is a form of fabrication that concerns itself with the forces of nature. Racial and group antagonism is a form of fabrication which concerns itself with the human factors in the environment. In both cases, the unconscious fabrication is the ignorant person's easiest way of fitting himself securely into the picture. When he wears a rabbit's foot as a protection against rheumatism, he has achieved that perfect assurance which passeth all understanding. When he turns a Jew out of a hotel, he has achieved that sense of God-given grace which makes him a kinder father and a more loyal citizen.

The same is true of the ignorant Protestant's attitude

toward the Catholics. Here, again, there is no intelligent attempt to learn the real character of individual Catholics. By means of an easy fabrication, an anti-Catholic complex applicable indiscriminately to everyone professing the Catholic faith is built up. That fabrication is then the truth, the kind of truth which gives the ignorant Protestant a more secure feeling of his complete superiority and a grander conviction of his chosen place in the eyes of the Lord.

Social snobbishness, again, is a prevalent form of fabrication. Here likewise is a trait that can be seen only at a distance; for none of us know ourselves to be snobbish. Again, this is so because our snobbishness is deeply hidden away in our unconsciousness, where it functions with the greater effectiveness.

Snobbishness arises out of an unwillingness to be critically honest about other people. That unwillingness, in turn, arises out of our own unrecognized wish to be securely superior. The combination of these two make us fabricate an inferiority in the other. Thus to have our own little set and deliberately to exclude others from our set gives us a continuing sense of power. This may be—and in most cases is—compensatory. We should like to be in a higher set, but cannot. We deliberately repress our disappointment into unconsciousness by the more rigorously excluding certain persons from our own set and so building up an "our set" complex. Here, again, it is only when we rise to persons who are fine in intelligence and wisdom that we find this compensatory trait almost absent.

The college fraternity, unfortunately, is often a breeding place for this kind of snobbishness-fabrication. Here the fabricator uses a typical form of rationalization. It would be too crude for fraternity members to say that they considered themselves superior to others, that they excluded those whom they considered inferior to themselves.   Hence the earnest statement that it is good for likeminded persons to be together, since out of the harmony of such likemindedness comes great social and spiritual good!   The characteristic of all rationalization, of course, is to give a perfectly acceptable reason for a motive which is itself perfectly unacceptable.[1]

### Ego Magnification

We find this fabrication habit taking all sorts of amusing forms.   Thus the member of an adult fraternal order who puts on his tinsel uniform and marches down the street before the eyes of his womankind is acting out his infantile fantasy of military heroism.   He is a hero returning from the wars.   All the city has turned out to greet him.   He rides in on his trusty charger.   There stands the girl he loves—and who has perhaps cruelly rejected him.   The crowd cheers; the girl, in a sudden rush of returning love and admiration, throws him a blossom from her bouquet. . . .

It is the dream stuff of which all our life is made; and if, when we are old and undistinguished, we grasp what sorry means we have to bespangle ourselves as heroes and to feel the creep of gooseflesh under the admiring eyes of our stout Susans and our buxom Janes, who shall deny us?

Unless, perhaps, there is here a subtle danger, the danger that our fabricated satisfactions will last over as realities and make us insensitive to unlovely things; or what is

---

[1] This will be treated more fully in the following chapter.

worse, intolerant of those who tell of unlovely things.   The characteristic of the inveterate "joiner" is that he is a "good fellow."   Is he not a "good fellow," perhaps, because he has found, in his naïve, fabricated way, how to fashion his world into a good world—for himself and his crowd?   Has he, in short, not found an unconscious way of easement, which releases him from all obligation to grapple with unlovely realities, and so puts him in the same class with the heaven-adoring religionist and the romance-reading nursemaid?

When, however, the tinsel uniform of the lodge member is exchanged for the ghostly and sinister uniform of the lyncher or the terrorizer, then the fabrication-habit leads to tragedy.   Here again, the same motives are operative.   Here is the magnifying of the ego in the easiest way, a magnifying that is by way of compensation for a minifying in ordinary life.   One does not find these terrorizing orders officered by distinguished scientists.   One does not find lynching mobs led by the Wells's, the Bernard Shaw's, the Masefield's.   One finds them led by men who, in ordinary life, have the basic craving for distinction; but who, by reason of mediocrity of their powers, are able to achieve distinction only by facing away from the realities and building up a fabricated structure of evil and hatred and infantile retribution.

Here again, all the well known processes of rationalizing self-deception are operative.   These men declare—and deeply believe it—that they are terrorizing for the good of the community.   They are wielding the scourge for an angry God.   They are cleansers; rectifiers; citizens burning with the flame of righteousness.   Here, again, the reason given is wholly acceptable.   It is, indeed, so acceptable that it completely hides from the perpetrators their real motives. And so crimes are committed in the name of justice, but in the unconscious service of self-glorification.

### New Moral Commandments

Some day, in our education of future adults, we shall pay more attention to this socially mischievous fabrication-habit. We are still very naïve and crude about our education. About the only form of deception that we get excited over is the overt lie. We are utterly abased if it is discovered to us that our children—or that we ourselves—have perpetrated this awful sin. But the overt lie, while indeed culpable, is harmless compared with these processes of un-recognized self-deception which daily and hourly shape our characters into the prejudices, intolerances, indifferences and complacencies that slacken our social efforts and hold us content with the world as it is.

There is every indication, however, of a very real and significant psychological awakening. Even the ordinary man today knows that there is such a thing as a rationalization; and while he may not be quite certain just what it is, he knows that everybody—himself included—has not infrequently an attack of it. He tends therefore, a bit uneasily, to watch himself for signs of the distemper. Also, he has a triumphant sense of detecting rationalizations in persons with whom he disagrees.

All this, elementary and confused as it is, is to the good. It means that the psychological subsoil is being turned up and that a new crop of social admonitions is in process of planting. Precisely as our automobile consciousness is being so awakened that we shall soon write with sternness: "Thou shalt not pass another car on a curve;" or "Thou shalt remember thy neighbor which is behind thee to wave him a warning when thou slackeneth they speed;" so we shall write, with even greater sternness: "Thou shalt not, in thine unconscious self, build for thyself an image of superiority, either of thyself or thy wife or thy children, thy race or thy social set;" or "Beware the happy romance when it enticeth; for it slackeneth the arm and weakeneth the heart, and maketh one to lie down in the folly of one's own imaginings;" or "Put not on the uniform, neither of grandeur nor of terror; for in the one case it maketh into a child tickled at its own vanities; in the other, into a fiend, that excuseth his indulgences in the name of the Lord."

The opposite of the fantasy-habit is the habit of grappling with objective reality. That form of fabrication which we call superstition has, thanks to methods of observation and objective control, largely diminished. The problem now is how to apply this same method of observation and objective control to the region of our personal and social judgments. The first step, apparently, lies in a rigorous objective analysis of our psychological selves. Such an analysis, no doubt, will eventually become as regular a part of the education of the young as the learning of the multiplication table. For every one to know how persistently his unconscious desires tend to twist and falsify his judgments, how they induce in him a fool's satisfaction of unreal superiority, how they breed intolerances, prejudices, social hatreds, is to make him at least alert to dangers and in a better position to correct them when they develop into too obvious mischief,

So the study of all human history will become illuminated. Instead of being seen as a neutral succession of events, it will be seen rather as the serio-comic play of men's unconscious desires magnified into the action of groups. Such a study of history will make, one would suppose, for a greater wisdom in the evaluation of the present conflicts and tendencies that have the same psychological rootage.

The recognition that social judgments are, in the main, subjective, in short, is the first step in social wisdom. The next step is not simply to distrust these judgments: that is the function of the social sneerer; it is rather to understand them. One may suspect therefore that the next great stage in human emancipation—physical science and technology having played the dominant part in the first stages—will develop through an objective understanding of the psychological conditions which shape our judgments. As that understanding becomes clear and secure, it will inevitably penetrate through to the training of the still immature. Only in that way may we hope eventually to achieve a social mentality less given to subjective illusion and more responsive to the demands of the environmental realities.

## Our Basic Problem

Our very basic problem then is to trace out in ourselves these fabricated forms of mental and emotional life. As a matter of fact, not only do we not trace out and try to understand them, but we make no effort to check their development in that period of life when they have not yet grown to large dimensions. We teach the multiplication table and spelling and geography. We establish habits of toothbrushing and politeness. We do not teach the basic facts of self-deception, self-excusing, self-glorification and evasion.

Can this be done? Can we, in short, develop habits of straight thinking? This is our next major problem.

## CHAPTER XI

## THE PROBLEM OF STRAIGHT THINKING

Our fundamental concern, then, is to build up habits of straight thinking. How is this to be done? Apparently, our educational systems exist for that purpose. Do they accomplish their end? If they did, one would indeed be put to it to explain the self-deluded terrorizers, practically all of whom are the product of our school systems; the race snobs; the lynchers; the breakers-up-of-liberal-meetings; the curbers of free speech; the war-rumor hounds; the "sic-em-Uncle-Sam" misguided type of patriots, the patent medicine and the gold brick victims.

Let us consider the technique used in the schools for inducing straight thinking. The chief and captain of them is the "drill" technique. 2 times 2 equals 4; e-a-t spells eat; Albany is the capital of New York; a sentence has a subject and a predicate; Columbus discovered America in 1492 . . . "drill, ye terriers, drill!" After a pleasant introductory season of play in the kindergarten, education becomes the serious business of learning by heart what one is rigorously bidden to learn.

Unquestionably, a noticeable degree of accuracy is thereby attained—in a few matters. But two questions arise: (1) Does this accuracy "carry over" into other regions of mental life? (2) Does the "drill" techinque inspire an ardent love for accuracy?

## No Transfer of Skills

Upon the answer to the first question, educational psychologists are now fairly in agreement: a skill attained in one mental pursuit does not necessarily "transfer" to other mental pursuits. Thus, for example, the power to be infallibly accurate as to multiplication tables does not, of necessity, make one an accurate-minded reader of history or of the newspapers. Accuracy in each of the latter regions seems to require a training of its own.

This conclusion has most profound implications. Let us note the kinds of mental accuracy developed in the schools. They consist of accuracy (1) with regard to the adding, subtracting, multiplying and dividing of numbers; (2) the spelling of words; (3) the forming and punctuating of sentences; (4) the learning of known facts about the location of cities, rivers, mountains, and about the population and products of cities and countries; (5) the learning of known facts about certain outstanding historic occurrences. Accuracy in these matters is practically the sum total of education as it exists in most of our elementary schools.

However, the accuracies required in our adult thinking go far beyond these. 7 times 9 equals 63 will not enable one to measure the amount of uncritical opinion contained in an editorial; "s-e-i-z-e spells seize" will not help one far in putting together the various arguments for and against Soviet philosophy. "Hoboken lies to the west of New York" will not be of great assistance in estimating the truth and the falsity in race propaganda. "Sentences have modifying clauses" will give one little critical accuracy in judging the philosophy of economic imperialism. In short, the accuracy developed in the classrooms, at best, holds good only for the very limited subjects studied and does not, of necessity, induce an accuracy of mind which operates in other regions.

Thus the elementary school system, with all its purpose to prepare for life, does little more than make of the pupils something rather less than good adding machines, fair atlases and rather poor outlines of history. Life, however, requires that they be far more than mechanical technicians and compendia of facts, for life is a continuous process of judging, weighing, balancing, drawing conclusions; not a process of reciting sums, dates and localities.

### Being Accurate and Loving Accuracy Are Different

In the second place, a "drill" technique, while it achieves in the pupils a kind of ready and limited accuracy, really precludes the development of the kind of attitude which would make the wider and more fruitful appreciation of that skill and accuracy possible. A boy may have learned perfectly to parse every sentence in his book and yet have a slumbering hatred for the whole business. He achieves grammatic accuracy at the profound cost of hating it. Obviously, then, he is in no mood to pursue accuracy as a fascinating life aim. This, of course, is the severest indictment of the prevailing educational methods. They get from the pupil the golden eggs of precise information; but they kill the goose that lays them. For however much a boy or girl may be induced to know accurately, if he or she has not learned to love the art of seeking to know accurately in all things, the mere knowledge is a barren thing.

## The Schools Even Encourage Inaccuracy

But this is not the worst. For it might easily be objected that not everything can be accomplished within a few elementary years. However, there would hardly seem to be an excuse for the kind of teaching which quite definitely encourages the inaccurate, the prejudiced and the dogmatic mind.

The greatest offenses are committed in the field of history. Only in the rarest cases, for example, is history studied from the point of view of more than one textbook. This is particularly unfortunate where the history is that of one's own nation; for in such a case the result is almost invariably a disproportioned and ofttimes distorted account which the pupil (for he knows no better) accepts as the entire truth. Whether the account in the single textbook be true or not, however, matters little; the method of learning history from one source induces an uncritical receptiveness of mind and a resultant dogmatism that carry forward only too fatally into adult judgments on historical and political issues. History, as we shall presently show, presents a rich opportunity for the development of the critical, weighing mind. It is an opportunity, however, which is in far too many cases completely neglected.

One might suppose that the teaching of science would show more favorable results. But, in the first place, the great majority of our population, who leave school at the end of the elementary grades, study no science! Or if, in rare cases they do, they do not study it scientifically. For to learn certain facts which are stated as science-facts is not by any means to study science; e. g., the distance to the moon; the fact that water is made up of Hydrogen and Oxygen. The essence of science is the scientific method. Scientific method involves accurate observation, careful experiment, cautious inference. Where the student simply learns science-facts out of a textbook, he is no more being trained in the true spirit of science than if he were reciting doggerel verse. That is perhaps why anti-science flourishes so unashamed in the land. The chief weapon against dogmatism, in short, is unfortunately too often presented in the schools (where it is presented) dogmatically.

We need not pursue the analysis. The schools doubly fall short on the ground that the "drill" technique tends to kill the very spirit of ardent pursuit of truth; while the actual inaccuracies taught in the schools and the dogmatic methods of teaching even facts, develop minds that are sorely unfit for the noble task of thinking straight.

### Again, the Associative Technique

How then shall we do it? Obviously we must concern ourselves with far more than these limited and specific kinds of accuracy. We must, if we can, develop the ardent love for accuracy, for straight thinking in all things. We must, in short, develop an accuracy-habit-system.

Our chapter on building habits has perhaps given us the clue. As human beings grow older, habits can be less and less effectively established by punishment techniques. We develop habits most strongly, it was noted, to the extent that we associate desired types of action with pleasurable feelings.

Let us report, here, in illustration, an actual proceeding in a third year class (Miss Katharine Keelor's) in one of the more fortunately organized schools, the Lincoln School of Teachers College, New York City. Out of a study of boats had grown an interest in historic discoveries. The discovery of America was discussed. The students went to all the books in the library on which they could lay their hands. They brought back the astonishing information that the books differed! Some books said that Columbus had discovered America; others said that Leif Ericsson had done it. The class was at first divided into heated partisans for their favorites. But the matter was not permitted to rest there. The whole class set to work comparing the different accounts (youngsters of eight!) and discussing the relative points of historic value. Some made an eager visit to the Museum of Natural History to find out what they could learn there. At the end they reached the conclusion, that the matter could not be decided and that they would have to wait for further evidence.

Crude and elementary as the whole procedure was, to be smiled at by austere historians, could anything have been more finely in the spirit of science!

Note, now, that these young students had not been "assigned" a lesson on the discovery of America. They were not "studying" a textbook. They were out on a hunt, a self-imposed hunt; and they were having thrilling adventures on the way!

Again, one day, in this same class, a child, whirling the globe of the world, was heard to remark that it was at least two thousand miles from New York to Oklahoma. Another child said it was over three thousand. Neither child knew how to measure distance on the globe. Each child was at the stage of "opinion." They brought their problem to the teacher; and soon they all knew about the accurate use of scales of miles on maps.    They had graduated from opinion to science.

In this same school, science begins in the kindergarten. Nor does it begin with a textbook, but with flower pots and aquaria.    The children observe, because they naturally love to observe; but their observations do not go unchecked. They are constantly checked up by the group.    How long was it before the tadpole changed into a frog?    One child has the glib ready answer of the guesser.    Another child has another answer.    "Why, we put it down on the calendar;" says another.    "Let's count up the days."    Observation; documentation; the will to be accurate!

In these children the desire to be accurate is becoming a fascinating daily habit.

Education, by and large, has not yet caught this central idea that what we need to develop in children is not so much a knowledge of facts as an attitude toward facts—an attitude which "refuses all substitutes."

In one of the advanced grades of the same school, conducted by Dr. Daniel C. Knowlton, the students read a weekly journal—usually the *Literary Digest*—and in each article selected determine exactly what are the facts presented and what are the opinions.    A year of that kind of training to distinguish fact from opinion works wonders with young minds.    Here, again, the assignment is not something to be learned and recited.    There is something to be discovered by the student and when discovered to be defended before the group.

### Exposing the Rationalizing Process Early

The fairly widespread awareness of the fact that there is a rationalizing process is rather a recent achievement.

As a matter of fact even many adults who talk glibly of this or that person's rationalizing often confuse it with a good many other things—usually with plain stubbornness. It is little wonder, then, that the exposing of its dangers has not yet penetrated to the earlier years. However, as its power for mischief becomes increasingly revealed, there is every reason to believe that before long warnings will be issued against it even in the early years of children's lives, precisely as we now issue warnings against the most awful error of computing 7 plus 5 as 13. It seems a pity that children must grow up to a college class in psychology before they can be made clearly aware of this insidious art of self deception.

Once we understand quite clearly what the rationalizing process is, it is not difficult to find numerous examples of it in the lives of children, as well as in the literature they read. Rationalizing, as we know, has its source in an intense desire—an "emotionalized system of ideas"—which is itself in conflict with another desire. Let us suppose, for example, that a married man has fallen in love with another woman. He may secretly visit her, in which case there is a perpetual conflict between his passion and his sense of what is right, or at least respectable. A conflict of such a kind is not pleasant. He may of course solve it by giving up the passionate love; or by deserting his wife. Either course will make him unhappy. Finally he discovers a most acceptable way to ease his mental distresses. He begins to argue that the sex conventions are really too narrow, particularly for men of a finer nature; and that extra-marital relationships are necessary for one's development. Pretty soon he has quite convinced himself of that. Then he goes on to argue that, of course, his wife will not understand, she being a woman; hence in order not to hurt her—for he really does not wish to hurt her, poor thing—he must keep it all quite secret. Now he is perfectly happy. He has supplied himself with an apparently indisputable reason for doing what he wants to do, a reason, of course, which is not the real reason at all. The real reason is his passionate desire for the other woman. His expressed "reason" is the means whereby he deceives himself into a standpoint which saves his own feelings of what is right or respectable and also permits him to have what he wants.

Now child life and child literature are full of examples of just this procedure. The fox wanted the sour grapes. He tried hard to get them but failed. "Bah!" he finally said and walked away; "They are only sour grapes!" Was that the real reason, the child might be asked. Of course not. What was it then? It was a make-believe reason. And why did he give a make-believe reason? Because he did not want to acknowledge that he could not get the grapes.

Or, again, the fox had lost his tail. He went about saying that it was much more stylish to be without a tail. Was that his real reason? Of course not. Why did he give it? Because he did not like to acknowledge that he did not have what the other foxes had.

A wealth of examples suggest themselves in child life. In fact, children are masterly rationalizers. It must be remembered, of course, that rationalizing is not overt and intended deception. The rationalizer really deceives himself. Thus the fox leaped so many times that bitterness entered his soul. He really believed after a while that the grapes were sour, or at least that he did not want them anyway; while the fox without a tail, as he surveyed himself in the mirror, actually became convinced that tails, after all, weren't so handsome, when you came to think about it.

So the child frequently deceives himself as to his true reasons. He wants something very badly,—to go to a week-end party, say. But he knows he has lessons to do. He can quite fervently convince himself that he can do his lessons much better if he gets up early Monday morning and does them when he is fresh. Or he does not want to wash the dishes. He can quite earnestly convince himself, that really, he has a lot of homework to do—oh, a lot— and half an hour later will be found reading a story. Or, in school, he does not wish to buckle down to his arithmetic; and he can quite eloquently explain that he really has to finish that boat he is making; he has a chance to use the tools now, etc., etc.

We shall not get very far if we introduce into the elementary grades lessons in the logic and psychology of rationalizing. But to get children on the still hunt for signs of self-deceptive reasoning in themselves and their fellows; to make a merry game out of it all so that it is not taken too seriously yet nevertheless gets into the habit-systems of the children, may work wonders toward bringing up a new generation less subject than the older generations, to solemn, self-justifying muddle-headedness.[1]

### What Shall We Do With the Older Generation?

But, now, what of the older generation? We touch here upon one of the profound problems of our modern civiliza-

---

[1] Child life is so full of the gentle art of "kidding oneself along" that it is a pity not to scotch the bad habit at the beginning. For when we grow old, the habit has become so much a part of us that we are often unable to distinguish between the still small voice of our own intense desires and the pretentious explanations we give to gratify them.

tion. Let us note the curious psychological situation in which an average adult in an average small city finds himself.

In the first place, supposing that he left school at about fourteen years of age, the mental training (outside of his specialized vocational life) which he has received was given him during his immature years. That rigorous mental training gave him command of a few necessary but quite elementary skills. Beyond these, his mental training was *nil*. Even if he was fortunate enough to have gone to teachers more richly endowed than usual with social insight, his mind was too immature to grasp full significances in matters social, historical, political, economic and moral. Hence, in the only period open to him for systematic and thoroughgoing training in the questions that most vitally concern human life, his mind was left unequipped.

He is now a man of between thirty and forty. He has read the newspapers and popular magazines; has gone to "happy ending" plays; perhaps to church; has learned to make a fair amount of money. He has never had the chance to subject his mind to a thorough overhauling as far as the really crucial matters of human life are concerned. His mind, therefore, is, save in rare cases, a museum of immature fixations, snap judgments, picked-up prejudices, and unverified "hand-me-downs." It is the mind of a child on the shoulders of an adult.

Today, he judges the affairs of the nation. He brings up a family; he selects or deposes a minister of his church; a respected and influential member of the board of education, he decides what shall and shall not be taught, and how. And he doubtless has already done his fair share of heresy hunting!

Again, let us remember that he graduated at fourteen. Or no, let us give him some "advantages." Let us have him go on to high school and to college. Now he belongs to the "intellectual élite." He has his sheepskin; and the world is his oyster!

How mightily that brain worked at college! Between Chaucer, and French verbs, and football and beer-busts it really developed! There was one professor who began to set his brain stirring. A rather upsetting young chap, the professor was. He did not seem to think that the world oyster was already long since opened and ready for the eating. The world was full of problems—"social maladjustments," "unjust exploitation" and other seemingly unlovely things which one did not mention in the society of papas and mamas. The young student's mind, filled with *clichés* and conventional fixations, was just beginning to stir, when the unconventional professor was asked to resign.

So his one chance was lost; and now our hero finds himself in middle age, stout, respectable, financially established, convinced that he has been "well-educated" and not averse to giving his opinions on politics, morals, economics, religion and the sad future of civilization to any reporter who will do him the honor of calling.

But note—granting even that he did receive adequate education in college, that was from ten to twenty years and more ago! The world, since then, has moved ahead so rapidly and so far that if one did not keep alive to it all, one was left quite measurably in the rear. That is what has happened to the very great majority even of college-bred men of twenty-odd years ago. Most of them have at best kept up with the intellectual and scientific times only through the newspapers and popular magazines. They really do not know the science—the physical or the social science—of today!

That sentence ought to be repeated every morning before breakfast by everyone over forty!

Now, when people fall behind in the intellectual race, they do not feel bubblingly happy about it. They feel vaguely disquieted. But the queer thing is that they do not, as a matter of course, put the blame upon themselves. They automatically invoke the gentle art of rationalizing and place the blame upon the new. "Things weren't this way when I was a boy." "All these new fangled ideas—what is the world coming to?" The older generation, mentally unequipped (for the most part) and now lagging far behind, sends out angry cries to the impetuous new world to stop and behave itself and settle down!

## Education Without Graduation

The foregoing analysis of the typical grown-up has seemed necessary in order to emphasize the great civilizational opportunity which is just opening before us. A new idea is beginning to gain ground, the idea of education as a process continuous throughout life. Old stereotypes still check the full emergence of this idea. There is the accustomed thought that life is made up of two stages: the stage of preparation for life; and the stage of living itself. This "two-stage" idea of life has, of course, already been thoroughly discredited in the newer philosophy of education. John Dewey and his followers have clearly shown that the life of children in the schools should not be regarded simply as a preparation for something to come later, but as a life to be lived. So, in like manner, adult life will eventually come to be regarded not simply as a putting-into-practice of education already received, but as a process of continuing-education-with-living.

At any rate, however the philosophy of it may be formulated, the actual development of this type of adult life is taking place all over the world. In all the leading countries of the world, adult education is increasingly to the fore. One need not pose as a very rash prophet, therefore, if one suggests that within another generation adult colleges will be found springing up all over the world. There was a time when even universal elementary education was not dreamed of. It is only recently that secondary education has come to be regarded as an essential part of the educational system. It is still more recently that college education for young men and women has reached out widely into all classes. The next stage of our educational advance is obviously the establishment of the privilege of systematic education for all adults—college bred and non-college bred alike.

Nothing short of this can have very wide social significance. Our laws are what our lawmakers make them. And our lawmakers are what their education and their vocations have made them. A generation of lawmakers ill equipped with minds to judge the grave social issues that confront us will make laws ill suited to solve the trying questions of our very trying days. Hence the quite fundamental importance of this movement forward into the systematic continuance of the education of those who have grown up.

Curiously enough, adult education is often thought of as education for those who missed the opportunity of education in their youth. On the contrary, it should be regarded, far more fundamentally and broadly, as the needed stimulus and training for all minds that have grown beyond the easy judgments and the rather superficial training of youthful immaturity. When age begins, education is then, in a profound sense, really possible.

## Concerning Freedom of Thought

One superlative advantage of an adult system of education is to be noted. Those of us who are concerned about freedom of thought in our colleges often fail to note that even in college classes there are vital questions of individual and social life that cannot be gone into with completeness. One reason for this—quite apart from the pressure of parents and trustees—is that college students, for the most part, lack the equipment of experience which makes it possible for them to pass judgment upon some of our trying social and moral problems. This, of course, would in no sense be true of adult classes. In adult education, then, we should at last possess a field of investigation and discussion in which speech need not be halted by the shocked protest that "My son John is too young to be told such things!"

From a broad social point of view this is a most exhilarating prospect. For as one looks over the present educational field, one finds not a single spot in it, save perhaps in the limited sphere of graduate work, where social and ethical investigation and discussion are really free! The situation would be utterly preposterous did we not call to mind what we have just intimated, that in no part of the educational system, with the one exception noted, is education carried on with minds that are really old enough to be fully free.

## The Issue is Fundamental

In the foregoing, then, we have indicated not one or more specific techniques for inducing straight thinking among adults, but rather a fundamental change of attitude and habit. Anything short of this is mere psychological tinkering with the problem. Adults think crudely because most of them have never systematically learned to think otherwise. It is no wonder then that in difficult days like our own the eager-minded of the younger generation despair of their elders. For the older generation, with few exceptions, have no acceptable philosophy of life to offer to the young. When, ever, or where, did they overhaul their minds thoroughly enough to clear out prejudices and false impressions and arrive at something that has even the semblance of being bed-rock and comprehensive? The older generation, learning in the much overrated "school of experience," contribute a philosophy of material adventurousness and social timidity!

There is no doubt that the removal of illiteracy among the masses has had a powerful effect upon human behavior. There is no doubt that the increasing utilization of the privileges of higher education has likewise had a powerful effect. Once adult education gets into full swing, we shall doubtless find that, in the same manner, its effect upon our social and ethical thinking will be of immeasurable importance.

## Summary

Effective training in straight-thinking-habits, we pointed

out, is one of our most profound educational concerns.   We
noted the inadequacy of the prevalent "drill" technique in
the schools, the fact that it develops only limited skills, and
fails to arouse that love of accuracy which is of the essence
of straight thinking.   We noted, then, that a better technique was to be found by associating accuracy of performance with pleasurable undertakings.   We noted, in particular, how the troublesome act of rationalizing might be ex-
posed and corrected even in the early years of life.   Finally
we noted that the great hope of straighter and more fruitful thinking among adults lay in the increasingly wide recog-
ition of the fact that education should not be confined to a
few preparatory years but should be a continuing process
throughout life.   The adoption in practice of the slogan
"Education without graduation" might have an effect upon
our individual and social life far profounder than any other
single change that could be wrought.

# CHAPTER XII

## DIAGNOSING THE PUBLIC

Some of the foregoing chapters should throw important light upon the difficult problem of influencing that mysterious entity which we call the Public. Let us recall the argument in our chapter on "How to Change Persons." If we think of the Public as a whole, as just a vast, unencompassable mass, we shall doubtless be staggered at the thought of affecting it in any profound sense. If, on the other hand, we think of the Public (any particular Public) as, like the individual, a more or less unified aggregate of habit-systems, we may, by making an intelligent diagnosis, find the opening wedge for bringing our intelligent influence to bear.

What we discovered in the case of the individual was that certain habit-systems are more important than others in that they are the determinants of a number of dependent habit-systems. We noted, for example, in the case of Alice, how the poorly developed reading habit-system was the key to her defective character. Once that habit-system was set right other habit-systems straightened themselves out. Now the same kind of diagnosis made of a people or of any other social group would doubtless clarify matters for us very greatly, and enable us to approach the "hugeness" of what we call the social problem with less of bewilderment and with a swifter and more certain effectiveness.

A Public, for example, like an individual, has bodily habits. We do not by that mean that there is a mystical entity called the Public which has body and bodily habits. We mean that in any particular Public there are bodily habits which prevail among the large majority of its members. Thus there was a difference, for example, between the bodily habits of the large mass of pre-war Russian peasants and the large mass of British farmers. The difference was great enough for us to note a sharp contrast. Now we might ask, do cleanly or uncleanly bodily habits have any noticeable effect upon other habits? Are they causes of other habits? Or are there other habit-systems which are causes of the bodily habits?

A Russian woman, speaking the other day of the hard-drinking habits of the pre-war peasants, made the following significant remark: "Because they could not read, they were lonely; and so, of course, they drank." Her implication was that the absence of a reading-habit-system was in large degree responsible not only for the drink habit but for thriftlessness (work and consumer habits); filth (bodily habits); quarreling, animosities (emotional habits).

Apparently, then, the defective reading habit-system was an important clue to the other defects in the Russian peasant Public, precisely as it was in the case of Alice. Following upon such a diagnosis then, we should be less inclined to trouble ourselves about the habit-systems which were only effects, and should address ourselves instead to the defective habit-system which was the determinant cause of the others. Or to put it a little more accurately, if we did concern ourselves with one of the chief effects (drinking), we should realize that the elimination of the drinking-habit was dependent upon the establishment of a reading-habit—

which doubtless might itself have been dependent upon the establishment of a still more crucial habit-system—let us say, the work-habit-system.

## Determinant Habit-Systems in the Emancipation of Women

Let us note a number of changes in the habit-systems of the American people. After several years of agitation, there has finally been achieved the political emancipation of women. This means that women have built up a new set of political habits. How was this new habit-system achieved? On the surface it appears as if direct agitation of the idea of political equality was the major cause. In one sense this may be true. Without the direct presentation of the idea of political equality, political equality would doubtless never have been achieved. But there were also a number of causes, it would seem, apparently far removed from direct agitation, which were doubtless as powerful, if not indeed more so, than the presentation of the equality idea.

It is obvious, for example, that no amount of preachment by an eloquent and fearless Mary Wollstonecraft in the days of Pericles could ever have brought about political emancipation of the Greek women of that era. There were habit-systems which would have completely nullified all her eloquence and courage. It is a question indeed whether a Mary Wollstonecraft could even have existed in those days.[1] Why? We have a mystical way of saying that the time was not ripe. What do we mean by that? What we really mean is that the major habit-systems both of women

[1] The emancipated women of those days were, in the main, what we should call "loose" women, women of too exceptional brilliancy to subject themselves to the seclusion-habits of married life.

and of men were such that the political-equality habit-system could not have been regarded as a possibility.

Again, in the "clinging vine" days in England and America, the preaching of emancipation could have had no real effect. A woman who laced herself to suffocation, who dragged acres of cloth over the ground, who wore impossible shoes, who screamed on every possible occasion and fainted with regularity into the arms of her male protector; above all, a woman who really knew nothing save a little French and music, was a bundle of physical, emotional and mental habits ill fitted to adopt or even to care for a habit of political independence.

In the past few decades a type of woman with different habit-systems has been developing. Three of these have been of particular significance. The first has been a new system of physical habits. Women, like all the rest of us, have been carried along by a new movement for the cultivation of vigor of body. It began a few decades ago with fresh-air crusades. People began to open their windows at night. Then they began to seek fresh air through walking, out-door games and bicycling (the bicycle itself had a powerful effect in developing new bodily habits). Then came bathing. First more frequent indoor bathing; then out-of-door bathing. I can remember in my boyhood when girls simply did not swim. It was not the "thing." If they went to a watering place, they put on long mother-hubbards and stepped gingerly and rather secretly into the water. Contrast the present day! Many of us can also remember when a bath once-a-week was the height of respectability!

These fresh air habits, these habits of out-of-door exercise, and these habits of joyous unashamed bathing have made of woman a new kind of creature. Long before any-

one preached political emancipation to her, she had begun to
emancipate her body.  Here, then, was a physical habit-
system without which, one suspects, women could not really
have become emancipated.

In the second place, with the growth of our industrial
system, women began in increasing numbers to change their
old domestic-seclusion habit-systems.  They learned to
work regular hours outside the home; and to receive regular pay for their own specific work.  They learned to
handle money and to spend it as they wished.  They
learned in short to organize their own economic life.  Here,
then, was a second powerful habit-system which was prerequisite to emancipation.  Had it never been formed,
women would, despite all possible preachments, still be in
the "Doll's House" stage—and would, for the most part
be adoring their Doll's House and making angry remarks
at their shameless sisters who "wanted to be like men."

In the third place, following upon the greater sense of
freedom brought about by the more vigorous bodily habits,
women began to change their old mental habit-systems.
French and music were increasingly insufficient.  Women—
fearfully at first and subject to suspicion and ridicule—
began to develop mental habits like those of their male pro-
tectors.  They went to the higher schools and colleges.
And so, finally, there emerged the type of woman whose
mental habits made her responsive to intellectual stimuli—
social, political, economic—to which formerly she had been
quite indifferent.  The little unenlightened doll, in short,
plaything of the man, was now increasingly a mind in her
own right.

Here, then, were the real determining factors in the
emancipation of women—new systems of bodily, economic

and mental habits.   It is significant to note that the women
who opposed the movement of political emancipation were
(so far as my own observation goes) in the main of the so-
called "feminine" type—the delicate, unathletic, well-taken-
care-of women; the economically dependent, seminary
trained women typical of the Victorian age.


## Why Are We Temperate?

Let us analyze another change which has taken place in
the habits of the Public.   Despite all the gloomy pronounce-
ments about bootlegging and our general disregard of the
law, we are a temperate people, far more temperate than
we were forty or fifty years ago.   Why?   The ladies of
the W.C.T.U. would proudly answer: "We did it!"
And the Anti-Saloon League would beg to come in as a
close second—or first!   One may be inclined to doubt these
estimable people.   Viewing temperance as a consumption
habit-system, one may quite safely regard it as the result
of forces far more powerful than any preachments.   In a
highly industrialized society any large amount of intemper-
ance is impossible.

What has happened, in short, since the Civil War in
America, has been the building up of new systems of work-
habits.   Mechanized industry requires regularity, steadi-
ness of hand and eye, swiftness and unerringness of execu-
tion.   A misstep or a mishandling is too costly to be permitted.   A drunken locomotive engineer is obviously not
to be thought of.   An intoxicated worker at the centrifugals would probably find himself armless or legless or
lifeless and the centrifugals wrecked, with possibly other
workers maimed and killed in the bargain.

Again, a commercial and banking system growing upon the active body of a highly industrialized system, requires keenness of mind, accuracy of attention, the habit of "being on the job." During the occupation period in Cologne, I came, to my dismay and great inconvenience, upon a drunken ticket-seller behind one of the station windows. Of course there was nothing to do but to wait until his substitute appeared. The thing was unprecedented in my own experience; and was due, of course,—a most significant fact—to the temporary superimposition of a military upon a commercial system.

Drunkenness as a prevailing habit, in short, cannot co-exist with the work-habit-systems required by a highly industrialized and commercialized society. Those genial old village scoundrels who drank themselves to death in our boyhood days, the cobblers particularly, and sometimes the hotel keepers and the lawyers, have disappeared—to the sorrow of our story writers. But not because the ladies of the W.C.T.U. preached them out of existence! If the ladies believe that, they are gentle sentimentalists!

We are a temperate people, in short—and despite our bootlegging forebodings—always will be as long as we are a highly industrialized and commercialized people, because our work-habit-systems are the determinants which imperatively govern our consumption-habit-systems.

### Analyzing Our Political Habit-Systems

Such analyses as the above should be of significance to a person interested in modifying the political life of the society in which he lives. In a recent copy of a liberal journal, a melancholy account was given of the unregenerate habit which the American people have of being quite willing, time after time, to be fooled by political charlatans. Why, the writer asked in despair, cannot the American people learn to guard themselves against the buncombe which is periodically "put over" on them?

"The lesson might have been learned after the Hard Cider Campaign of 1840, when a political party without an issue and with only a mediocre candidate got itself elected by wheeling log cabins and rolling cider barrels through the streets of an America eager for any sort of a substitute for reality. By 1876 it was fairly well established that the temperance principles of one candidate availed more than the intellectual preëminence of his opponent, and in 1896, the 'free silver' buncombe of Bryan was brought to naught only by the even more preposterous buncombe of the McKinley campaign with its hysterical predictions of disaster. The insincerities of 1920 and 1924 are of too recent and painful memory to require amplification; but they, too, point to the truth of our major premise, which is . . . that you can—with enough money and a good press agent—fool enough of the people all of the time."

What are we to do about it? And the following is this writer's mystical answer! "We need a 'passion for souls' to call us to the battle for the preservation and spread of 'culture,' tolerance, decency and the critical spirit. The bravest Wesleyan zeal is the one thing which can save—not so much George F. Babbitt from the sloughs of Philistia—but you and me and even H. L. Mencken, from jail or hanging. We must burn with a tremendous passion for the evangelization of Demos or we shall lose our precious freedom to enjoy our own evangel."

Is it not precisely this kind of writing from the pens of forward looking minds, which makes the whole task seem so hopeless! Suppose one wishes to start out with a "passion for souls," what, actually, does one do? Or suppose one starts out to spread "culture!" Do we not know of the most socially and politically benighted minds who cry culture from the housetops? And what, pray, is this "evangelization of Demos?" Words, words!

As a matter of fact, so far as the practical direction of our intelligent energies is concerned, the article tells us precisely—nothing. We all know of the strange aptness of the masses to be politically fooled. *But what can we do about it?*

Perhaps there is really nothing we can do about it. But perhaps, if we keep our heads and refuse to lapse into vague sentimentalism, we may proceed to analyze our American public into its major and minor habit-systems. If we do that, we may at least discover what are the determinant habit factors. When we have discovered these, we may be able with some heart to go about building up habit-systems which will correct what is now defective. Of course, we may find the whole situation quite beyond our feeble tinkering. Or we may find that more powerful forces are already at their corrective work. In any event, such an analysis is the first prerequisite to the understanding both of the problem and its solution.

### Agricultural Work Habits as Determinants

It is significant at the outset to recall this fact: farming populations are normally conservative. They are conservative in religion, in economics, and in politics. The predatory interests that deceive them must, therefore, appear in the guise of defenders of the *status quo*. Radical philosophies, in short—like socialism, communism, etc.—have never gained any extensive hold upon the rural populations. To be sure, flash-in-the-pan radicalisms, like Mr. Bryan's preposterous free-silver doctrine, momentarily captured the western farmers. But the very fact that so patently absurd a financial doctrine could win the suffrage of farmers was itself a symptom of the mental-habit-system which we wish to analyze.

Now in any issue of national importance, it is the rural population, who, by their weight of numbers, decide. When we despair of "the people," therefore, we must remember that the great majority of "the people" still live in that habit-system which we call rural.

What, now, is the typical mental-habit-system of the farmer? (Let me emphasize the word "typical," for of course there are many notable exceptions.) In the first place, the farmer, in his productive activity, is subject to forces which are quite beyond his control. He contributes his labor, to be sure; but the outcome is so predominantly not his work that he constantly is face to face with the fact of his own littleness and dependence. The wind bloweth where it listeth. So does the sun shine as it lists and the rain pour. All the work-habits, in short, are conditioned upon an acceptance of blessings beyond his own power to produce.

In the second place, his work enforces upon him a relative isolation. He may labor with three or four or a dozen in his fields; but never with a hundred, five hundred, a thousand. Hence the range of his associations through continuous human contacts is distinctly limited.

In the third place, he is far from the swift give and take of commercial transactions. His crop is six months or a year in ripening. He makes one long meditated transaction, or two. Other than that, his transactions are concerned with petty matters of household provisioning.

The work-habits above described must inevitably have a profound influence upon the farmer's mental habits—his ways of thinking about the universe, his human fellows, politics, economics, morals and the rest. We have much that substantiates this. In the first place, the farmer is ever the outstanding pietist. He is in the hands of God; and so to God his thoughts naturally turn. Also, he is the outstanding individualist. It is with awkward difficulty that he joins with his neighbor farmers even in coöperative ventures that are for his own benefit. He creates few of those voluntary group associations that flourish in cities for the sharpening of minds and the widening of horizons. His sole voluntary association usually is pietistic—his church. Also, in the third place, he is the outstanding example of the "slow" type of mind. He may indeed be profoundly sure, in his limited way; but the very absence of the daily give and take of more active modes of life, makes his mind move cumbrously to its conclusions.

Now here is a psychological pattern in which the work-habit-system is the preëminent and controlling factor. It is no wonder that the farmers of Tennessee vote to oust evolution from the schools. They are—to be sure, to a greater degree than usual in America—rural pietists. It is no wonder that the great bulk of Presbyterians and Baptists throughout the country are against the New York modernists. Nothing else is to be expected of the hundreds on hundreds of simple minded country congregations. Nor is it to be wondered at that vigorous new social philosophies of economic reconstruction and of political internationalization find no countenance among farmers. In the isolated, individualistic self-sufficiency of rural life, farmers rarely develop any sense of the subtle and far reaching inter-relations of human enterprise.

The root of our difficulties with our farm population, in short, is not that they are poor creatures easily fooled by political charlatans. The real difficulty lies in the typical rural work-habits. In certain European countries—notably in Denmark—where the farmer lives continuously a more integrated group life, his general intelligence, his political and his economic acumen are notably higher than in the rural districts of America. He is interested in adult education; he works harmoniously with the group; he forms his coöperative producing and distributing associations. In short, he has industrialized and socialized himself.

Here, then, apparently, is one clue to our American problem. It is the work-habit-systems of the American farmer that need changing. Once that change could be accomplished, other important things would follow. If, in short, the American farmer could learn to live more continuously and actively in the group (the automobile and the union district school are helping him to this); if he could enter upon the coöperative production and selling of his products (become, in short, industrialized and socialized), we should doubtless find his intelligence rising and his proneness to be the tool of designing politicians increasingly less in evidence.

It should be obvious, then, that the political salvation of the farmer cannot be accomplished through verbal means. Therein lies the mistake of most political idealists. What the progressive political thinker does is to harangue the farmer, scold him, cajole him, plead with him to wake up and cease being deceived. Such techniques, however, save on momentary occasions, are really futile for the simple reason above noted that the most powerful force shaping the mental outlook of the farmer is his work-habit-system. It is that which must be changed; and no amount of verbal exhortation is likely to do it. Hence the person who can, for example, induce farmers to organize coöperative producers' associations is probably far more effective in changing the mind of the farmers than all the earnest generations of political persuaders.

### Diagnosing Jingoism

We have made the above analysis merely for the sake of indicating what we believe to be the true technique of social diagnosis. If this were a sociological treatise we should now proceed to further analysis. Our purpose, however, being purely psychological, we shall content ourselves with the single example. Also, we are aware that there may be disagreement as to the details of the analysis. We are not really concerned about that. What we are concerned about is to point out how persons who are interested in modifying the Public must approach their problem if they are to find an effective entering wedge. The essence of that technique apparently lies in regarding a Public as a more or less unified aggregate of habit-systems and in finding the one or more habit-systems which are determinant of the others.

Suppose, for example, we take a typical instance like the following of the kind of talk which actually influences the

Public today and ask what the habit-systems are which make it possible for such talk to be effective.

"For an example of the sort of jingo folly to which we refer, one could ask nothing better than some remarks young Mr. Cornelius Vanderbilt, Jr., recently uttered in the San Francisco *Illustrated Daily Herald,* one of several popular picture papers of which he is the owner. When the American fleet arrived at the Golden Gate on its way to Hawaii a few weeks ago, he welcomed it in an article over his signature in which he said (italics his) ; [1]

" 'The *next war*—and that war may *not be so very far distant,* if we are to believe reports seeping out of Tokyo and Washington— will be a *sea war.* . . . Today, 145 vessels of *war* lie in the bay, aboard which close to 50,000 men are quartered. *There is a reason why this fleet lies in* San Francisco waters *today.* That reason will be forthcoming before many months pass by. In 1914 another great armada lay in the waters of Portsmouth harbor, Great Britain. One month later the world was embarked on its greatest war-making venture. That is not synonymous; it is simply exemplary.

" 'Should trouble eventually occur in the Pacific—and there is *no reason why that trouble should not occur,* it is a probable certainty that the nations bordering the South Pacific, feeling as they do at present, and the nations bordering the Northeast Pacific, British Columbia in particular, would be drawn into the conflict on the side of the nation whose fleet lies with us today.' " [1]

Why is it that such inflammatory writing gets any audience at all? We have noted the quite elementary character of the intellectual habit-systems of the farmer. That the farmer should be aroused by primitive fears and animosities is not at all surprising. What of the typical

[1] *The New Republic,* June 3, 1925.

business man? Is it perhaps true that his prevailing habit-system has been, in his business enterprise, a fight habit-system? Certainly commerce seems always to have had a rather intimate connection with war; while art and science, on the contrary, have been the crossers-of-boundaries, the uniters-of-peoples. Is it true that the typical habit-system of business technique is greatly different from the typical habit-system of art and of science? If so, then the hope of diminishing the power of such anti-social statements as we have quoted above must lie in changing the typical habit-system of the millions of men who make up our business population. I mean by this that the change in business attitude from one of competitive and predatory self interest to one of productive social serviceableness is fundamental to any real change in world outlook. One may suspect, then, that the most important movement toward the elimination of war which is at present taking place among business men is the movement toward making business socially serviceable.[1]

Where that movement is weak or not yet begun, the war mind is bred like rank weeds. Where that movement grows strong, the war habit of mind is increasingly weakened; and an interest in the productive harmonization of human enterprises takes the place of the older interest in destructive antagonisms.

### Summary

The reader will find it a valuable aid to social insight to analyze, in the manner above described, the particular

[1] See the author's chapters in "The Scientific Foundations of Business"; edited by Henry C. Metcalf.

Public with which he is familiar.   He will probably agree that it has hitherto not been his custom to regard the Public as an aggregate of more or less unified habit-systems. He has, like most of us, regarded the Public *as a whole,* a kind of mysterious, unapproachable entity.   Let him, however, begin to make a habit analysis of the Public and he will find a sudden increase in social illumination.   If, then, as he proceeds with his analysis, he will attempt to discover those habit-systems which control subordinate habit-systems, he will hit upon the only really effective clue to the difficult task of influencing a people's behavior.   Thus the problem of social and political advance becomes fundamentally a problem of discovering the crucial habit-systems of a people and of devising the means for changing them.

# CHAPTER XIII

## TRAINING THE CREATIVE MIND

The technique of experimentation may be regarded as the high-water mark of human achievement. Where the primitive mind is acceptive, taking the world as it superficially finds it and fitting itself to its rude requirements, the highly civilized mind is creative, taking the world as it more deeply discovers it—in its basic laws—and readjusting the superficial order of things to suit its own needs.

In primitive life, the experimental habit of mind was long hindered in its development by the tribal *tabu*. The *tabu* was a "strictly forbidden," rooting usually in some supernatural belief. Thus to introduce an innovation in the form of a new weapon, or a new utensil was to go counter to the sacred customs of the tribe. The inventor was a heretic. The only true piety was faithful conformity to the practices which had descended from immemorial, sacred antiquity. If variations occurred, therefore, they occurred by accident or by slow, imperceptible changes; seldom, if ever, by conscious design.

It was not, in short, until this "piety" motive was removed from the realm of tool making and tool use, that the inventive powers of man rapidly developed. One may doubt whether it is even as yet completely removed, for one recalls the absurd objection urged only a few decades ago against the use of the umbrella as a setting up of the

217

prideful human being against the manifest ordinances of God; also, the outcry against the application of anaesthetics in cases of childbirth. Here, as in primitive days, the reason given was supernatural. God had ordained woman to suffer; therefore let not man seek to relieve her of the pain that is divinely her due. One still hears persons object to the removal of tonsils and appendices on the ground that it is natural to have them. One must not do what is unnatural. So, a curious old book on homeopathy, written somewhere in the 80's, advises most earnestly against shaving off the beard on the double ground that it is bad for the throat and that God evidently intended it for man's use and adornment. The striking contemporary example of the fight between the supernaturalistic and the naturalistic habit of mind is found in the controversy over birth control. Now and then one finds an opponent of birth control arguing upon serious physiological and sociological grounds. For the most part, unfortunately—for, in this matter, serious physiological and sociological wisdom is needed—opposition is confined to supernatural grounds. Bearing children is an act of piety not to be invaded by the spirit of inquiry.

### Explanation of Social Pietism

One is tempted to explain this *tabu* habit of mind psychologically. The impulse to such an explanation is given by the disconcerting experiences one has even now-a-days in trying to introduce labor-saving devices. One has these experiences not only with unintelligent domestic help but with intelligent housewives. The power-driven washing machine has still to make its difficult way against the suspicious dislike of servant and mistress, even where, in the case of the latter, there is no financial obstacle in the way of purchase. In most cases the electric iron has won its way into use. But in many a household the oldfashioned broom is still preferred; while over the length and breadth of the land, hand-washed dishes still triumphantly rule in the kitchen.

As one listens to the reasons given for not using or even not experimenting with new devices, one is tempted to see in these reasons an unconscious rationalization of a very elemental force in life—the force, if one may call it such, of psychological inertia. Habit, we know, is an energy saver. A new device is a breaker of old habits. It therefore calls for conscious effort of readjustment. But conscious effort is precisely what, if we possibly can, we avoid.

In the sharp competitions of industry and business, effort cannot be avoided. The competitor must be alive to discover ways that are more successful than those of his rivals. Hence the male mind, in business and industry, has developed a readiness to scrap old devices and adopt new ones; more than that, it has developed a habit of working hard to find new and more successful machines, new and more successful types of business and industrial organization.

The household, obviously, is subject to no such competitive pressure. Hence it has been a fertile field for the growth of strong inhibiting habits. The housewife-mind, in fact, is *par excellence* the "inertia" type of mind. Innovations invade her realm of pious fixity only with difficulty, and against the unconscious resistance of a mind not

trained to the efforts of swift and continuous readjustment
along the lines of the most efficient utilization of materials
and energy.   The housewife is notoriously the type of
worker who still uses the most energy for the least result.
Nor is she resentful of this.   There is for her a kind of
pious glorification in the fact that while a man's work
(thanks, of course to his inventive hospitality) is from
sun to sun, a woman's work (thanks, chiefly, to an inventive inhospitality of which she is not herself aware) is
never done.

Perhaps the supernatural reasons given by the more
primitive peoples against the introduction of new devices
or the adoption of new customs were rationalizations of
this sort.   Resort to the supernatural was the easiest way
for primitive peoples.   Hence the deep, unconscious desire not to change habits would most easily justify itself
by reference to the only causes of which the primitive was
aware, namely, the ancient and honorable order of the
Unseen.

It is significant in this connection to note that among
primitive peoples, customs tend to change, with the greater
rapidity, as group competition develops.   No one cause,
perhaps, contributed more to the modification of primitive
*mores* than war.   War forced the effort of readjustment;
forced into the forefront the necessity for achieving the
greatest results by the most effective means.   Primitive war
was the only striking means of breaking in upon the seemingly ineradicable inertia-tendency of the human mind.
Apparently, the problem of modern societies is to find
means, more compatible with their civilized motives than
war, of stirring themselves out of their social inertia.

## Pietism versus Use-Value

The "piety" habit of mind has well nigh disappeared from the region of mechanical use and invention. Experimentation in that field, therefore, is no longer regarded as a commerce with the devil; no longer an insult to the sacred traditions of the tribe; no longer, therefore, something to be visited with social disapprobation. The fruitful thought has developed, rather, that to understand the material world and to organize it still more effectively to human uses, is the really high function of man. Therefore the inventor is now an honored benefactor. He is held up to the admiration of the young. The entire educational system swings in strongly behind him, supporting his peculiar type of reconstructive iconoclasm and developing in its young charges a hospitality towards experimental procedures.

All this, however, is true only of the region of mechanical use and invention. In the region of social relationships the "piety" habit of mind still prevails.

Thus any attempt to consider the finality of monogamic marriage as an open question meets with the shocked outcry "immoral," "indecent;" any suggestion of a different mode of breeding and nurturing children is greeted with "unnatural," "monstrous;" any attempt to examine the basic claims of the private property system is opposed by the heated outcry, "revolutionary," "subversive;" any serious suggestion that the constitutional organization of one's own land is basically at fault, is met by the most inflamed cry of all —"disloyal."

All of these are "piety" terms, terms that root not in

an impersonal examination of the use-value of these relationships, but rather in an emotional acceptance of evaluations handed down from the elders.

So far as our social intelligence is concerned, in short, we are very much at the same point as was the primitive when he sternly reprobated any change in the accustomed shape of his utensil. To the enormous benefit of the race, we have advanced beyond that stage. May we not venture to guess that the next really significant civilizational advance will be in the direction of freeing social relationships altogether of the "piety" motive and making them subject to the same naturalistic inspection and experimental reorganization as now prevails in the physical and mechanical field?

## Developing Social Experimentation

The problem, for those who see the trend of things, is to find out how this is to be brought about. It may be objected, however, that it is not to be brought about at all; rather, that it will, in good time, come about. But that is itself to renounce the naturalistic habit of mind, is to sink back into a kind of civilizational passivity—really a civilizational mysticism—which is the very reverse of naturalistic. For the naturalistic, experimental habit of mind is one which is convinced of the possibility, through observation and conscious experimentation, of controlling and therefore of redirecting its world.

As a matter of fact, modern civilization has developed one instrumentality of conscious control which has already proved to be of very real effectiveness. The educational system now successfully molds young minds in ways acceptable to the societary standards. To be sure, those standards, in social, political and economic matters, are still so powerfully pietistic that any overt opposition to them —as when a teacher questions the prevailing economic system or suggests the feasibility of another type of sex relation—meets with instant and overpowering opposition. Nevertheless it is not impossible to conceive of ways in which the instrumentality of education may be used for the purpose of developing a more consistent and far reaching naturalistic and experimental habit of mind.

The mistake of social radicals in education, one suspects, is that in the face of a pietistic public opinion they attempt to teach anti-pietistic *views* instead of attempting to develop an anti-pietistic *habit of mind*.

After all it is the basic habit of mind that counts; and it is with that—not with specific views—that education should mainly be concerned. So the problem of a progressive education comes to this: how can the minds of the young be made as fearlessly experimental in their attitude towards social matters as in their attitude towards matters physical and mechanical?

The first answer, one suspects, is that the mind of the young must be made more experimental even in physical and mechanical matters. Education has indeed been hospitable to the experimental habit of mind; it has not as yet been as successful as it might be in developing that habit in its young charges. Education is still notoriously an authoritarian process. Students come to school to learn the facts. The facts are all there ready to be memorized. All that is needed is submission to authority and patient industry.

Students, in short, are not supposed to come to school to

find the facts—for themselves—much less to find new facts. Textbooks are written to supply the available information. Teachers are there to see to it that the information is faithfully reproduced.

One would suppose that in the teaching of science it would be different. But it is not so. Science is experimental; science teaching is, in almost entire degree, authoritarian. This even extends to the so-called experimental or laboratory work in science. Here, with a few exceptions, the whole matter is cut and dried for the student. He is directed to do thus and so, and to note that a result, thus and so, will follow. Cook-book science, it is sometimes called. Or he is directed to work back from a result and discover the (already well-known) stages by which it was reached.

There is no margin of uncertainty in all this; no trying and failing; no independent and individual venturing; in short, no actual experimentation. There is at most only a repetition of the experiments of others—which is a widely different matter.

Now it should be obvious that the experimental habit of mind can be developed only through experimenting—actual, *bona fide* experimenting—not through this shadow-boxing that is so largely carried on in the school laboratories.

One may illustrate the difference in method and result by comparing the teaching of electricity to small boys by the stereotyped method of set experiments, and by the method of letting the small boys construct electrical devices for themselves. When a boy starts out (because he chooses that) to build, let us say, a motor-driven truck, with his Meccano set, he first of all, sets his own problem. That is primary. In the second place, since there is no textbook to supply information, he works out his own plans and proceeds to execute them to the best of his own ability. That is equally essential—an exercise in independence and initiative. In the third place, he probably makes mistakes. That is almost more essential—for that is precisely the type of experience which makes for flexibility—as well as for persistence of mind. In the end, if he has succeeded after a number of trials and failures, in building a truck that runs, he has developed a vigor and acuteness of mind and a workable knowledge of mechanics and electricity that is far more important than the most exemplary memorizing, from textbook and teacher, of the facts.

One may illustrate likewise from a non-mechanical field of education. Art, in the schools, has very largely been taught as an exercise in learning certain skills with pencil and brush. The process has been to get the student to do certain things—things, of course, that others had done many times before. Cook-book art. In recent years new methods have begun to be introduced. Despite his lack of technical proficiency, the young student is asked to create. Thus, for example, the child in the kindergarten is not directed laboriously to copy squares and triangles and circles and color them acccording to directions. He is asked to draw what he pleases, or to illustrate some suggested idea. Here again, the emphasis is placed upon initiative, individual planning, trying and failing, and trying with increasingly greater success. This method is interestingly in evidence in the training in design. Here the student is given certain elementary forms, like straight lines, curves, and circles, and asked so to compose them that a beautiful design results.

The effect of such training, as over against the old authoritarian training, is to develop a certain habit of mind—

the creative, exploratory, experimental habit rather than the passively acceptive habit.

These two illustrations will doubtless be sufficient to point the moral, namely, that there is a vast difference between welcoming the experimental mind when it happens to appear in a few rare individuals, and making a conscious effort to develop that habit of mind in everyone.   It should be clear that when once the habit is developed of being individual, of striking out on one's own, of trying new ways of doing old things, and of projecting new things in new ways, an exceedingly significant change will have been brought about in the attitude of the ordinary mind.   No doubt this willingness to try will eventually penetrate to other regions of life. The compulsive, uniformitarian attitudes in social matters, the pious acceptances, and the horror of non-conformity will perhaps begin to disappear; and experimentalism in the field of social judgments will increasingly lose its menace.

### Utilizing the Evolutionary Idea.

It is interesting to remember that there was a time when man was regarded as a fixed type, indeed the highest type in the universe.   In those times ideas that now are almost a commonplace had no existence—the ideas, for example, embodied in the study of eugenics.   It is, of course, the evolutionary habit of mind which has made it possible to conceive of improvements in the human type to be brought about by selective control.

The ordinary attitude towards social institutions is much like the attitude of a century ago towards *homo sapiens*. So powerful are the pietistic compulsions that it is difficult for the ordinary person to think of the particular social institutions in which he lives—marriage, the state, private property,—as not final, but as distinctly subject to modification by selective control. The problem is how to induce in the social region an evolutionary habit of mind as strong as has been formed in regions biological.

Obviously social evolution is to be studied through history; and if an evolutionary habit of mind is to be developed it must be through such a study of history as emphasizes the factor of progressive societary modification. This, of course, in the past, has not been the way in which history has been studied or taught. It is only in recent years that history has been regarded as a study of the social life of the past. Previously it had been regarded rather as a picturesque account or calendar of dynastic intrigues, wars, successions, and other singular events.

There is every reason to believe, however, that a new impulse has come into the study and teaching of history. Societary life is now increasingly an object of serious investigation; and social evolution is a phrase that is increasingly comprehensible to the mass mind. When one realizes that this development is a matter of only a few recent years, that the vast resources of history have hitherto been untapped save for the few stories they hold of uxorious kings or designing queens, one can understand why it is that the ordinary person is still non-evolutionary minded when it comes to the institutions with which he is familiar. One may venture to guess that within the next five or six decades the study of history will have become as powerfully evolutionary in the social field as the study of life forms has become in biology. It is not rash, therefore, to prophesy that through the increasing power of the evolutionary idea (its power is shown in the frantic outcries of the anti-evolutionists) the pietistic attitude toward social institutions will be gradually displaced and social institutions will be regarded as much a part of the whole developing order of things as the atom or the protoplasmic cell or the living organism.

### Must We Simply Let Things Take Their Course?

With this more comprehensive development of the evolutionary habit of mind, a future age will no doubt be as eagerly engaged in trying out new social experiments as the present age is in trying out new chemical or mechanical experiments; and it will welcome the social experimentor as eagerly as now it welcomes the inventor.

There are those, however, who are too impatient to wait for this blessed consummation. For such the way is undoubtedly open to teach history from an evolutionary standpoint, as an account of the origin, growth and progressive modification of social attitudes and institutions. There is every reason why such teaching should bear fruit. The rigidities and intolerances of moral absolutism tend to be broken down as one studies morals in evolution. So likewise do the rigidities and intolerances of political, economic and religious absolutism. The teacher of history who is vividly aware of the mischief wrought in all these regions by the pietistic habit of mind undoubtedly has it within his power, by uncovering the past as the progressive modification of social attitudes and institutions, subtly but strongly to develop a habit of mind alert to the inadequacies of the present societary order and hospitable to efforts towards progressive modification.

Necessity, however, is still the mother of invention. We are led, in the main, to think in new ways, because of the compulsion of the situation. Undoubtedly this is what is happening in the region of our social pieties. The egoistic, nationalistic state simply will no longer work. Some modification of it apparently must be discovered if civilization is not to wreck itself. We are passing at present through a more or less conscious, more or less reluctant period of political trial and error. Old political habits are, willy nilly, having to be broken and new habits of thought and of loyalty are having to be formed. The same thing is true in the economic order. Experimentation in modified forms of economic organization is of the order of the day —not, indeed, because we love economic experimentation, but because we are forced to it by the necessities of a very troublesome situation. The same thing is true of the relation of men and women; of the place of women in the world; of the relation of children to parents; of the form and function of family life. We live now within a rapidly changing order, an order indeed, so rapidly changing, that change begins to lose its terrors. And as change begins to lose its terrors, the way becomes increasingly open for the conscious study and control of change.

All this means a preparation of the soil for the growth of the socially experimental mind.

### The Power of Psychological Insight.

But perhaps one of the most powerful ways in which to undermine the socially pietistic habit of mind is through a study of the social processes of the mind itself. Modern psychology—particularly the psychology of the unconscious—is beginning to address itself to the important task long ago set by Francis Bacon, namely, to purge the mind of its uncritical prepossessions, or "idols," as he called them. Bacon grouped these into four classes: Idols of the Tribe, the Market Place, the Theatre, the Den. Idols of the Tribe were those prejudices which unconsciously took shape in us by reason of our human, or racial, or tribal outlook upon the world; Idols of the Market Place were the confusions that were engendered out of the easy acceptance and use of ambiguous or ill defined terms; Idols of the Theatre were the views or theories which were uncritically accepted as if they were facts; Idols of the Den were the peculiar personal attitudes that arose out of our individual dispositions, environments and nurture.

The point which Bacon was trying to drive home was that most of our thinking is not straight, logical thinking at all, but is thinking colored and confused by all kinds of racial, group, environmental, and individual inheritances. Modern analytical psychology is confirming this in striking ways. It shows the "complex" to be at the root of much of our prejudiced thinking and the "rationalization" the means whereby such illegitimate thinking plausibly shapes itself into the seeming pattern of truth.

A vivid acquaintance with these distorting psychological factors—particularly an acquaintance with them in ourselves, which was what Bacon desired—tends inevitably to make one less sure of one's ardent loyalties or of the ardent loyalties of one's particular group. It tends to make one critical of the manner in which social judgments are formed, and so lessens the easy reverence which one is inclined to pay to the social convictions of one's age or group.

One may confidently look, then, to the new developments in psychological analysis which have taken place in recent years, as a powerful stimulus to a more objective study of social institutions and practices; and one may venture to guess that as this analysis becomes a part of the everyday knowledge of young minds—as it is increasingly becoming —much of the impenetrable sacredness that has hitherto surrounded our societary forms and functions will be dissipated; and there will be applied to social institutions the same rigorous experimental analysis and control that now prevails in regions physical and mechanical.

## The Next Enterprise

The great enterprise to which the humanistic spirit may in the next decades most fruitfully address itself, then, is to assist in the development of a new habit or trend of mind. Particular views, as we have said, count for little compared with the basic quality or attitude of minds, with the ways, in short, in which minds "go at" things. That desirable attitude we have called naturalistic and experimental, meaning thereby the willingness to accept as truth only what is verifiably observable, the willingness also, not only to accept what is observable, but to control, and if necessary, redirect it to the most effective human uses. We have noted that the human mind is still backward in its judgments and activities wherever its trend towards experimentalism continues to be hindered by the drag of pietism. We have seen likewise not only that there are forces inevitably making for the development of the socially experimental mind, but that there are instrumentalities and methods whereby this development may be consciously accelerated. No doubt an enlightened system of education will increasingly incorporate these instrumentalities and methods, so that, without overtly going counter to the sensitive pieties of its age, it will imperceptibly but powerfully change the mind-habit of its age and in that way bring about the condition which will eventually lead to a more reasonable and flexible handling of social perplexities.

## Doing It Differently

In the foregoing we have traced some of the deeper conditions affecting the experimental and creative mind. Let us now betake ourselves to more practical considerations. How can the reader himself—if he is not that already—become a creative mind?

Here again, we are confronted (1) by mystery and (2) by poor early conditioning. Creative is one of those awe-inspiring words which we use with a kind of reverent surrender of our clear thinking. We do not seek to analyze. A creative mind is just—creative. It is a gift of the gods. Bow low, all we of lesser breed, and worship!

The chief cause, no doubt, of this mystical reverence has been our early conditioning in the schools and at home. We learned about the "great" inventors, the "great" discoverers, artists and poets. Consequently, the human race came to be divided into two sharply contrasted classes: the few great and the multitude of lesser ones. Of course, with our powers still in the bud, and with our juvenile habit-systems causing a fair amount of annoyance, no teacher ever suggested that we might be as these breath-taking great ones were. At the most, we might (if we were male) become Presidents. But creative geniuses! The latter always, it seemed, were born somewhere else.

All of this has been most unfortunate, for it has

developed the view that inventiveness is a power with which a few rare individuals are endowed at birth.   Since we find no strong symptoms of this power in ourselves, we simply take it for granted that we are not destined to belong to the ranks of the inventors; and so, quite naturally, we make no effort to develop such latent powers as we may possess.

Let us suppose, however, that in another generation we should become convinced that inventive or creative power, in greater or lesser degree, is possessed by everybody; moreover that there are ways of stimulating and of training it which are capable of increasing it far beyond its latent condition.   One suspects that if once such a conviction were widespread, education would be revolutionized. Instead of serving, as education now does, chiefly as a technique for the transmission of past information, its major energies would be directed towards the arousing and training of the inventive powers latent in all its children. For it would realize that a society alive with inventive power would, on the whole, be the most powerfully progressive society.

No such recognition, however, can come until the mystery is removed.   What, after all, does the creative or inventive mind do?   Stated in the simplest terms it breaks up old habits of association and establishes new ones.   Let us take as an example the invention of the fountain pen.   Generations of men and women were quite content to live within the fixity of a certain system of writing-associations.   Writing meant: pen (here), inkwell (there).   There was no questioning of that association.   It was taken for granted, as final; precisely as most of us take many things for granted today; e. g. an unwashable man's suit of clothes; unremovable, uncleanable pockets, etc.   The first step in the act of invention was to doubt the finality of that pen-inkwell association.[1]    Why must it be necessary to have the pen here and the inkwell there?    Once that doubt was aroused, the next step was not difficult.    Why not a new relationship of pen and inkwell?    What new relationship? The questioning mind might at this point have found no solution.    It might have hung suspended in doubt.    But it might have gone on to ask:    Why not the inkwell *with* the pen? *in* the pen?

If the reader will analyze a number of simple inventions —like the detachable collar, the wrist watch, the washing machine,—he will note that the above is the typical process: (1) a questioning of the habitual relationships (e. g. watch in the pocket); (2) a working out of new possible relationships (watch on the wrist).

Thus the mystery completely disappears.    No doubt there is a difference in our natural endowments, although we are as yet, and perhaps always will be, completely unable to measure these differences.    (Hence there is practically no use talking about them.)    But however near some of us may naturally be to the heights of genius, however humbly others of us must remain on the levels of mediocrity, it is possible for every one of us to question some of the habitual relationships in our world of things and institutions.    It is also possible for every one of us to keep asking himself, in this situation and in that: how may it be done differently?

Some time ago the writer was engaged in the laborious task of entering grades upon a number of sheets of paper. Inasmuch as the sheets had to be shuffled, each notation had

[1] This doubt may actually have been so swift as not to be recognized; but swift or slow it must have been there for anything to follow.

to be blotted.    This meant picking up and putting down the blotter many times, with a fair amount of hunting for the elusive article when it became lost beneath the shuffle.    The writer hates to confess on how many occasions he performed this task before it occurred to him to cut a small piece of blotting paper and snap it with an elastic on to his left hand.    Thereafter hundreds of needless motions were saved; and his inventive soul was exalted.    This same device was independently discovered and reported later by one of the members of the writer's adult class.

The following is from the manuscript of a forthcoming book by a member of the writer's class (Anna G. Noyes):

### "An Invention"

"During the war, we had ten barrels of corn on the cob, our chicken food for the winter.    To get it shelled we used the scheme of Colonial days, a corn shelling bee.    Boys and girls, dressed in overalls and aprons, were paired off. Each couple was provided with a large pail and a pile of corn ears, and at a given signal all would start shelling. At the close of thirty minutes each couple's output was weighed and appropriate prizes awarded . . . Fingers flew, and corn shot gaily around the room.    One girl tried her teeth; several blistered their fingers.    At the second party one of the boys exhibited a corn sheller of his own make.    It consisted of a board with a hole in it large enough to admit the stripped end of a corn cob, and was surrounded by a close row of projecting brads.    Holding this in one hand and the corn cob in the other, he twisted the cob through the hole; the kernels were loosened off and then dropped.    The invention appealed to the others and soon half a dozen like it were in operation. Then the inventor found that the plain board was difficult to hold, so he fitted it with a handle, and that was copied. Then to prevent the kernels from flying around the room, he put a hood on the device. And soon, in one way or another, he improved upon the original invention five times."

This little tale indicates admirably the psychological steps in inventing. First the difficulty, the lack, the shortcoming. (Necessity the mother of invention.) Then the question: need it be done in this way? The next question: how can it be done differently? Once the first step in the solution is reached, other steps suggest themselves, until the invention swings along to a finished device never dreamed of in the beginning.

### Taking the Matter Into Our Own Hands

The whole matter is so simple, one wonders that education has made so little of it. There are hundreds of objects about us of each one of which we may ask: May this not be made differently? There are scores of undertakings—games, conferences, dinners,—of each one of which we may ask: May this not be done differently? In fact, one might say that the really alive mind is one that every now and then is asking itself such questions. Most of our minds are simply too lazy to ask them—too lazy, and also, never yet made adequately aware that these questions are the "open sesame" to invention.

It should be obvious that there is no more fruitful task which a society can set itself than that of increasing the inventive power of its citizenry. For in social life, as in biological, the effective variation is the key to progressive evolution. It is true that transmission of information must ever remain a chief function of education, for the simple reason that without a background of established fact, no very fruitful creation of new fact can be expected. But transmission should be instrumental, never an end-in-itself. It should be instrumental to the production of that questioning, experimental, creative mind which is the greatest asset of any civilization.

But we need not wait for education to capture this idea. The matter is within our own hands. We can decide now to "do things differently"—things mechanical, domestic, social, political, economic. Out of our decision may come results that can quite easily be of vast moment to ourselves and our society.

# CHAPTER XIV

## CONFLICT AND INVENTION

In one sense all life is conflict and all conflict is good. We have to struggle to keep ourselves alive. Out of that struggle has come most of the intelligence we possess. Were we spoon-fed by Nature we should doubtless be Nature's morons. No one, therefore, who is wise to the peculiar human genius for mental "slumping" would wish to get rid of conflict. Conflict is our gad-fly. We fret and fume at it; but in the end we must acknowledge that it keeps us on the move.

And yet there are forms of conflict which even those of us who are not averse to mental movement deplore. For example, there is a widespread feeling, that war is a kind of conflict which is tragically stupid. Much incidental good, indeed, comes out of it, but so much more harm, that we seek to eliminate it altogether. Are we in error about this? Is the view sounder and wholesomer, said to have been expressed some years ago by Theodore Roosevelt, that "war makes for the manly and adventurous qualities?" Was Heraclitus justified when he wrote: "War is the Father of all things?"

Is not the same to be said of industrial conflict? When there was no conflict, most of the population were the obedient slaves of the few. When the slaves organized and fought lustily, they won for themselves some measure of

238

freedom. Must not the good work go on? Is he not a sentimentalist who deplores class conflict, who urges that the economic lamb should lie down in company union with the economic lion?

Is not the same to be said of race conflicts? Has not the entire history of man been a wholesome fight of races each for its own supremacy? Who would wish the magnificent Nordics to have established peaceful matrimonial relations with the despised Yellows? To have produced a mongrel breed! Must not the good fight still be fought —with the weapons of bitterness and violence? If God indeed moves in a mysterious way his wonders to perform, is it not perhaps best shown in this instance, where out of hatred and contempt for others is born the fine flower of our chivalric and world-serving Nordicism?

It seems, at first sight, a difficult problem to solve. Unquestionably there is no form of conflict which does not eventuate in good. It is quite erroneous therefore to oppose conflict as such. The very opposition is itself a form of conflict which believes itself to be good. On the other hand, it would seem equally erroneous to grow mystically ecstatic over conflict. The very fact that most of us, even the ardent advocates of war, or of class conflict, or of race supremacy disbelieve in clubbing our wives into submission, is sufficient indication that we believe that there are fight techniques which at least are not in good taste. Perhaps we may even go farther and acknowledge that there are fight techniques which are highly intelligent and others which are tragically stupid.

And so we are again at the point where we must analyze our meanings. It should be obvious that we are here concerned with one of the most crucial problems of in-

fluencing human behavior.   Conflict still plays a major rôle
in our life.   How we are to behave with regard to it depends fundamentally upon what we are to believe with regard to it.   It is important then that we clarify our ideas.

## When Is Conflict Intelligent?

We speak of the struggle to survive as if it were wholly
a matter of fighting enemies.   And yet, if we regard our
civilized life, with its various equipments for food, shelter,
clothing, learning, etc., we note that it becomes successful
precisely to the degree, not that we are able to oppose the
so-called forces of Nature, but to the extent that we can
understand them and work with them.   It may, of course,
be said that gravitation is the deadly foe of the airplane
and that our aspiring life is in conflict with this down-pulling
force.   And yet the down-pulling force is that without
which the up-flying mechanism would be quite impossible,
precisely as it would be impossible for the bird to fly were
there no resistance of the air.   Our metaphor of conflict
in this connection is then largely erroneous.   Our human
task is not just to fight Nature; it is rather to understand
the natural conditions of our life so thoroughly and in such
detail that we can utilize and enjoy them—live with them,
in brief,—instead of breaking our stupid heads against
them.

What then has the so-called struggle with Nature meant
for us?   It has given us the impulse to find out about this
supposed enemy of ours and to devise ways in which to
join our forces with its requirements.   It has, in short,
been the stimulus to both our intelligence and our invention.

One might at the outset, then, venture the following hypothesis: conflict is civilizing when it involves an effort (1) to understand the opposing factor; and (2) to invent a means whereby the opposition is succeeded by fruitful coöperation.

### Conflict Within the Individual

Accepting this hypothesis for the time being, let us examine some of the typical conflict situations in our life in order to determine, if possible, when it is that conflicts are carried on stupidly and when intelligently. Let us consider first the conflicts within the individual life. Our most illuminating example perhaps will be found in the type of conflict brought about by a suppression. Freudian analysis has made us sufficiently aware of these psychological antagonisms within ourselves; it has shown us how deep-seated they often are and how they eventuate in various more or less serious conditions of disease. What is the psychological situation in such conflicts? The strong emotion—it may have been an infantile fear, or a powerful sex attachment,—has been, as the Freudians say, suppressed into the unconscious. The conscious part of us refused to face it. It hid it away, so to speak; pushed it off; would have nothing to do with it. It treated it as a foe that must be cast out completely. But, as we know, our efforts thus to suppress the enemy usually achieve only this, that the suppressed emotion lives on without our knowing it, and in a most puzzling way, breaks up the harmonious integration of our life.

Thus, in this case of conflict within the individual, mere opposition does us no good. Note now what happens when we apply the therapeutic technique devised by this new school of psychologists.   The disturbing cause has long since been pushed out of consciousness; we have quite forgotten it.   The object of the analytic technique is to find the foe, face it and understand it.   The understanding is as fundamental as the finding and the facing.   The remarkable thing about this technique is that it makes the understanding of the foe—not the defeat of the foe—the chief prerequisite for the wholesome resolution of the conflict.

Once the disturbing cause is found and thoroughly understood, a new relationship is made possible within the individual.   The individual now adjusts the opposing emotion-systems to each other and so devises a new mode of life wherein both may function.

Here then we have the resolution of conflict by the process (1) of understanding; and (2) of forming a new integration.

The foregoing account of what takes place in the psychoanalytic process is altogether too little understood.   As a matter of fact it is quite simple.   That a skilled psychologist is necessary to carry the process through is only incidental.   The process is really one of bringing a detached and repudiated portion of our mentality into the full light of our conscious intelligence.   To understand, in this case, is to reconcile.   Why?   Because, with understanding, a new relationship can be established between factors hitherto so completely at odds that no reconciliation has been possible.[1]

[1] Recall Chapter VIII.   The Freudian analysis is a striking example of the possibility of straightening out the entire life of an individual by the reconstruction of a single habit-system.   The analyst suspects in the patient an emotional habit-system wherein a suppressed factor plays a continuous

## The War Psychosis

Let us now pass to that state of intense individual and social arousal called war. We find in war a most significant symptom. When war begins, all the avenues of mutual approach between the warring peoples are instantly closed and are kept closed. Those avenues, in modern times, are so numerous; so much passes over them from land to land and people to people—science, art, commerce, literature, friendly correspondence—that, in times of peace, they make of the various nations an integrated world. By that we mean that no part of the world lives in isolated independence of the rest. Each land or people both gives and receives. Each therefore is, in quite a vital sense, organic with the whole.

In time of war, on the other hand, this wholesome inter-penetrative unity becomes a split-in-two. Each combatant builds a psychological wall about itself, shutting out the other. Upon normal, organic association, in short, there supervenes (except for destructive relationships) a complete dissociation. We all know well enough what happens. Within each self-enclosed area there are bred the intensest hatreds of the enemy. These hatreds are fostered by rumors, ignorant exaggerations and outright lies. The outright lies are condoned on the ground that any means is justifiable which builds up the morale (note the irony of that word!) of a people at war.

And now the curious thing happens. Should some one in nation A, let us say, desire honestly to find out the real and perhaps justifiable grievances of the enemy people, B, he is cried down as disloyal!

and disastrous part. The uncovering of this factor breaks the habitual relations and makes possible the formation of a new habit-system.

The chief war technique, in short, is to preserve each member to the conflict in darkest ignorance of the other.

Far more fundamental and powerful than the force of armies, in short, is the force of censorship and propaganda. Were there no censorship, even propaganda, one suspects, would be relatively harmless. Were there neither censorship nor propaganda, mere armies would be powerless to carry on a conflict, for the simple reason that war can go on only through a refusal to understand.

Now what is significant about this is the sheer split-in-two which this attitude accomplishes. In the case of the individual, as we have seen, a sheer split-in-two of the integrated organism is a sign of disease. We find such a split in the insane person. The lunatic is so dissociated mentally, that the identical person is at once a King of England and a humble petitioner for a pipeful of tobacco. The hysteric is a dissociated personality who, in each successive state, is quite unaware of the preceding state. Now all our therapeutic effort in the case of the dissociated individual is to bring about integration of the personality. Disintegration—the Dr. Jekyll powerless to understand and control the Mr. Hyde—is the major symptom of a personality-disease.

Apparently war, in the social field, is likewise this type of disease. We are not here pretending to an analogy between society and the individual. We are simply, in each case, analyzing the facts. War means a relatively complete psychological dissociation between conflicting groups.

It is no wonder, then, that war employs the technique of suppression. The foe must be trampled upon; as nearly as possible annihilated. The victory of the one must mean the utter defeat of the other.   The other side is all wrong; it must be put completely out of business.

Now there are two things that must be said about such a form of conflict.   In the first place we may suspect that any form of conflict which deliberately repudiates that which is the most precious achievement of our whole human history, namely, the truth seeking attitude, can hardly be otherwise than deeply disastrous.   To say that war makes for manly virtues and for many other fine things is to say no more than that an attack of typhoid makes for the sympathy of one's family.   But to seek to develop sympathy by inducing an attack of typhoid would be a most Chinese method of burning down the house in order to roast the pig.

In the second place, conflict, to be really fruitful, must eventuate in a discovery.   Consider primitive man standing helplessly on the shore of the ocean.   The ocean is a foe. It places an irrevocable bar to his advance.   Here, then, is conflict.   Let us suppose that the primitive man cries out in his rage, calls his magicians and bids them order back the offending waters.   Not even a primitive would be as stupid as that.   What he proceeds to do is to find out about this offending thing; how he may come to terms with it. And he does come to terms when he is intelligent enough to build a boat.

### The Substitute for War

Conflict is fruitful when it is the stimulus to a new way out.   War is really no way out at all—at least no fruitful way.   What, then, shall we substitute for war?   The extreme answer is, let us substitute loving kindness, the brotherhood of man. If we can, well and good. But one suspects that life is hardly to be reduced (or lifted up) to so simple a formula. Life is inevitably a conflict of interests. Our substitute for war, then, must be not an absence of conflict but a handling of conflict in such a way that it becomes the opportunity for a new creative achievement.

That, of course, is what is happening, for example, in Geneva. Sweden and Finland are in conflict over the Aaland Islands. From the point of view of Geneva the conflict is an opportunity. A neutral commission is appointed to find out all the facts. The commission makes a report which gives to neither contestant a full victory over the other. On the other hand it does not simply infuriate each by giving each less than it desired. It invents a new way out.

Such, undoubtedly, must be the fertile technique of the future. With it will go that chief abomination of the older, war technique, secret diplomacy. Secret diplomacy, with censorship and propaganda are the unholy trinity that have brought most of the distresses in a world struggling with difficulty to be intelligent. The substitute for war must involve a technique of openness, understanding and invention.

### Labor and Capital

Much the same analysis can be made of the conflict between labor and capital. The traditional form of conflict has been that of an outright fight—either in process of being fought out or in preparation for being fought out.

The two parties to the fight have held themselves rigorously apart—again, a condition of complete dissociation, a split-in-two. Neither party has tried or wished to know the real grievances or the real difficulties of the other. The morale of each has been maintained by its own system of propaganda: employers' propaganda in the meetings of merchants' and manufacturers' associations, to which the terrible foe are never, under any circumstances, admitted; employees' propaganda in union meetings, to which the hated employing class are never invited.

Hence there have been two self-enclosed groups hating each other because not knowing and not seeking to know each other. It is no wonder that the typical technique of the labor fight has been the war technique, the victory of one over the other. And here, too, the unholy trinity has been operative: secret diplomacy, censorship and propaganda. For let a worker within his own group speak a kind word for the employer, or let an employer propose friendly relations with workers—instantly the war-cry of the infuriated pack!

Conflict, we have maintained, may be of great human value, but never when it repudiates our most precious human achievement, the will to know the truth. What is the substitute for this traditional technique of the labor fight? The outlines of it are already discernible. In a little office in Rochester, three mornings a week, representatives of the employers and of the employees in the garment trades gather together. They still sit on opposite sides of the room; and doubtless there is still a fair amount of glaring at each other. But between them, behind a desk, sits an impartial chairman chosen by both parties. The task of the chairman is to adjudicate difficulties as they come up.

No sooner does an irritation arise in the shops than it is brought out into the open. It is discussed by both sides; then decided by the chairman; and the decision thereupon is in black and white for all the world to see.

Here then is a technique which stresses openness; the wish to find out and face the facts; and the willingness to devise new ways out of difficulties. In other words, conflict, here, is an opportunity for (1) intelligence and (2) invention.

### Racial Enemies

"Prejudice," writes Dr. Sheffield in his enlightening little book, "Entering Into Public Discussion," "is a defense reaction of ignorance. You're apt to be 'down on' what you're not 'up on.'" No doubt race antagonism can chiefly be reduced to this. Each race counts itself superior because it knows itself and does not know the other. Each race makes a show of proving that other races are inferior. No single one of these proofs, however, has as yet any standing in sober science. They are at best the rationalizations of our own deep wish to be superior.

The curious thing about race antagonism is that it does not arise out of a conflict regarding matters that are really basic.[1] It springs rather out of the trifling surface differences between peoples. Thus it is blackness of skin that arouses the virtuous indignation of the Southerner. The heart within the skin may be whiter than the white Southerner's, and the brain within the black skull may be infinitely more capable. Nevertheless beyond the skin covering the Southerner will not go. For the race-inflamed

---

[1] Race, of course, is quite an inaccurate word, typical of the inaccuracy that invades this entire field.

anti-ethiopian, in short, the rather curious philosophy holds (it is, of course, the philosophy of infantilism) that "the appearance *is* the reality."

Race prejudice is the sorriest of our human mal-achievements. Is there a way out? Again, we offer our hypothesis: a conflict is fruitful precisely to the degree that we apply our intelligence and seek a new way out.

On Morningside Heights in New York City is a structure called the "International House." There—if the reader is not Nordically squeamish—he may dine with men and women of more than forty nationalities. He may sit in the lobby and discuss Omar Khayyam with a Persian, or Lao Tze with a Chinaman, or Ghandi with a Hindoo. It is, as it were, an "asylum of refuge" from the furious racial prejudices of the everyday world. Does it bring social disaster? It is too soon to predict what this, and other places like it, are to mean for our race-rationalizing world; but for those who have grown the habit of meeting men and women of other colors on a level of personal equality, the experiment is a challenge to our traditional ways of handling the conflict of race. It is a deliberate effort to face the conflict by understanding the other party and, through such understanding, working out a new relationship.

## Creating Our Own Conflicts

The four types of conflict above discussed—conflict between emotional states within the individual, conflict between nations, between capital and labor, and between races—are not staged by us for our own pleasure. They arise, somehow; and we do the best we can with them. To be sure, our best has been fairly inadequate; but it can hardly be said that we have deliberately set about to wish these conflicts upon ourselves. It is different, however, with the type of conflict which we are now to discuss. We deliberately create it, and come out in crowds—fathers and mothers and sisters and aunts and all the rest of the noble citizenry—to admire our handiwork! Nay more than that, we solemnly instruct our young folk that to engage in such a conflict—we call it a debate—and to come forth victorious is to be well on the way toward success.

It is only in a very special field that we are still able to continue this thing. If we go into the chemical laboratory and ask that a public combat be staged on the possible outcome of radium research, the chemical professor will shake his head: "We don't stage combats here. We try to find things out." If we go into the biological laboratory, we get the same subtly ironic answer. The biologist will admit, if pressed, that there are indeed conflicting views in biology—between mechanists and vitalists, for example. "Ah, then," we say, "let us stage a combat—a great public combat—affirmative and negative; with judges to decide who wins and who gets defeated; and an audience to go wild with enthusiasm at the oratory." The biologist will shake his head. "That is not the way we scientists do things. Long ago, when science was still learned out of Aristotle, scientific men argued themselves hoarse;—disputations, they called such verbal orgies. No more of that now. Our task, as scientists, is not to see who can argue the most cleverly, but who can really find things out." Then, if he is a good friend, he may whisper in our ear: "Go to those who deal in social questions. They still do that mediaeval thing!"

Of course, if we are a bit huffed, we may reply: "Why so highty tighty? Is not an oratorical combat a most effective way to find things out? Doesn't every question have two sides?"

"Yes, indeed, and sometimes three, sometimes four, or five, or a dozen!"

"Oh well, but it has two sides at least, and if we get those two sides well fought out. . . ."

"My friend," the biologist may then reply, "have you ever studied a real problem?"

"I've—I've studied chemistry and physics."

"No, no! I don't mean have you learned to reproduce what is in a textbook. I mean have you ever studied a *problem,* a real problem, like the question how to make synthetic sugar, or (to go into that region of nebulous hypothesis, sociology) how to fit young ladies into their proper sphere in life? Well if you have, then you will be aware that when you start to run down a problem there are no clearly defined sides at the beginning. As you pursue the problem to its solution, you may have to take a position at the end which you never even dreamed of taking at the beginning.

"Chasing down problems in science is like that. Each new step is a discovery. You chart your way as you go along. And when you have reached your conclusion, you may look back at the tentative positions you held at the beginning and smile at all that you did not then know.

"Now that is why all this Yes-No business; Affirmative —Negative; God-for-me—the Devil-with-you; I'm White —You're Black; I'm going to Win—You're going to

Lose—what you call 'debate'—(which, you remember comes from *debatuere,* to beat, to thump)—that is why no real scientist will have anything to do with it. It is not science, it is sophistry."

Those are hard words for the ancient and honorable tournament yclept debate! But is not our scientific friend right about it? Is not debate a left-over from a military age, when the chief object in life was to be the hardest hitter, the chief cracker of skulls? A debate is never a "Come let us reason together." It is rather a "Shake hands; now ready—Gong!"

## Reversing the Scientific Process

As one writer has recently expressed it: "Now what kind of process is this? Students meet, and agree to discuss a problem. The latter is generally of a political, sociological, ethical or philosophical nature, and one they know little or nothing about. Whatever it is, they have yet to make a careful, thorough and systematic study of it. But their ignorance does not prevent them from determining that this or that proposed solution is or is not practicable. Having come to a conclusion, they proceed to find the facts and justify it!

"As a process, this is the very reverse of that dictated by logic and by science. Yet it is one of the objects of our schools to train students in the art of approaching problems with minds free of any bias toward a preconceived solution. It is also the object of the science courses in particular to impress upon the pupils the importance and the necessity of arriving at even tentative conclusions, or rather hypotheses, only after a careful, thorough, systematic and impartial examination of all the available data relating to a given problem." [1]

Debate, then, is deeply in conflict with the scientific spirit of our age. It is militarism in the intellectual life. It is mediaevalism in modernity. By teaching young minds to start with their conclusions and then find the facts to justify them, it is the great aider and abettor of the noble art of rationalizing.

## Constructive Debate

But it is always a little dangerous to cast out the baby with the bath. Perhaps there is something that can be salvaged out of this verbal bellicosity. Let us recall our hypothesis about conflict. Conflict, we said, was civilizing when it was accepted as an opportunity (1) to understand the opposed side; (2) to find a new way out. Debate, as hitherto conducted has been carried on like war, namely, with the deliberate refusal to understand the other side, and with the sole aim, not of a creative way out, but of a smashing victory.

Let us suppose, however, that we keep in mind our creative view of conflict.[2] Let us also grant to our debating friends that there are social, economic and political problems with reference to which, in a more or less general

[1] "The Competitive Debate"; by Arnold H. Kamiat. *School and Society,* vol. XIX, No. 488; May 3, 1924. See also the writer's two articles: "Reason and the 'Fight Image,'" *New Republic,* Dec. 20, 1922; and "Forming First Habits for the International Mind," *Progressive Education,* vol. II, No. 2; 1925.

[2] A valuable analysis of this view is to be found in the book already cited, "Creative Experience," by M. P. Follett.

way, two opposed stands can be taken.   Suppose now that we say to our young minds: "It is fair to give each side its strongest defense; let us first do that.   It makes no difference whether you believe in the affirmative or not. If you defend it valiantly, we all know that you are simply doing your chivalric best to say what can be said in its favor.   But now, after we have done our best for affirmative and negative, let us take off our disputatious habits and don the habit of the scientists.   Let us, in short, now consider together what we are going to do with the whole question.   We shall now not debate; we shall discuss.   We shall try honestly to understand each other.   Above all, we shall hope not to end with the affirmative-negative deadlock with which we began; we shall rather hope to find a new way out."

We might call this "constructive debate," implying by the term the spirit of the upbuilding scientist rather than the spirit of the down battering militarist.

### "Where Two or Three are Gathered Together"

"The way we generally strive for rights is by getting our fighting blood up; and I venture to say that that is the long way and not the short way.   If you come at me with your fists doubled, I think I can promise you that mine will double as fast as yours; but if you come to me and say, 'Let us sit down and take counsel together, and, if we differ from one another, understand why it is that we differ from one another, just what the points at issue are,' we will presently find that we are not so far apart after all, that the points on which we differ are few and the points on which we agree are many, and that if we only have the patience and the candor and the desire to get together, we will get together." [1]

All this is in line with our more civilized techniques. Open diplomacy, the leaguing of all nations, international conferences, fact-finding agencies, boards of adjustment—all these operate in terms of the hypothesis above expressed for the handling of conflicts. The militaristic mind is the either-or mind; the black-white, god-devil mind. It is essentially, therefore, the static and destructive mind. The new type that is increasingly developing in our social affairs is the neither-and-both mind; the gradations-of-color; the neither-you-nor-I-am-God-or-devil; the come-let-us-reason-together mind. It is therefore essentially the evolving, creative mind.

Some day we shall doubtless realize, more than we now do, the profound psychological significance of the biblical sentence: "Where two or three are gathered together in My name there am I in their midst." That has hitherto been taken only in a religiously mystical sense. Psychologically interpreted, however, it means that in every coming together of minds that are serious in the effort to understand, there is something more than the sum of minds. There is the Creative Plus which no one mind by itself could achieve. And even when the two or three are in conflict together, if the intent to understand and to find a new way out is there something creatively new emerges.

This is the secret of civilized conflict which is slowly but quite certainly being learned in our times. The day of destructive fight is passing; the day of constructive fight is ahead of us.

[1] From a speech of Woodrow Wilson at the dedication of the A. F. of L. Building, July 4, 1916. Recall the homeogenic technique, Chapter I.

# CHAPTER XV

# THE TECHNIQUE OF HUMOR

Why, it may be asked, do we now take up so apparently trifling a subject as humor? But humor is not trifling. It is that blessed quality which pervades or should pervade all our techniques for influencing human behavior.

So many books have been written about humor that even a short chapter might seem superfluous. Our only excuse is that we have a special object in view. Knowing that humor is a powerful factor in influencing behavior, we wish to ask not what humor is but how it can be cultivated. Does this seem a preposterous question? But to assert that we ought not to ask it is to take the obscurantist position that humor is a kind of mysterious gift. In that case, if one has a sense of humor, let him thank the good gods; if he has it not, let him be brave, poor soul, and try to bear up under his sorry affliction. But in the present day, when we successfully feed thyroid to cretins, and regenerate senile functioning by transplantation, we should be little inclined to make a final judgment upon any human lack whatever, particularly, in the matter of a sense of humor, about which we know so little.

## Why is Humor Effective?

We might begin our analysis indirectly by asking why humor is effective as a technique. Doubtless there are many answers to this question. The following answer may perhaps lead us to some fertile conclusions. When a person uses humor, he implies that his respondent possesses a sense of humor. Now that implication is one of the highest compliments which he can pay him. Conversely, it is almost the greatest reproach to tell a person flatly that he has no sense of humor whatever. Tell him that he is disorderly, or lackadaisical, or homely, or awkward; he will bear up under these. But tell him that he has no sense of humor; it is a blow from which even the best of us find it difficult to recover.

People have a most curious sensitiveness in this regard. That is why, no doubt, the humorless person actually builds up for himself the belief that he has a sense of humor. He must have it if he is to retain his self-respect.

Why is there this all but universal wish to be possessed of humor? We are now treading obscure paths; and what we have to offer by way of explanation must be accepted only as tentative suggestion. However, our approach may yield something of value.

## What a Sense of Humor Implies

Apparently, the possession of humor implies the possession of a number of typical habit-systems. The first is an emotional one: the habit of playfulness. Why should one be proud of being playful? For a double reason. First, playfulness connotes childhood and youth. If one can be playful, one still possesses something of the vigor and the joy of young life. If one has ceased to be playful, one writes oneself down as rigidly old. And who wishes to confess to himself that, rheumatic as are his joints, his mind and spirit are really aged? So the old man is proud of the playful joke which assures him that he is still friskily young.

But there is a deeper implication. To be playful is, in a sense, to be free. When a person is playful, he momentarily disregards the binding necessities which compel him, in business, morals, domestic and community life. These binding necessities, for the most part, encompass our lives. We have to submit to them whether we wish to or not. We *have* to go to work—no play about that! We *have* to pay our rent, to watch our moral step, to obey the policeman, to be circumspect in our diet. Life is largely compulsion. But in play we are free! We do what we please. *We* make the rules. And if we lose, there is no harm done; while if we win, there is no sadness at having brought distress to another.

Apparently there is no dearer human wish than to be free.

But this is not simply a wish to be free *from;* it is also, and more deeply, a wish to be free *to.* What galls us is that the binding necessities do not permit us to shape our world as we please. They hand out the conditions to us. We must take them or leave them. What we most deeply desire, however, is to create our world for ourselves. Whenever we can do that, even in the slightest degree, we are happy. Now in play we create our own world. Omnipotent as God in Heaven may be, He never played football. We made football! Thereupon a new world was created; and ever since, we have sat in the grandstand and pronounced it good. *Our* world!

So when we play, we function happily within our own created world. To be sure, play is not our last word in creation. Play is evanescent creation. In art—which is our more serious play—we create for permanence. Here, too, we are free. In art and play, then, we are most happily ourselves. All our other activities—industry, business, even science, save when they are themselves play —are but instrumentalities to meet the hard necessities and give us room for freedom.

To imply, therefore, that a person has a fine sense of humor is to imply that he has still in him the spirit of play, which implies even more deeply the spirit of freedom and of creative spontaneity.

## Poking Fun at the Respectabilities

In humor this spirit of playful freedom gets frequent expression in delighted digs at "necessary things." Why be so oppressively respectable? To be sure, we have to be respectable. We cannot do certain things. But at least we can take it out on the solemn respectabilities by saying certain things. This is what Freud calls "escaping the censor." We all like to be a little wicked just because virtue is so uppish about it—and so confoundedly necessary!

It would almost seem as if the willingness and the wish to be somewhat flippant toward the solemn respectabilities —of state and church and sex and family—were a prerequisite for a sense of humor. For apparently the person who submits himself utterly to the social and moralistic compulsions can hardly possess that gay freedom which delights in building a world for itself; which delights, therefore, every now and then, in knocking the long-faced respectabilities endwise.

We all remember the irreverent way in which Dean
Briggs handled the social respectables of Boston:

> "I dwell in the city of Boston,
>     The home of the bean and the cod;
> Where the Cabots talk only to Lowells,
>     And the Lowells talk only to God."

That was far more humorous, because far more daring of
the censor, than the self-congratulatory, though also cleverly
humorous reply of Dean Jones of Yale:

> "I hail from the town of New Haven,
>     The home of the truth and the light,
>         Where the Lord talks to Jones
>         In the very same tones
>     Which he uses to Hadley and Dwight."

Perhaps one of the best instances of slyly escaping the
censor was the case of the young curate who had quarreled
with his vicar and was due to leave.  On the Sunday of
his departure, he preached his farewell sermon.  "I shall
take as my text," he said, "those words from the moving
story of Abraham:  'Tarry ye here with the ass while I
go yonder.'"

## We Blunder

Not all humor, however, seeks to poke fun at the respectabilities.  Much of it is concerned with our blunders.
Now we can have the habit of taking all blunders seriously;
then we condemn them.  Or we can have the habit of playing with them.  One of our newly-rich mothers made her-

self famous some years ago by declaring with great earnestness that she was looking up the best schools in Washington for her daughters, because, she said, she wanted her daughters to be well macadamized. Stupid woman, says the serious person; she ought to have learned better English!

It is, among other things, in the power to see blunders and to see them with laughter in one's soul that the human creature differs from the lower animal. Dogs do not appear to laugh at each other. Perhaps they do in their own way; but I seem to see one dog sitting quite solemnly, without the twinkle of a smile on his flexible nose, while another dog blunders around trying to disentangle himself from the rope that has got, most mysteriously, wound about his legs. Perhaps the solemn dog is just solemn, and the tangled dog is just tangled, simply because a dog always has his nose right up against the facts. The solemn dog simply hasn't a rope about his legs. The other dog has. If the solemn dog were roped, he would himself make frantic efforts to become unroped; but being at the present moment serenely unroped, sufficient unto the moment is the comfort thereof. By which we mean, I suppose, that the dog has not the imaginative power to see around facts. He does not, for example, picture to himself his companion dog's state of mind immediately preceding the snarl—the proud independence of his soul, his calm self-assurance, his cocksure way of marching ahead with uplifted tail as if the world were his own private ham bone. He has, therefore, no sense of the amusing contrast presented by this depressed and irritated and very much bewildered creature tied up in a hard knot.

To see the humor of a situation, therefore, apparently requires not only the ability to blunder and to see blunders —we all possess that—but the ability to blunder and to see blunders with a certain detachment. The deadly serious person is all wrapped up in what he is doing. The crusader, for example, is never humorous about his crusading. If he were, he would doubtless not crusade. In order to get himself properly worked up, he has to put his soul right up against one deadly, detestable fact and hold it there. He must see nothing else, particularly nothing that will mitigate the one fact. In the same manner, a person may put his soul so immediately up against himself, or his troubles, or his ambitions as to see nothing else in the universe. He then is said to take himself too seriously; and any joke made at his expense is not a joke but an insult.

## Humor is Not Censorious

But the humorous person is blessed among us because he has the habit of taking other people's blunders rather lightly. He is not a perfectionist. There are few more deadly persons than perfectionists. They take the joy out of life because what they require of us is so dolefully beyond our powers. The finely humorous person, on the contrary, is felt to be one of us. He is not offensively our moral superior. He knows our weaknesses; but he rather suspects that he has similar weaknesses himself. Hence, when we are with him, we are comfortable. We know that he will not pry too severely into our shortcomings. He will not draw a long face and threaten us with eventual damnation.

## Humor is Unexpected

Again, the humorous person is not completely predictable. At any moment he may say and do precisely what the logic of the situation did not call for. He makes a logic of his own, which is far more interesting at times than the humdrum logic which marches with due precision past all the well-known milestones. A rather pretentious fellow met the artist Whistler one evening. Pretentious Fellow: "I passed your house to-day, Mr. Whistler." Whistler: "I'm much obliged."

One suspects that there is so much greater joy over one sinner that repenteth than over the ninety and nine good and virtuous citizens for the reason that the whole thing is so unexpected. Logically, the sinner belongs in the other place. All his friends had told him that he was going there; the angels expected it. Then suddenly he turned a trick; and stands grinning before St. Peter! Meanwhile the good and virtuous citizens have been trudging with their Baedeckers in hand, straight and solemnly to the appointed hotel.

Thus the humorous person is always something of a mystery, a wonder. We never quite know what he will say or do next. That is why humor, apparently, is so utterly essential in the long years of married life, and why the very best advice to the lovelorn is: "Be certain that he has a sense of humor—and that you have one yourself!"

## Why We Like Humorous Persons

From the foregoing brief analysis, then, it should be clear why—other things being equal—we like persons who have a sense of humor. The humorous person has a number of delightful qualities: he is playful; free; creative; not priggish, nor fanatic, nor bigoted; he is not afraid of laughing at the too solemn respectabilities; he is not censorious; above all he is everlastingly and refreshingly unexpected. Therefore we like to live with him. And so because, by implication, we deny these delightful qualities, we offer the direst insult when we jokingly say to a person: "You're all right, my friend; but you haven't a grain of humor in you." We mean that he had best not be around too much!

### Can We Cultivate Humor?

And now we come to a difficult question: how can this fine quality of humor be cultivated? The foregoing analysis should cast some light upon the problem. Humor, we said, exhibits itself in a number of typical habits. Can we cultivate these? In the first place there is the habit of being playful. If we vaguely suspect that we have not a noticeable degree of humor, we might ask ourselves: Are we ever playful with serious things; or is it our habit always to take serious things,—our work, our soul's salvation, the salvation of our neighbors or the world—with prodigious solemnity?

The Puritan may cry out against this, but serious things apparently have to be taken with a touch of playfulness if we are not to surrender the freedom of our spirits. Why, for example, if we are scientists, be so deadly in earnest about our researches in chromosomes? Chromosomes are valuable, no doubt; but there are other things in life. Besides, there is even a possibility that one may be mistaken about one's blessed chromosomes and that a later scientist may have a good round laugh at one's expense. Or if it is not chromosomes, then vegetarianism, or antivivisection, or fundamentalism or birth control. We can get the habit of being playful with our serious concerns. We can knock them about a bit; be irreverent towards them; consider them temporary nuisances. We can refrain from scowling when people disagree with what we hold certain or sacred; and we can heroically restrain ourselves from passing laws to compel them to bow the knee to our beliefs.

Are we timid towards the respectabilities? Then we can learn to poke fun at them. We can realize that the world is still in the making and that the last respectability has not been cast into the mold of eternity. We can at least be proud of our ability to be free spirits and can genially make faces at that ofttimes royal pretender, Convention.

The first thing, of course, that we have to learn is that humor is something far more than making jokes. It is an attitude. If we are of that unfortunate number who can never remember the right joke at the right moment, we may rest easy. There are more things in the heaven and earth of humor than made-to-order jokes. The important thing is that we begin to be free with our utilitarian and conventional concerns—playfully free; that we renounce the slavery of a too strict allegiance and take mental and spiritual holidays. The effect is much like an actual vacation; we come back a little boisterous and contagiously happy.

Again, have we developed the habit of heresy hunting? Are we terribly hot against bolshevists? Have we formed an association to suppress the reading of Russian novels? Are we storming the women's clubs to cast out the menace of the cross word puzzle? It is good to disagree about things. It is also good to be in earnest about our convictions. But not too earnest. Humanity has had a long, hard march. It is often tired and blunderheaded. Apparently there is no use getting too wrought up about the mistakes it makes. Things straighten out far more quickly in the presence of the genial and understanding mind than in the presence of the mind all ugly to condemn and to crucify.

If our lack of humor exhibits itself in a constant habit of censoriousness, have we not a remedy? The trouble about this matter of censoriousness is that it is invariably treated from a solemnly moralistic point of view. "Judge not that ye be not judged." Rather, "Judge not, lest ye lose the fine power of indulgent laughter."

## The Problem of the Unexpected

But now comes the difficult problem. The unhumorous person may mend his ways in all the above respects; but if he is one of those terribly predictable creatures who bores us by the very regularity and inevitability of his processes, what can he do about it? Can he solemnly say to himself: "Now is the time to be unexpected"; and turn a somersault?

There are of course innumerable ways of being humorously unexpected. The lowest way is the way of the pun. We would not suggest it, but one can actually train one's self to the unexpectedness of pun making by keeping a constant lookout for double meanings in words. It is a low way of humor, however, since it is so bereft of ideas, so lacking in a fine quality of philosophic vision. Humor, most deeply, is a playful sense of those contrasts that we call incongruities. An incongruity is something out of proportion, out of its true relations. To see things in proportion is wisdom. To see things in their lack of proportion and to be playfully aware of the incongruity is the wisdom of humor.

There is no doubt that we can develop the habit of observing incongruities. When we can (1) note an incongruity, and can then (2) raise it to laughable conspicuousness, we perform that unexpected creative act which brings the delighted laugh. Recall the stanza about the Lowells, the Cabots and God. That is sheer unexpectedness. The raw material of it was a certain aloofness from the common herd. Dean Briggs might have said: "The thing one notices about the Lowells and the Cabots is that they consider themselves superior to their fellows." That, besides being commonplace, would have had a touch of asperity. No, he remarks the incongruity, the quite disproportionate aloofness; but he does more; he raises it, by exaggeration, to laughable conspicuousness: "And the Lowells talk only to God."

That, one suspects, is the secret. Life is full of all kinds of incongruities. People are constantly exaggerating their own importance; saying one thing and doing another; making mountains out of molehills. Most of us solemnly note these incongruities; get irritated at them; condemn them; scoff at them. The humorist, on the other hand, gives a flip of exaggeration; and the irritating situation is transformed into laughter!

One of the best examples of this playful exaggeration of incongruities is found in Donald Ogden Stewart's "The Haddocks Abroad" (Doran). I cannot forbear quoting the following passage from the book, since it illustrates so aptly the power to note incongruities and raise them to the level of laughter.

"I'm so excited," said Mrs. Haddock, as the time for departure drew near. "I've never been on a boat before."

"You'll be very seasick," said Aunt Flora. "The Quetches were never good sailors except your half-brother Edmund who was drowned at that picnic thirteen years ago next July fourth."

"Drowned people can be raised to the surface by firing guns over a river," said little Mildred.

"People who are drowned at sea," said Aunt Flora, "are never recovered."

"I should think," said little Mildred, "that if you fired a big enough gun over the Atlantic Ocean you could bring a lot of interesting things to the surface."

That was the way little Mildred's mind worked and she was already becoming known among the simple folk of the town as the Joan of Arc of 453 Crestview Ave.

The last week before sailing was full of problems. There was first of all the question of whether or not to take Mr. Haddock's winter pajamas.

"It might turn cold," said Mrs. Haddock, who, man and boy, had had forty-nine years of experience with weather and ought to have known what she was talking about.

"Nonsense," said Mr. Haddock. "It won't turn cold in June."

"It was in June," said Aunt Flora, "that your brother Samuel took pneumonia and died—June twenty-sixth."

"That wasn't in Europe," said Mr. Haddock, who had once thought of taking up the law.

"Weather is the same the world over," said Mrs. Haddock.

"It isn't," said Mildred. "In Abyssinia the average mean rainfall is 13.4 inches."

"But we aren't going to Abyssinia," said Mr. Haddock plaintively.

"We might," said Mrs. Haddock, and so she packed the pajamas rather triumphantly (for pajamas) and asked Mr. Haddock to sit on the lid.

"I don't see why you packed my dress suit," said Mr. Haddock. "I'm not going to any banquets."

"At the Opera in Paris," said little Mildred, "full evening dress is *de rigueur.*"

"You see," said Mrs. Haddock.   "Mildred, talk some more French for your Aunt Flora."

"I won't," said Mildred.

"Please, Mildred," said Aunt Flora, "talk some French for your Aunt Flora."

"Mildred," said Mr. Haddock, "you talk some French for your Aunt Flora or you don't get any Toasted Fruito for dessert to-night. Papa means it."

"All right," said Mildred.   "Ou est l'encre?"

"You see," said Mrs. Haddock proudly.

"What does that mean, Mildred?" asked Aunt Flora.

"Where is the ink?" translated Mildred obediently with a pretty toss of her curls.

"She will be a great help to you," said Aunt Flora.

"Especially if we need much ink," said Mr. Haddock.

Note the quite disproportionate concern of Aunt Flora about seasickness.   How it looms!   And drowning!   And note the delicious irrelevancy of little Mildred's mind, which meets every situation with a text-book futility.   And the seriousness of the discussion of winter pajamas in summer. We find people like that all around us.   We hear discussions of exactly such profound triviality.   But for the most part we take no particular notice.   The cultivation of a sense of humor lies in sharpening our attention to the incongruities that are about us and then in learning how, by a slight exaggeration, to raise these incongruities to laughable conspicuousness.

Some day, no doubt, we shall begin to train our young people in this art. For the noting of incongruities is the first step in wisdom. Most of us are clever enough to see the things that can literally be seen. Fewer of us are clever enough to note the subtle contradictions that lurk within ideas and situations—the pedantry that protests its liberality; the conservatism that loudly proclaims its progressiveness; the timidity that makes a boast of its own courage. We do not really observe human life until we have learned to see it in terms of these subtler inconsistencies. When once we achieve that power and can at the same time preserve our kindliness, we are well on the way to humor.

### The Crucial Test

But now we come to our real test. It is fairly easy to laugh at the incongruities in the behavior of other folk; it is not so easy to laugh at the incongruities in our own behavior. Have we been disproportionately wrathful at something that really, in the long run, amounted to little? And has our life-companion rather caustically remarked that we seemed to have lost our sense of humor? To be sure, life-companions should not be caustic in such crises. Far better if husband and wife agreed beforehand on a non-irritating signal to be given on all such trying occasions. But even the mildest and most kindly-intentioned signal might only infuriate us the more.

We had best, therefore, in time of fair weather prepare for storms. We might do well then to remind ourselves fairly frequently that the most liberating ability possessed by man is the ability to laugh at himself. With sufficient self-reminding, it is not impossible to build up a laughing-at oneself habit.   Our irritations, frustrations, disgusts and angers would take on a most delightful sporting quality if we began to watch ourselves under stress and to note the precise moment at which, our sense of proportion completely vanishing, our humor went into the discard.

## Summary

A sense of humor, then, is not to be regarded as a mysterious gift with which some fortunate individuals are endowed.   It is a system of prevailing habits, habits which it is apparently within the power of all of us to develop. Primary among them is the habit of playfulness.   Expressed briefly, this is the habit of taking things out of their conventionally accepted relationships, as, for example, when we use a good utilitarian pillow for a pillow fight instead of for a nocturnal head-rest.   So the punster plays with words when he departs from the accepted utilitarian way of holding each word strictly to a single meaning.   So, again, a contest becomes play when it is agreed that losing is bereft of its conventional meaning of disaster.

To be playful, in short, is to re-create our world of binding necessities, to do with it what is not conventionally expected or required.

It seems reasonable to assert that there is no fixed or inherited degree of playfulness in each of us, but that once we are aware of the basic relation of playfulness to humor, the degree to which the former operates can be noticeably increased.

So we can learn, with moderation, to play with the serious things of life.   We can play with people's blunders.   We can overcome our habits of undue censoriousness. Above all, we can grow the habit of noting incongruities, noting them, however, without bitterness and raising them by exaggeration to laughable conspicuousness. Finally, precisely as we can direct this fine playfulness towards others, we can direct it towards ourselves, learning the salutary habit of not taking ourselves too seriously.

Humor is so powerful a factor in influencing human behavior that we may well believe its cultivation to be a major concern. If, now, we regard the sense of humor not as a mysterious endowment, but as a system of habits, we may, with fair confidence, assert that it is possible for us to refashion one after another of the habits that make us unhumorous. We may, in short, actually develop a sense of humor where apparently it does not exist.

# CHAPTER XVI

## THE INDIVIDUAL AND HIS WORLD

"The sermon now ended,
Each turned and descended;
The eels went on eeling;
The pikes went on stealing;
Much delighted were they,
But preferred the old way."

Perhaps that is how the reader now feels. We have talked of influencing human behavior——our own and that of others. Can we actually do it to any important extent? Do not the vast impersonal forces sweep us along, paying scant heed to our aspirations or techniques? Spinoza tells the tale of a stone shot from a catapult. In mid-flight it awoke to consciousness. "Aha!" we can hear it say, "see how swiftly I am pushing myself along! Not many stones can do what I am doing!"

In modern days we express our human impotence biologically. Note the paramecium swimming about with apparent freedom, we say. Now introduce a beam of light. Instantly the paramecium makes for the illuminated spot. Does the creature freely choose its direction? Not at all. A force stronger than itself informs its muscles and compels its direction. A tropism! And thus, many of us conclude, it is with human beings. We are physicochemically determined; and despite all our psychological techniques, we shall be what we are to be and go whither we are destined to go. How absurd, then, to believe that by taking thought about it, we can add one new psychological wrinkle to our make-up!

It is possible, however, that we have been a little overawed by these new biological observations. Paramecia and tropisms and the rest have not yet become part of our daily régime, like chairs and tables, bank checks and breakfasts. Hence we still receive them into our company a little bashfully, admit them with perhaps too uncritical a deference. But two things are worth our noting: first, that the human being is apparently the only animal that asks questions such as the above; second, that the human being is apparently the only animal that not only can ask questions about the so-called natural processes, like birth, struggle, biological determination, racial distribution, but also can actually control these processes. The human individual, for example, decides that he will have no more than four children to his mating, and is able (despite the laws) to carry out his decision. He decides that only so many individuals shall migrate from one portion of the earth to his own particular locality; and again he carries out his decision. In short, the human being is not only subject to the laws of biological evolution, he himself, within limits, subjects those laws to his purposes. In this respect he is like no other animal.

Profound, then, and unmistakable as is our identity with the world of animal life, equally profound and unmistakable is our difference. We human beings have somehow emerged to a different level, one on which we can turn back upon ourselves, can see' ourselves in relation to events and processes and can exercise upon them our selective control.

## Our Three Objectives

In the foregoing chapters we have discussed very briefly some of the ways in which we can thus selectively control our human situation. We have called the particular type of control in which we are here interested "influencing human behavior." Roughly speaking, we discovered that we influence human behavior in three ways: first, through various methods of capturing attention, arousing interest, making ideas stick—thereby getting some measure of desired action. To be able to do these things, we found, is the first prerequisite to the possession of any real power among one's fellows.

In the second place, we influence human behavior through the ability to change individuals. We noted how individuals are to be regarded not as mysterious entities, but as more or less unified, more or less modifiable groups of habit-systems. He who can find the crucial or determinant habit-system in a person—or in that collectivity of persons called the public—and can set about, by adequate methods, to alter that controlling system, has a power over the human situation which is indeed profound.

In the third place, we can influence human behavior by deliberately setting about to develop—in ourselves and in others—the creative type of mind. The creative mind is the active variant. It puts new things into the world. They may be mechanical things, like automobiles, which bring about changes in many of our habit systems; or they may be social things, like republics or leagues of nations, which effect even wider and more significant changes in our habit-systems. Even the most tough-minded determinists, who speak slightingly of man's supposed power to change his world by his ideas, make one exception. In so far as man can invent, they agree, he is in truth a transformer. In other words, he is then not merely a looker-on at Nature's processes; he himself is actively a shaper of those processes.

Hitherto, as we saw, the creative mind has been accepted simply as a kind of inexplicable gift to the human race. There is, however, every reason to believe that this supposed gift need no longer be waited for, humbly, and accepted with gratitude when it comes. By intelligent understanding and direction, it can actually be stimulated into growth. He who can develop the creative mind, whether in himself or in others, produces an effect upon the human situation which is so endlessly wide-reaching as to be in reality incalculable.

## Our Basic Enterprise

Here, then, are three important ways in which we may set ourselves to influence human behavior. The fascination of it is that no one of them is closed to any single normal individual. As a matter of fact, it is to be hoped that the day is not far in the future when education along all three lines will be part of everyone's training. It is most astounding when one thinks of it, that in these issues which are really at the root of both our happiness and our human progress, we leave the whole matter largely to hit or miss. Nowhere have we set about systematically to instruct ourselves in this art of all arts, the art of influencing human behavior.   A significant beginning is to be noted in a course recently projected at Vassar College, called Euthenics, a course in the science and art of improving the human race by securing the best influences for the physical, mental and moral development of the individual.   It is noteworthy that this effort to secure the improvement of the individual, and thereby of the race, is made not by devout aspiration, but by a thorough and systematic study of the physiological, psychological and social techniques necessary for wholesome living.   It is to be hoped that out of a small beginning like this will grow a wider interest in the problem which is really basic to our entire human enterprise.

The past centuries—when not otherwise occupied—busied themselves with searching out the chief "end" of human life.   They paid little attention to the means whereby this chief end might be attained.   It remains for our century, already expert in devising mechanical aids to more wholesome living, to search out the psychological and social means to a more adequate human life.   Eventually the problem of influencing human behavior to this end will become the major concern of education.

# THE LISTENERS SPEAK

The foregoing has been cast in the form of a typical professorial monologue. The lecturer has not permitted himself to be interrupted. When, however, the course was given, of which these chapters are in part the substance, questions and answers and vigorous discussions were the order of the evening. Many a point was hotly contested; and new points were suggested by the class. It has been quite impossible to reproduce the liveliness of this continuous give and take. The reader may be assured, however, that something of it has found its way into the text through the effect of the discussions upon the lecturer himself. For the course exemplified in a striking manner that circular process of which mention has been made in these chapters, in which the movement goes both ways, from speaker to audience and from audience to speaker.

In the following pages some of the more considered reactions, as given in letters from the members of the class, are recorded. These are of particular interest not so much as comments upon the lectures but rather as suggestions of further points of view that might well be developed. They constitute only about a fifth of the material received. In all cases, except in the reference to a forthcoming book, the name of the writer has been omitted. This was the custom adhered to throughout the course.

## Doing Favors

"By this time I suppose you have considered the technique of letting-the-other-fellow-do-you-a-favor. I am much impressed by its usefulness as a means of breaking the ice with a child to whom one is about to give a psychological test. When he has been asked if he will carry some of the games and puzzles upstairs for the examination, has eagerly complied, and has been warmly thanked, it seems very easy to secure his cooperation for the testing. It is just as useful with adults."

## Fixations

"The first fixation in my young life was the certainty, established before I was eight, that all really respectable families were Baptist, Republican, and Homeopathist. Various members of my family still cling to one or another of these innocent delusions, so that I am long accustomed to being the only truly emancipated member.

"My own pet fixation is the conviction that no real business person, male or female, could ever be a kinspirit of mine. I might make a doubtful exception of such souls as cruel circumstance had forced against their better selves to abandon a chosen vocation for the pursuit of filthy lucre, but the genuine, enthusiastic business man or woman—never! This conviction has possibly been reinforced by the notable absence of evidence that business persons recognize a kinspirit in me. In view of this mutuality, is it worth while to unfixate it?"

## Breaking Fixations

"Fixation: 'When I have the money.'
"Substitute: 'As we journey through life, let us live by the way' (poetic version).
     'The kingdom of God is within' (Jesus Christ).
     'Do it now' (business man).
"Fixation: Debating society attitude: argue against what was advanced with which we do not agree; look out for weak

spots. Fighting activities and emotions aroused. Motive: desire for recognition.

"Substitute: Find points of agreement. Amplify and illuminate what is advanced with which we agree. Look for strong spots. Altruistic activities and emotions aroused. Motive: desire for response. If this substitute can be made, it will greatly improve the quality of discussion. The point is for the group to try to find a consensus of opinion and develop it.

"Fixation: Being frank. 'Tell the truth and shame the devil.' 'Call a spade a spade.' Trying to cure faults by discussing them with the person to be cured. Giving (unsought) advice. Smoothing the fur the wrong way, thus lowering bodily tone.

"Substitute: Flattery in the non-invidious sense. Rubbing the fur the right way, thus elevating bodily tone. This change will add more to human happiness than anything else I know of."

## "I Seen Me Opportunities and Acted Accordin'."

"Perhaps one of the most harmful series of fixations is that which blocks our seeing our opportunities and acting accordingly. Booker T. Washington said this: 'If we will do our level best every day, we will be surprised at the unexpected opportunities which will come to us.'

"The other day I was thinking of this in connection with the 'when I have the money' and 'when I have the leisure' fixations. To-day I am reading Robinson's *The Humanizing of Knowledge* and am thinking of the waiting for the creative intelligence to do or say something fixation. Robinson himself has the right answer. It is this: we must fumble; and by chance we may make a success. If we do we shall have the creative intelligence. The creative intelligence is something that exists after the event (success). Did not William James fumble? Was he not a successful teacher? Did he not print the results of his fumbling and the fumbling itself? Was he not then recognized as a creative intelligence? Where was the creative intelligence before he began fumbling?

"Anybody can fumble and fumble at anything. Perhaps the diference between those with and those without creative intelligence consists of this: those with it try to do something they can't (yet) do; and the others have the fixation that one has to learn to do something first, otherwise there is no use trying to do it. Perhaps the term creative intelligence is an evil stereotype. Perhaps the very words artist, poet, writer, musician, inventor, and so on are evil stereotypes preventing people from trying to do what artists, writers, poets do. The stereotype we all need is the idea embodied in the statement 'function makes faculty.' This statement should be rewritten in terms of modern psychology, in forms that will stick."

## Fabrication Defended

"While considering the fabrication habit from the standpoint of your talk, would it not be wise also to consider the value of phantasy under some conditions of life?

"To be forced to live always in the midst of depressing conditions and yet to be able to at times dream oneself into a life of beauty or joy, is, I think, to gain a real stimulation that makes for mental and physical health. A sense of humor with the power of controlled day-dreams has kept many a lonely woman human and sane. Of course this implies the power to snap out of the phantasy and face reality at the proper times.

"You spoke of the Christian with a fixed prejudice against the Jew. May not *one* of the forces that has made the Jew survive such prejudice and the centuries of persecution which accompanied it, be almost a race power of fabrication as you use the term? Even when forced to live in a ghetto, wear a prescribed garb with a yellow badge, and often literally be 'spat upon,' the Jew feels himself of 'God's chosen people' and therefore superior to his persecutors. His home, a hovel, was happy; for the Jew has never been other-worldly. He has lived wholly in the world that tortured him, dreamed he was superior, and survived. To-day the poorest, most ignorant Jew still has that superiority complex and still drives on to give his children a chance to show what they really are. They firmly believe it is what they are and always have been; they do not believe it is what they may be or will become.

"While I realize it is only in a limited number of conditions that superiority dreams, which have no foundations in material reality, are of value, I do think it unwise to overlook the imaginative symbolism in even the worst crude dreams of limited minds and the stimulation such dreams can bring to depressed or miserable lives."

## Good Will Technique

"At one time I determined to read through the Gospels and see if the cure for social evils was to be found in Christ's teachings. I read till I came to the golden rule and then stopped. I said to myself, 'Yes, here it is. It hasn't been tried.'

"It seems to me that the consideration of the golden rule should not be isolated from the numerous sayings of Christ's which are summed up in the doctrine of non-resistance to evil. In sum these sayings advocate the attitude of good will. Christ meant that good will should be displayed whole-heartedly, as illustrated in the saying 'if a man compel you to go with him one mile, go with him two.' The situation here was that the Roman soldiers by law had the right to impress subjects to carry their baggage 1000 paces. Christ advocated doing more than was required to show that it was done ungrudgingly.

"The point is, then, that we are to show good-will, and we are to do it, even when the other fellow does not show it. As such it can be examined as to how and why it works as it does. These two statements seem to be facts: (1) We tend to feel the emotions we overtly display. Darwin's work on the expression of the emotions seems to prove this. (2) We tend to induce in others the emotions which we ourselves display."

## Simulated Disinterest

" 'Simulated disinterest' may briefly be defined as pretended indifference. Several very painful personal experiences have taught me that simulated disinterest is a technique which, if applied to love affairs, results in quick and downcrashing disaster. Even when applied to those relatively less sensitive associations we term friendships, it leads only to the slow but none the less inevitable evaporation of the friendship—no breakage, no sharp recriminations; 'evaporation' seems to be the word.

"On the other hand, very pleasant experiences have taught me, though with mild and dubitable emphasis, that simulated disinterest is a technique which often proves surprisingly successful in obtaining a sanction of a business proposition. More than one very desirable position has been obtained by the applicant at the end of his resources, by the simple process of pretending an indifference to such a barely desirable position! On at least three occasions he has obtained worthwhile jobs by this means. He has also sold several difficult propositions by this means."

## The Unexpected

"The unexpected is desired! Perhaps someone with a deeper insight than mine can tell why. In the days of my youth when thoughtful people were fed on Spencer's evolutionary philosophy, the answer was that it is due to inheritance. Our ancestors lived in a dreadful state of uncertainty, whether in the next moment they would happen on a square meal or themselves be eaten. They became used to it, and we miss what they were used to. I don't believe this.

"The unexpected is desired! Hence arousing expectation of the unexpected can be a technique for influencing human behavior.

"This is not just the same as novelty. It must involve curiosity plus something. This something is we know not what, but something wanted and important."

## The Use of a Story to Put an Idea Across

"The great exemplar of the use of stories to put ideas across was Christ. One of the women students told me she was going to read the Gospels through again to see what Christ's techniques were."

## Literary Clinics

"A professional or perhaps, even better, a general discussion group might function quite effectively as a clinic for the examination and testing of literature directed toward the influencing of behavior. Doubtless you know how fashionable such clinics have become among public health workers in the last few years.  Perhaps the idea grew out of such thorough studies as Watson, Lashley, and Achilles made of the effectiveness of the educational pamphlets of the American Public Health Association.  The Committee on Publicity Methods in Social Work have held a number of quite successful public clinical examinations of sample circulars submitted by different organizations. The knife has generally been wielded by one or more advertising men, psychologists or expert printers."

## Including the Reader

"Having but a poor grounding in the elements of English prosody, I opened Professor Bliss Perry's book to see what I could learn, and in the chapter on rhythm and metre, I found a delightful example of the technique you described.  He 'puts it up' to the reader by ingenious use of the device of reviewing the subject as 'something that we all learned in college.'  In this way, inserting a parenthetical 'so our instructors taught us' in almost every other sentence, he succeeds in a few pages in summarizing and driving home all the rudimentary facts which readers like myself are looking for, while politely indicating in each new paragraph, that of course we all went to college and learned all this!"

## The Importance of What We Are About

"A 'crank' has been defined as a man of one idea.  Wilson said that he (Wilson) had a 'single track mind.'  He also said he was descended from covenanter ancestry and would fight for the League of Nations.  He died of fighting for it.  There are people who believe that it is the 'cranks' who put new things across.

"What is peculiar about 'cranks' and those of 'single track minds' is that they think that what they are about is of *great* importance. If this belief can be made infectious, the means of making it so becomes a productive technique for influencing human behavior."

## Nuisance Technique

"Besides those techniques already mentioned for gaining attention, there seems to me to be another one, very effective and very widely used, and that is the nuisance technique.

"It is used instinctively from childhood on. When a baby wants something it cries. If refused at first—louder and louder crying brings results. The little girl sulks. 'I'll take my doll clothes and go home' is an easy way to get what she wants. The bad boy throws things or punches. Another kind whines.

"I was present at this scene. A mother with a child by the hand was talking to a neighbor on the sidewalk. An ice-wagon drew up beside the curb. The child asked the mother for a piece of ice. The mother said, 'No.' Then the play began. After a slight pause, the child said again, 'Mama, can I have a piece of ice?' No answer. Then, 'Mama, can I have a piece of ice?' 'Mama, can I have a piece of ice? MamacanIhaveapieceofice,' etc., etc., etc., for ten minutes without pause. No temper, no accent, and no cessation, until finally the dropping water wore away the stone and she got the piece of ice.

"The little boy who pestered his mother for a drink of water after he was put to bed, until he was told that if he asked once more he would be spanked, then called down stairs, 'Mama, when you come up to spank me will you bring me a drink of water?' was a master of nuisance technique.

"Teachers know this technique and can generally name each gray hair after a nuisance-child. . . . Mr. Everett Dean Martin tells about a man who worked in a factory out West where he was foreman with some two hundred men under him. He was a poor worker, was the most insolent, the most pugnacious and the foulest-mouthed man he ever came in contact with. He was the bane of his existence throughout a very hot summer. But in looking back over the experience after some years, that man is the only one he can remember. The man got his personality across by nuisance.

"Beggars are trained to employ this technique. Anyone who has travelled in Italy recalls a much keener sense of annoyance than of pity. I remember vividly an experience in China which is illustrative of this. Getting off the train at the place where one starts to walk up to the Great Wall, one is met by a swarm of Chinese men and boys who are poised for so much prey. I was in a small party, vastly outnumbered by the jabbering mob. One toothless old man was especially solicitous. He wanted to help us over the rocks and show us the way—very intimately—until one person whom he had made his particular charge called out to the guide, 'I don't mind the rest of this gang but I will give this one two dollars if he will just *go away!*'

"Most argumentation is based on nuisance. Someone has said that very few men have been convinced by argument—no women. It is true that the one who can talk the loudest and the longest and make the most nuisance is generally the one who wins. I talked recently with the manager of a successful and much travelled debating team. He told me that after hundreds of debates, they had come to the conclusion that very few decisions had been upon logic at all; that no matter how carefully selected the judges, the decisions turned on other points. Not the least of these was the above-mentioned technique. When argument fails, the nuisance technique is often very effective. Ghandi is trying it in India. The Irish put it over in Ireland and the Suffragettes in England. If men won't listen to reason, throw stones, break windows, attack policemen, wreck, ruin, grow hungry and die before the public. In a word, make a complete nuisance of yourself and you win.

"Not only hunger strikes but all strikes are based on this government by nuisance. When Labor becomes impatient of being heard before justice through orderly procedure and argument, Labor strikes. Then, right or wrong, it is heard. The game of politics is full of this technique of nuisance. A great deal of advertising is based on it. And through the ages it has been woman's most used weapon—tears. The weeping woman is usually not crying to make you sad or sorry for her, but because she knows that where all other resources fail, that is the one effect that will wear down the resistance—of a man. It is everywhere the tyranny of weakness."

## Inducing an Imagined Experience

"A life insurance agent had been unsuccessful in persuading a farmer to provide an educational policy for his daughter. The conversation shifted to the subject of the farmer's garden, especially to some particularly fine looking rows of beans which ran along the fence. The farmer spoke of the profit which he made on beans each year. 'About how much do you make on each row?' asked the salesman. The farmer gave a rough estimate of the amount. 'Mr. Williams,' asked the salesman, 'wouldn't you be willing to cultivate two more rows of beans to make sure that if anything happened to you, your daughter would have the education that a bright girl like yours should have? It would be an easy way of paying for that education, in any case, wouldn't it?'

"The sale was made."

## Inducing an Imagined Experience

"Some years ago I was arguing with a young Republican, who was quite satisfied with Roosevelt's régime.

"I must have argued rather well, for my opponent seemed to have exhausted all his stock of objections and was simply repeating himself. Then to wind up, he said:

"'You know what another fellow would do to you if you talked that way? He'd punch you in the jaw.'

"He was a few years older, a few inches taller and some pounds heavier than I was, and my only thought at the time was, 'What shall I do to be saved?' In the twinkling of an eye I decided that on account of his proximity to me at the time, my safety lay in making him feel that he was not that other fellow. Hence, with an air of seeming detachment, I retorted: 'I have no doubt at all that there are a number of men so utterly devoid of knowledge or the power of reasoning that they must resort to fistic measures when anything is said with which they don't agree. But fortunately you and I, my dear fellow, can discuss ideas we are utterly opposed to, with some warmth, of course, but with no ill-feeling in the end. After all, we do agree in essentials, don't we? We both want to make this country the best in the world, and we only differ on details. Well, regarding the means, who knows? Maybe some day you will discover that my way is the best, or I will discover that your way is the best. And naturally, the only way we can learn the real value of ideas is by exchanging ours with those of other people, and by crystallizing the best out of them. Isn't that so?'

"He had to admit that it was. By the time I had delivered myself completely of this philosophy, his features had relaxed, his fists had become unclenched, and God was in His heaven."

### Challenge

"Clarence had to have iodine put on an abrasion for the first time.

" 'Do you know how I can tell how old you are when I put iodine on this bruise?'

" 'How?'

" 'It will tickle you a little. Might even hurt some. If you scream and kick I shall know you are a baby only two years old. If you cry and fuss, you are just four years old. But if you merely say, 'Ouch!' and laugh and dance the iodine dance that goes something like this (making appropriate gestures, ridiculous enough so that he laughed) you might be as old as SIX!'

" 'Now we'll see if you are two or four or SIX!'

"Clarence was four.

" 'I'll bet you're only two.'

"Tense moments. Then—'Ouch! Ouch! OUCH!!!' and hilarious laughter and dancing sparkling through tears.

" 'So big? So soon? How did you do it?'

" 'O—I yist grewed up.' "

*From a forthcoming book by Anna G. Noyes*

### The Interview

"In trying to analyze my contact with people I believe I follow three more or less definite steps.

"First, I try for a 'transfer,' to make the person I'm talking with, feel my genuine interest in him; by

(a)   concentrated attention with the impression that my time is his entirely for as long as he wishes;

(b)  establishing some bond of common interest or experience;

(c)  finding something about the person's looks, manner, or experience that I can conscientiously admire.

"Second, I try to have him feel my desire and ability to help or advise him; and

"Third, I try to make him feel I believe in him and make him believe in himself.

"My chief failures have come when I was fatigued, and when it became an effort even to simulate interest. The person talked with felt the break, the effort; and the responsive chord was not awakened."

## A Symptom

"We all have numerous ideas, beliefs, and attitudes which have been 'wished on us' by others—hand-me-downs of the group or groups in which we have been reared. One of our problems is to get rid of such stuff as will not stand the light of critical examination. We should be skeptical towards every old belief and idea we have, simply because we know from our studies in psychology that the chances are that we harbor an immense amount of error.

"Mr.—— has suggested a very good piece of technique for judging our assurance of the validity of our ideas on any subject. Do we get excited when these ideas are challenged? We frequently think we are not excited when we are. Mr.—— says that it is a sure sign of lack of well-considered basis for our ideas if we raise our voice, get hot under the collar, or speak like an oracle passing out judgment. When these signs appear, it is time to be skeptical."

## Learning How To Do It

"I shall go a long way off for my illustrative case, to China. The impact of Western Civilization has given China a staggering, almost a death blow to her civilization. Whether China can be reconstructed is of vast importance. This matter arouses intense interest among Chinese students. They think (for a time) that it can be done. But they become pessimistic. Speaking of this pessimism, Pearl S. Buck, for many years a professor in one of the Chinese universities (Art. *Chinese Student's Mind, Nation,* October 8, 1924) in part has this to say: 'A second reason for this attitude of pessimism may be their apparent lack of ability to preserve in any line of action in attacking their problems; this is partly youth and partly an inherent facial characteristic. They start off with fire crackers, speech making and a high sounding name, and then impetus seems to be dissipated, and the attention drawn off to other things. Possibly it is lack of deep seated convictions. They do certainly tend to lack convictions. Whatever the cause, they are incorrigible promoters. They are forever starting agricultural societies and mutual improvement societies and anti-Japanese societies and dozens of others. Most of these die of general inanition, and then are reorganized with more fire crackers and speeches into something else. Magazines have sprouted up like weeds all over the country—radical magazines, so-called scientific magazines, literary magazines, short-story magazines —a fascinating kaleidoscopic mirror of student mind and thought. These magazines continue with great fervor for a short time and then they are no more. Three months seems to be the average life time. Again part of it is youth; part of it is lack of sufficient technical knowledge; part of it is natural lack of stick-to-it-iveness.'

"I present this quotation because in it are all the elements—importance, devotion, conviction that something can be done; but the one thing lacking is knowing what to do and how to do it. I can imagine the kind of education these Chinese students have been getting is the kind that was given to Negroes in the institutions of higher learning for them in the South soon after the Civil War; the curriculum of colleges: English, Latin, mathematics, philosophy, history, and some smattering of science. The professors thought they were preparing the boys for life. The results were similar to those described in Buck's article.

"These students did not learn what to do and how to do it. They were left in a state of puzzled confusion. The same is apparently the case with the Chinese students. Buck explains it as youth and lack of stick-to-it-iveness. I don't know what he means by this.

What they need is not knowledge alone but *the habit of doing*. There is no such thing as a natural lack of stick-to-itiveness. Buck, in short, does not put his finger on the right spot. These Chinese students have not been prepared in college for meeting the problems that have to be met. Above all, they have not learned to do by doing."

# INDEX

absolutism, breaking down of, 228
accuracy, training in, 186, 190
adult education, 138, 166, 194 ff.
advertising, psychology in, 34, 36, 70
antagonistic approach, 3, 18
apperception mass, 23
architecture, influence of, 60
argument, technique of, 49, 249 ff.
art, 57, 58, 61, 63, 89, 92, 96, 259
   of life, 3
   teaching of, 225
association-constants, 164
associative techniques, 159 ff.
attention, 4, 9 ff., 22, 30, 57, 60, 87, 118, 125 ff., 275
   limits, 24, 85

Bacon, Francis, 230
Butler, Samuel, 42

cartoon, 57
censor, escaping the, 259
challenge technique, 21, 289
changing persons, 143 ff.
character, building of, 158, 166
   conflicts, 154 ff.
chase technique, 13
choice, act of, 47
circular response, 76, 279
citizenship, training of, 32
clichés, 93, 132 ff.
Cody, Sherwin, 22 n.
Colcord, Joanna C., 15
Coleman, McAlistor, 112 n.
Comenius, 28
commerce, psychology of, 215
compensatory habits, 169 ff., 177
compulsion techniques, 44, 47, 48

Comte, Auguste, 122
concreteness, 4, 64, 115
conditioned reflex, 159
conditioning, early, 88, 232
conflict, 121, 238 ff.
   argumentative, 249 ff.
   between nations, 238, 243
   character, 154 ff.
   industrial, 238, 246
   racial, 176, 239, 248
   within the individual, 241 ff.
coöperation, 213
Corbett, Arthur T., 51 n.
creative mind, 255, 258, 276, 281
   training of, 217 ff.
   use of, 253
Crothers, Rachel, *Expressing Willie*, 154

Dalton method, 14, 21
Davenport, Professor F. M., 66
day-dream, 169 ff.
Dearborn, G. V., 68
debate, 249 ff., 280
   constructive, 253
Dewey, John, 4, 22, 197
Didactic, The Great, 28
discipline, 47
dissociation, 244, 247
dramatic quality, 13, 93, 94, 113, 115, 122
drawing, teaching of, 62
dullness, 14, 93, 95, 118, 121
duty techniques, 32, 46 ff.

education, 44, 62, 88, 91, 163, 167, 181, 186, 190, 197, 200, 222, 277
   adult, 138, 166, 184, 194 ff., 231
ego magnification, 179

293

ethics, 5, 46 ff.
ethnocentrism, 175, 248
euthenics, 277
evasions of reality, 171 ff., 179
experimentation, 46, 217 ff.
  social, 222, 228
expository method, 20, 29

fabrication habits, 169, 282
facts, appeal to, 29, 30
familiar in unfamiliar, 24, 75, 93
fixations, 280, 281
Follett, M. P., 77 n., 253 n.
France, Anatole, 103
freedom of thought, 198

Galsworthy, John, *Forsyte Saga*, 104
Ghandi, 21
good-will technique, 283

habits, 146 ff., 275
  building of, 159 ff., 253 n.
  compensatory, 169 ff., 177
  consumption, 206
  experimental, 223
  evolutionary, 226
  fabrication, 169
  jingoistic, 213 ff.
  in humor, 257 ff.
  new, in women, 203 ff.
  of doing, 292
  perverted, 157
  rural, 209 ff.
  significance for politics, 208 ff.
  social, 201 ff.
  unlearning, 61
history and the experimental mind, 227
Hobhouse, Leonard, 102
Hobson, John A., 116
homeogenic technique, 15, 74, 164, 255
human nature, 144 ff.
humor, 42, 78, 257 ff., 282

Ibsen, 112, 119

ideas, 90, 125, 275
imaginative experience, 64
inaccuracy, encouragement of, 187
incongruities, observing, 267
inducing an imagined experience, 64 ff., 68, 288
inertia, psychological, 219
infantilism, 170, 173, 178
inferiority feeling, 20, 76, 78
influencing the public, 201 ff.
intellectualism, abstract, 43
interest, 45, 55, 75, 87, 275
  dead-line, 110 ff.
internationalism, 12, 245, 249, 253 n., 255
invention, 126, 221, 241, 245, 248, 276
  psychology of, 232 ff.

James, William, 21, 126
jingoism, psychology of, 213
Joy, B. Franklin, 111 n.

Kamiat, Arnold H., 253 n.
Keatinge, Dr., 28, 29
Kennedy, Margaret, *The Constant Nymph*, 105
kinetic technique, 12, 82, 112, 115
Korzybski, 89

*Landerziehungsheime,* 167
League of Nations, 11

mannerisms, in speaking, 80
means and ends, 4, 5, 277
Mencken, H. L., 114, 119
mind, the, 28, 83
  and verbal expression, 136
  of the child, 46
motivation, subtler, 42
movement, 12 (see also *kinetic technique*)
Munro, Professor William Bennett, 127
music, error in teaching, 88

names that stick, 125 ff.
novel, the, 70, 113, 115, 174
novelty, 23, 42, 94, 118
Noyes, Anna G., 235, 289
nuance, in words, 96
nuisance technique, 286

obedience, 44

pain techniques, 161
parent, the, 2, 4, 15, 29, 44, 48, 70,
    75, 164
Pascal, 43
Peirce, Charles, 126
personal appearance, 80
personality, 2, 14, 47, 107, 144 ff.,
    152, 158
persuasion, 69
philosophy, of life, 199
    psychology of teaching, 117, 122
phrasing, 83, 97, 99, 127
phrases that stick, 129 ff.
picturizing, 51 ff., 58, 61, 63
pietism, social, 217 ff.
playfulness, in humor, 257
prejudice, 248
    race, 248 ff.
problem, our central, 1, 278
progressivism, techniques of, 68
Proust, Marcel, 113
psycho-analytic process, 242
public, influencing the, 201 ff.
putting-it-up-to-you technique, 18 ff.

racial antagonism, 176
rationalizing, 178, 190 ff., 230, 248,
    253
reason, appeal to, 32, 33
reflex, conditioned, 159
reformers, techniques of, 4, 127
response, 16, 32, 72, 73, 87, 94, 160
    circular, 76, 279
rhythm, 84, 93, 101 ff.
Robinson, James Harvey, 21, 281

Sayles, Mary B., 149 n.

science, 75, 117
    spirit of, 189, 251
    teaching of, 187, 190, 224
sculpture, influence of, 60
selective emphasis, 57, 59, 61, 96
self-excusing, 171, 190 ff., 248, 253
sex habits, training of, 154 ff.
Shaw, Bernard, 121
Sheffield, Dr. Alfred Dwight, 248
shock technique, 120
situations, portraying, 115
slogans, 128, 129
snobbishness, 177
social pietism, 217 ff.
speaking, psychology of, 70, 71 ff.
Stewart, Donald Ogden, 268
story, the, as technique, 13, 78, 284
straight thinking, training in, 184 ff.
suggestion, 65
Sumner, William Graham, 122
superiority feeling, 20, 76, 78, 175,
    178, 248, 282
teacher, the, 2, 15, 43, 75, 152, 164
techniques for influencing behavior,
    accuracy training, 186, 190
    appeal to duty, 32, 46 ff.
        to facts, 29, 30
        to reason, 32, 33
        to wants, 28 ff., 33, 43, 45, 48,
            163
    associative, 159 ff.
    association-with-pleasurable-expe-
        rience, 159 ff.
    attention limits, 24, 85
    authoritarian, 225
    challenge, 21, 289
    chase, 13
    circular response, 76, 279
    constructive debate, 253
    creative, 126, 217 ff., 221, 232 ff.,
        241, 245, 248, 253, 255, 258, 276,
        281
    doing favors, 279
    dramatic, 93, 113, 115, 122
    evolutionary teaching of history,
        227

experimentation, 46, 217 ff.
exposing rationalizing process, 190 ff.
expository, 20, 29
good will, 284
habit analysis, individual, 143 ff.
  social, 201 ff.
homeogenic, 15, 74, 164, 255
humor, 42, 78, 256 ff., 282
inducing an imagined experience, 64 ff., 68, 288
interest dead-line, crossing of, 110 ff.
kinetic, 12, 82, 112, 115
names that stick, 125 ff.
novelty, 23, 42, 94, 118
nuisance, 287
pain, 161
phrases that stick, 129 ff.
picturizing, 51 ff., 58, 61, 63
psychological analysis, 229
putting-it-up-to-you, 18 ff.
selective emphasis, 57, 59, 61, 96
simulated disinterest, 283
speaking, 70, 71 ff.
straight thinking, 184 ff.
writing, 87 ff.
yes-response, 16
thinking, straight, training in, 184 ff.
thought, freedom of, 198
  instrument of action, 49

transfer of skills, 185
tropisms, 273

unconscious, the, 43, 172, 175, 177, 181, 229, 241
unpredictability, 13, 264, 285
use-value, 221

Van Waters, Miriam, 154
variation and evolution, 236
Vassar College, 278
verbal expression, 90, 97, 132, 137
visual-mindedness, 50, 52
visual images, 50 ff.
vividness, techniques of, 50 ff.
voice, psychological effect of, 15, 79, 164

wants, appeal to, 28 ff., 33, 43, 45, 48, 163
  fundamental, 34 ff.
  organizing of, 48
war, psychology of, 238, 243
Watson, John B., 148 n.
Wells, H. G., 21
Wilson, Woodrow, 11, 14, 107, 254, 285
Winans, James A., 121 n.
words, 96 ff., 125 ff., 138
writing, psychology of, 87 ff.

yes-response technique, 16